MALCOLM FORBES

MALCOLM FORBES

FORBES

PERIPATETIC MILLIONAIRE

ARTHUR JONES

HARPER & ROW, PUBLISHERS

NEW YORK, HAGERSTOWN, SAN FRANCISCO, LONDON

1817

For Alice and Les, my parents,
hoping they'll get a good chuckle
out of it

For Peggy Morrison, hoping she
knows how much her friendship has
always meant to me

MALCOLM FORBES: PERIPATETIC MILLIONAIRE. Copyright © 1977 by Arthur Jones.
All rights reserved. Printed in the United States of America. No part of this book may
be used or reproduced in any manner whatsoever without written permission except
in the case of brief quotations embodied in critical articles and reviews: For information address Harper & Row, Publishers, Inc., 10 East 53rd Street, New York, N.Y.
10022. Published simultaneously in Canada by Fitzhenry & Whiteside Limited,
Toronto.

FIRST EDITION

Designed by Sidney Feinberg

Library of Congress Cataloging in Publication Data
Jones, Arthur, 1936–
    Malcolm Forbes: peripatetic millionaire.
    Includes index.
    1. Forbes, Malcolm S. 2. Businessmen—United States
—Biography. 3. Capitalists and financiers—United
States—Biography. 4. Forbes magazine.
HC102.5.F67J66 1977   338.7′61′0705720924   [B]
ISBN 0–06–012204–8   77–6885

77 78 79 80 81 10 9 8 7 6 5 4 3 2 1

Contents

Acknowledgments   vii

1. Emperor Malcolm   1

2. Cunnieknowe   13

3. The Immigrant   28

4. The Forbeses of *Forbes*   38

5. Malcolm and BC   64

6. Malcolm and Bruce   87

7. Malcolm, Michaels and the Magazine   100

8. The Not-So-Eccentric Eccentric   126

9. The Balloonatic   157

10. The Sun Never Sets . . .   196

Index   205

A section of illustrations follows page 116.

Acknowledgments

Blame this book on Helen Egan. Helen sent me my first copy of *Forbes* among a batch of magazines she thought I might be interested in when I was job hunting.

I read magazines from the back and work forward. The *Forbes* "Thoughts on the Business of Life" struck me as a delightful anachronism, but it was the page of readers' letters (continued to the rear of the book from up front) that most intrigued me.

No matter what the readers wrote—subscription canceling, threat-gurgling missives some of those letters were—the editor, and someone labeled "MSF," stuck to their guns. Great.

When I eventually reached the masthead to read who put out this tightly edited magazine on a dull subject—rendered bright by clever writing—I found there was a Forbes at *Forbes*. And there was an editor named Michaels—to whom I wrote.

Michaels hired me. That same day I met Malcolm S. Forbes for the first time.

I was at *Forbes* just about five years and left to write this book. To me the work at *Forbes* was stimulating and challenging. My first book, *The Decline of Capital*, is very much a byproduct of those *Forbes* years.

When five years later I decided to write this book, I told Malcolm, who had agreed to cooperate, that my attitude would be "detached and objective," and that I would be paying my own way. He was annoyed at first because I insisted on paying my own hotel bills when I traveled with him. He was bewildered, but finally got used to the idea, that though I might fly with him on his private airliner,

The Capitalist Tool, for interviews, I would insist, either the outward journey or the return journey—to Fiji, Morocco or elsewhere—be on a commercial flight at my own expense.

Malcolm was extremely helpful. He gave openhanded access, encouraging me to use his own and his father's papers and scrapbooks, the *Forbes* magazine library files and the magazine itself. Whenever he came across items in his own correspondence, or other files he thought I might use, he would forward these with a cheery note. During hours of interviews, usually at 33,000 feet, Malcolm was candid about some things, absolutely close-mouthed about others—especially money.

This book went through three drafts. Malcolm saw part of the first draft to check facts only he knew for sure so that I could get his reaction to statements I was making—again usually about money, or family relationships. Because he was not permitted to see subsequent drafts, Malcolm would not provide family or corporate photographs for inclusion in the book.

Nonetheless, Malcolm's willingness to cooperate made the project possible and, one hopes, successful in describing the characters as they are. Thank you, Malcolm.

To Gertrude Weiner, the late Bertie Charles "BC" Forbes' secretary, friend, gin-rummy companion and former *Forbes* treasurer, I have a special "thank you." Gertrude played a special role. She would tell me nothing unless I had the facts wrong because, as she said in retirement in her Palm Springs home, "I sit here surrounded by the good memories. I don't want to remember the rest."

I have the fondest memories of days spent in Buchan, Scotland, exploring the locale of BC Forbes' childhood. John Webster, a great guide and a good companion, with me in tow, toured the crofts and farms, the kirks, schools and fine houses, meeting people who had known BC and picking up the little incidentals that helped flesh out the early years of *Forbes'* founder.

To those good people in Maud and New Deer—including that marvelous ninety-four-year-old who, as Janet Fowlie, had been at school with BC (and who, the evening before we took tea together had taken a small slam at bridge)—my thanks.

For the details of her grandfather, Gavin Grieg, my thanks to Nell Arno also.

To Jack Webster of the Scottish *Daily Express,* and to all others who know Honeyneuk:

> We maun haud a carefu' memory o' the road
>   back again;
> An' o' friendship an' o' kindness we'll often
>   tak a fit,
> An' come rinning' back to say: Yes, the
>   house is warm yet.

Many former and present *Forbes* employees, plus people who knew Malcolm at school and college, or knew BC, were especially helpful. But unless they are quoted by name in the book, they didn't want their names mentioned.

To Wilf Thompson and his colleague, thanks for finding out which train BC took from Maud in 1894! To the folks of Malcolm's many establishments—the ranch, the chateau, the island and the palace—thank you for your time and hospitality.

Of the immediate Forbes family, Mrs. Roberta Forbes, Steve, Bobby, and Kip were the ones I interviewed. My thanks to them.

To my *Forbes* colleagues of old, the folks in the library, many thanks for your help. Among my constant encouragers and friends I cannot help but single out two people: Jean Blake, my indefatigable critic and researcher, and Dero Saunders, my literary godfather, without whom, it seems no book of mine would be complete.

My own family has suffered through another book. I've been gone, whether absent in the study or lost in thought, for days and weeks and months on end.

Whether a long weekend in the George Arendts Research Library at the University of Syracuse—to that library, too, my thanks for access to BC's papers—or weeks gone to the South Pacific, it was absence.

There are some family compensations. En route to Santa Fe we all stopped off at Malcolm's Trinchera ranch—while I interviewed—and saw our first elk.

Another compensation: My wife, Margie, from past experience, usually won't travel with me when I'm working, even to exotic spots. But she agreed to accompany me to Morocco.

For that reason, my thanks to her—and to Malcolm and to Wimmer, Joe and Bill of the *Tool*—for the Moroccan interlude and interviews, and for three days in the Palais Mendoub.

To Chris, and Mike and Ian, this has meant more postcards for the collection, and a lot more stories for around the dinner table. Thanks, kids.

AJ

Prairie Village, Kansas, 1975–1977

MALCOLM FORBES

1

Emperor Malcolm

Don't give him an island.

Don't give him a ranch—he has a 240 square-mile spread in Colorado.

Don't give him a Fabergé egg—he has about $4 million worth.

Don't give him a 19th century toy boat—he has the largest collection in the world.

Don't give him a lead soldier—he has a collection of 5,000, all deployed in dioramas of historic battlegrounds.

Don't give him a castle in Normandy built by Mansart, or a palace in Morocco, or a Christopher Wren house in London, or a house in Far Hills, N.J., or a fishing lodge in Tahiti, or a plane or a yacht or a balloon.

And don't give him a magazine—he owns one of those, too.

Ted Morgan
Signature magazine
August, 1976

The purple-inked advertising slogan thumbtacked to the editorial bulletin board proclaimed: "One in every 24 *Forbes* readers is a millionaire."

Forbes editors and writers commuting in that morning saw the same purple-ink slogan at every train stop. In black and white it was all over the back page of the morning's *New York Times*.

At the office, even before the Schrafft's coffee-cart lady rang her 10 A.M. bell on the black-and-white marble editorial landing, someone had scrawled under the slogan: "Only one in every 204 *Forbes* employees is a millionaire."

Malcolm Stevenson Forbes, editor-in-chief and owner of *Forbes* magazine, howled with delight when he heard the story. He knew exactly who they meant. He didn't mind a bit.

Malcolm had reacted the same way when senior editor Hal Lavine told him: "Malcolm, you're the only 50-year-old adolescent I know." Lavine, describing the incident later in his Arizona *Republic* column, added: "I was a serf then on *Forbes* magazine. It's presumptuous for a serf to speak lightly of his master (and it can be dangerous, too) but Forbes only burst into laughter. He considered what I had said a compliment."

Ceaseless mirth is not the hallmark of working for Malcolm Forbes. Malcolm demands of his employees what he wants. What he wants he gets. One year Malcolm wanted his sailing yacht *Laucala* to call at the Galápagos Islands as he sailed to his Tahiti fishing camp that once belonged to Zane Grey. The Ecuador government was refusing visits to Galápagos. Malcolm called his Washington bureau chief and told him: "Fix it." It got fixed.

Another time, Malcolm was looking for a freighter to carry building materials from Viti Levu, Fiji's major island, to Lacaula, his own private island and coconut plantation. The *Forbes* London bureau chief was told: "Find me one." Within days three ships had been crawled over by the bureau chief, and Malcolm was in Europe looking at the most likely one.

Malcolm had decided to have an impressive gathering on his 174,000-acre Trinchera ranch, in Colorado. Malcolm's ranch foreman protested that if Malcolm held a barbecue in August the guests would be eaten alive by mosquitoes. "Spray," said Malcolm. The foreman said it wasn't simply a question of spraying the immediate area, the entire meadow valley would have to be sprayed from the air. "Then do it," said Malcolm. The guests picked at their steaks with scarcely a mosquito for miles.

In London one time the telephone rang. "How are *you?* Have you seen the current issue of *Connoisseur?* There's a sunburst of Scottish swords advertised. Call and find out how much they want for them. If you can get the price down a bit, buy 'em."

As Malcolm rules like an emperor, travels like a king, spends like a prince and besports himself like a maharajah, not just his employees, but business acquaintances, too, are drawn into his often impromptu scheme of things. Malcolm decided to have a "garden party" at Old Battersea House, his reputed Sir Christopher Wren mansion on the south side of the Thames. He doesn't own it. He rents it from the local council for a peppercorn a year—provided he refurbishes it, at a cost initially estimated at around $250,000 and now reaching three times that amount.

The house looked like the setting for a movie about the London blitz. The entire interior of the house had been gutted. Dry-rotted panels and beams were gone. Plaster had been chiseled from the ceilings and walls; laths and brickwork showed through.

When caterers from Fortnum and Mason, the posh London department store, came to reconnoiter the premises they thought someone was playing a practical joke. It took several phone calls and some financial guarantees before they agreed to turn up on the Sunday as arranged.

That Sunday was one of those biting English March days when the temperature doesn't get out of the low forties, and the cold damp air makes everyone's face blue. Malcolm had flown in from New York on his private airliner, *The Capitalist Tool,* carrying friends and business colleagues.

London celebrities, a few dignitaries, and as many journalists as would come began to crowd into the mansion. The front garden approach to the house was a cross between a rubble heap and a builders' yard. Stiff-lipped Britons in their Sunday best stepped gingerly on the planks laid through the mud to reach the door. There, with sheets of plastic across windows and laid on the floor to protect the wood, chemical toilets in various anterooms, the garden party got under way. Forced-hot-air heaters struggled with little result against four centuries of Old Battersea House dampness. The guests' noses turned blue as they drank their champagne and nibbled their smoked salmon.

The afternoon temperature dropped. The guests switched to Scotch, and as their noses turned red, the conversation became animated. Malcolm, who never removed his raincoat throughout the entire bash, spent ten minutes telling the bewildered garden-party goers—many of the women elegantly gowned—how much the rebuilding was costing him.

Malcolm gave an eighteenth-century book on dry rot to the

British architect. There was some circulating among the crowd, a little chitchat, and Malcolm was gone. The *Tool* had another destination: the warmer and far more organized Forbes palace in Tangier, the pristine Palais de Mendoub built on the edge of the Mediterranean and looking out toward Gibraltar.

When Emperor Malcolm makes the rounds of his tax-deductible, globe-girdling empire, his ghillies are at the ready at every establishment. "Mr. Forbes likes things just so. And when he wants things, that's when he wants them." Cooks and cowboys, bag boys and balloonists, curators and cleaners, plantation managers and coconut-tree climbers, chauffeurs and sailors, flight crew and master mariners —all are on hand when the master alights. All are there to serve. So, in their own way, are the editors and writers of *Forbes* magazine in the Forbes building on New York's Fifth Avenue.

The splendid foyer of the magazine, at 60 Fifth Avenue on the northern edge of Greenwich Village, looks like that of a bank. And well it might. The revolving doors, set in the middle of four two-story-high Ionic columns, lead to a black-and-white marble reception area, where the illuminated bullet-proof boxes built into walls house the largest collection of Fabergé Easter eggs outside the Kremlin.

The Imperial Russian flag stands in one corner and, at the other side, a wide marble stairway leads toward the mezzanine. A collection of letters signed by the U.S. presidents flank the visitor who begins the ascent. A uniformed guard watches politely, but carefully.

On the mezzanine landing, beneath David Burt's mobile *Capriccio,* a doorway leads into the *Forbes* magazine research department. Researchers, proofreaders and teletype tapecutters see the stories through to publication.

Those stories, like the building, concern wealth, money and success. The *Forbes* readers know, or want to know, about such things.

The broad staircase sweeps around to the right and on up to the second floor, the editorial floor.

The second floor of *Forbes* is carpeted. The quality click of heels on marble gives way to muffled steps in paneled corridors. A row of offices from which senior editors can look down onto Fifth Avenue takes up the front portion of the floor. The corridor wall opposite the office doors holds mementoes from the magazine's sixty-year history: B.C. Forbes, the founder, cartooned; Malcolm caricatured in a kilt;

awards; photographs of dinners, of Bruce Forbes with former president Herbert Hoover aboard the first Forbes yacht, *Highlander,* of Malcolm, always on the move.

Malcolm travels by hot-air balloon, on any of the dozen motorcycles he owns, on his $2 million oceangoing motor yacht, *Highlander II.* He is chauffeured in the luxury sports cars and limousines in his auto stable. Once he could jet around the world at whim in his personal airliner, the gold-colored DC-9, *The Capitalist Tool,* but the $3,000 a day in operating costs proved too much even for millionaire Malcolm.

The media often depict Forbes as fun-loving. *New York* magazine called him "The Most Happy Millionaire." He has been referred to as "the last of the fun millionaires." The words, respectively, of Suzy the gossip columnist and the *Wall Street Journal,* describe him as a "modern renaissance man" who lives amid "a display of splendor seldom seen this side of royalty."

He is as audacious in print as in person. His audience usually loves him for it. His magazine editorials, "Fact and Comment" are fun, *furioso* and far-fetched grammatical contortions that arouse the readers to anger, laughter, disbelief and, occasionally, to canceling their subscriptions. That *Forbes* audience has combined assets conservatively estimated at $120 billion, a clout that exceeds the external borrowing powers of most European nations combined.

At the main corridor's southwest corner, with his windows looking out onto both Fifth Avenue and West 12th Street, dwells James Walker Michaels—an editor with a touch of acid in his ink.

Oriental carpeting leads from the Forbes office block into the adjoining early nineteenth-century New York townhouse—the second floor of which is Malcolm's office. The one step down into the townhouse reveals a magnificent room with two fireplaces, oak-paneled walls hung with a Rubens, several Utrillos, three capes for honorary doctorates, a Norwegian track suit, family photographs and a few mementoes.

The Rubens is on the north wall. At the room's southern end, seated behind a mahogany desk with his back to windows that look out onto West 12th Street, sits Malcolm Forbes, editor-in-chief and owner—lock, stock and masthead. He starts his day at 7:30 A.M., hosts at least three townhouse business lunches each week, writes two pages of his personal column, "Fact and Comment," each issue, and dreams up schemes that have turned a once-struggling magazine into a business that gives him millions of dollars a year to spend. And spend he does.

Handsome, with gray hair closely cropped, wearing a restrained but modern blue-and-white-striped shirt with white collar and white cuffs, a subdued tie, Malcolm rises to his feet.

He walks around his desk. He is a tall man, broad-shouldered, and he rocks back slightly on his feet before he swings his right shoulder into the handshake as he sticks out his hand.

"How are *you?*" he asks, emphasizing the "you," and with a slight roll to the *r* in "are"—the lingering inflection inherited from a Scots-born father who never lost his brogue.

Malcolm's eyebrows rise, creating a concertina of creases up to the hairline. The slightly receding hairline accentuates the sloping forehead—but it is the eyes and the mouth that capture the attention. The eyes, behind thick-lensed spectacles—heavily framed as is everything about the man—glint with merriment, perhaps the mock malevolence of a melodrama villain. The smile cracks into a wide grin that spreads along the side of his mouth, revealing his teeth.

The effect is that of a good-natured Big Bad Wolf temporarily distracted from the more serious task of pursuing the Three Little Pigs: power, money and prestige.

The handshake is firm. The first-time visitor is impressed with the easy aura of command Forbes exudes, an aura no less attractive because his late-fifties ruggedness has a touch to it of the outdoorsman quality much sought after by billboard advertisers.

The conversation doesn't get a moment to stall or lapse into embarrassed silence with Malcolm on his feet. He turns to some object in the room, perhaps the Norwegian track suit: "Neat, doncha think?"

The visitor may comment on a copper model of a hot-air balloon on the desk, or refer to a recent ballooning, motorcycling or journalistic escapade that has involved Malcolm or the magazine. The conversation will be easily sustained until the visit is over, or lunch is announced.

Malcolm Forbes started off as a journalist. He has, as Margaret Lane said of author-playwright Edgar Wallace, "the opportunism of the born journalist." His instincts are visceral, not cerebral.

In his columns and speeches, Malcolm often cheerfully explains that through "sheer ability, spelled i-n-h-e-r-i-t-a-n-c-e, I have become Editor-in-Chief of *Forbes* magazine, and President of Forbes Inc."

But, no matter how cheerfully he uses it as a throwaway line, there is more than a touch of bitterness in the statement. It was not what he wanted, and not the way he wanted it. He had not wanted to inherit success. He had wanted to earn it.

Malcolm wanted to be recognized for himself.

Malcolm's range of material possessions and his ability to promote and keep track of them all require initiative, organizational ability and unflagging energy. His durability comes not from drugs (he pops a couple of Vitamin C pills each morning)—or drink (though outside of office hours he often has a glass in hand)—but from the same wellspring that drove and goaded his father, Bertie Charles "BC" Forbes, the magazine's founder.

In the nineteenth century men scratched for a living in Buchan, Scotland. "I early learned that if I didn't work, neither would I eat," BC was apt to say. It was true, and at an early age he had developed a prodigious appetite for work out of sheer necessity: to survive. And he had equally early decided that life was more uncomfortable and less desirable lower down the social and economic ladder than higher up the ladder.

Malcolm Forbes, Princeton class of '41 after Hackley and Lawrenceville, all three of them names that mean something to aspiring families that want that something, started on the social ladder at a level his father called success.

Malcolm wanted more. Just as his father had worked himself from obscurity to security and a sense of achievement, so Malcolm was anxious to do the same. Malcolm is first-generation American. At Princeton, being the son of a self-made Scots journalist—BC by that time also was William Randolph Hearst's best-known financial columnist and a magazine owner in his own right—was relatively small potatoes.

There were second-, third- and fourth-generation names at Lawrenceville and Princeton, with second-, third- and fourth-generation money. Just as BC had learned, on the neighbors' farm where he had been forced to tend cattle on Saturdays, that there were two classes of farmworkers, the foremen and the rest, so Malcolm was learning there were two classes of people: the rich and the rest.

The lesson was not lost on him.

Malcolm certainly was a young striver. He got his first typewriter at eight; launched his first household ditto newspaper shortly afterward. By the time he was an Eagle Scout, publishing the *Eagle Scout,* he was a fifteen-year-old with three newspapers, family, school and scouting, to his credit.

Malcolm produced newspapers at Hackley and Lawrenceville. At Princeton he launched the *Nassau Sovereign* "the campus *Fortune,*" which not only survived, but finally put out of business the long-established Princeton *Tiger.*

In 1941 graduate Malcolm bought a weekly newspaper in Lancaster, Ohio. From it he hoped to build a political and financial base from which to launch himself into national politics. But red ink flowed, and Malcolm instead went into khaki. The newspaper folded. His father settled the few remaining debts.

In the late 1940s, Malcolm again launched into publishing. But *Nation's Heritage,* while it still holds the world's record as the most expensive magazine ($35 a copy, $150 a year), was not the world's most successful. In less than a year, after producing eight glamorous fifteen-by-twelve-inch volumes, *Nation's Heritage* became museum pieces only. The venture took with it what remained of the new Mrs. Malcolm Forbes' dowry—used to provide her with a 25 percent interest in the venture. BC paid off the outstanding bills.

In the 1950s, as a freshman state senator in New Jersey, Malcolm Forbes made two determined assaults on the old-line Republican party in an attempt to become governor of New Jersey. He still had his eye on the White House, just as he had had fifteen years earlier in Lancaster, Ohio. But two defeats took the energetic and independent-minded Senator Forbes out of politics for good.

There was still the job on Father's magazine, just as there had been after World War II and after *Nation's Heritage,* working for a father who had always told his sons: "I never met a rich man's son who was worth a damn."

Malcolm Forbes had failed at many of the things he most wanted to do, but he succeeded beyond his wildest dreams with the one thing he least wanted—his father's magazine. No, perhaps not beyond his wildest dreams, because it is his wild dreams that have brought him the success, the riches and the flashes of satisfaction that have turned him, wittingly and willingly, into a unique, late-twentieth-century adventurer. He is a character *because* he luxuriates in the material goods and comforts *Forbes* magazine's income spins off.

The magazine, adventurous and gutsy itself, is the product of people other than Malcolm; nonetheless he is the personification. Skilled at picking clever and talented people—sometimes slightly underpaid, but never undervalued—to run his magazine, and handle his finances and possessions, Malcolm Forbes has sought, and still seeks ways to make his taste for luxury, his romanticism, his flights of fancy, pay their way.

Malcolm has his own, tax-deductible monarchy. He has—among his many other possessions—that palace: the Palais de Mendoub in Tangier, white, set in formal gardens on the Moroccan edge of the Mediterranean.

Malcolm is personally well-suited to entertaining Arabs. In the Islamic tradition, hospitality is one of the major marks of individual worth (public oratory is the other).

These demands sit well with cordial and hospitable Malcolm Forbes, and his ability to afford them stems as much from the Internal Revenue Service's justifiable allowances as it does from the tremendous cash flow generated by the highly profitable *Forbes* magazine and his Sangre de Cristo ranch land development in Colorado.

Malcolm Forbes is both the epitome and a parody of the American dream.

He is the son who took what BC, the immigrant Scots journalist, had started, *Forbes* magazine, and built it into a one-man empire. Without his inherited audacity and ability to gamble for ever higher stakes, *Forbes* magazine would not have made the big time.

He has never been short of audacity and daring, a highly developed flair for promotion and a wickedly humorous way with words.

Malcolm is a man with many jewels. In the most literal sense there is that collection of Fabergés the *Wall Street Journal* has described as the Forbes "collection of trinkets made for the royal family of czarist Russia."

Malcolm told that *Journal* reporter that the costs of the Fabergés and paintings are worth it because the magazine, "like other corporations, can deduct the prices from taxes as a business expense and thus reduce the tab by some 50 percent or so." As Patrick O'Higgins wrote in *Town and Country:* "Forbes is quite dotty for anything that is tax deductible."

The magazine can claim a wide variety of business expenses for Malcolm Forbes. He *is* the magazine. He *is* the sole owner. But his success has taken more than tax breaks—every business has those. It has taken flair and ambition. It has taken the hungry ambition of the almost newly-arrived.

Invalided out of World War II with a Bronze Star and Purple Heart, machine-gun sergeant Malcolm Forbes joined his father at the magazine. BC was sixty-five. Wartime newsprint rationing had kept *Forbes* magazine going, but by his own admission *Forbes* was in bad shape. The magazine was in a rough postwar fight for survival among New York–based magazines, most especially *Fortune* and *Business Week*. *Forbes'* circulation was a scant sixty-thousand. But *Forbes* survived and grew as a triumvirate: Malcolm, brother Bruce, and BC (Duncan had died as a teenager). It was a partnership, Malcolm and Bruce, after BC died in 1953. The old man had left his four—by that time—sons a debt-free magazine. Gordon never joined the magazine, Wallace did. Both were minority stockholders.

With BC dead, Bruce and Malcolm were in an uneasy partnership: Bruce as publisher, Malcolm—spasmodically during his years in politics—laboring uncomfortably alongside as editor-in-chief. Bruce, the easygoing sportsman, affable and good company; Malcolm, more introverted, shrewder, more business oriented, and ambitious as hell. But they jarred on each other. Then, in 1964, Bruce died of cancer. He was forty-six.

Having been placed by fate at the head of the once-struggling magazine, Malcolm gambled with imagination and audacity. He entered the East Coast media jungle and emerged with a magnificent trophy: the modern *Forbes* magazine, a punchy, highly profitable, easy-to-read mass-circulation business magazine devoted to money, wealth and success.

He and his editor, Michaels, know what turns the reader on. So does Paul Erdman, who, in *The Silver Bears*, wrote: "The entire essence of America is the hope to first make money—then make

money with money—then make lots of money with lots of money."
Forbes magazine is about people who do that well, or do it badly, or
who try to do it and fail.

Left with *Forbes* magazine to run as he saw fit, Malcolm's first
hope was to make money. There was but one way to do it—with the
magazine. And he did it. Then his hope was to use that money to
make more money. The planes, the castles, the jaunts, the adventures, all cost money.

But, as any entrepreneur, adventurer, capitalist or promoter will
admit, the toughest trick is first of all making the money.

Malcolm Forbes is a self-created public image. He wants to be
recognized; he likes to be considered an eccentric; he wants to appear to be having the time of his life—and often he is; he wants to
appear brave and daring—and he is; he wants to make it all look easy
—which it isn't; and most of all, he wants it to be called "fun."

It is easier to visualize Malcolm Forbes in nineteenth-century
rather than Edwardian or twentieth-century terms. He is like late
Victorian architecture—bold, brassy and overembellished. And yet,
like Victorian redbrick, he conveys the same massive presence: you
don't have to like it, but you can't ignore it.

As an entrepreneurial capitalist, Malcolm is an artist, the sort of
artist G. K. Chesterton talked about, an artist "in using every circum-
stance that comes along." His balloon escapades are one such circum-
stance. Ballooning is the kind of whimsical and romantic nineteenth-
century pursuit Malcolm willingly identifies with.

In ballooning, Malcolm is drawn to a sport that allows him the
freedom to play the variations on his actor's personality.

Balloonist Anthony Smith, in *Jambo,* could have been describing
Malcolm Forbes: "The balloon somehow invites mockery . . . a figure
of fun . . . a piece of light-heartedness deserving to be treated with
equal levity."

Malcolm, publicly playing the clown, attracts mockery and deri-
sion at times. His life appears to some to be just like ballooning: "It
is destiny without a destination."

And yet, like ballooning; "it is pointlessness which gives great
purpose. It is enchanting. It is funny. It is idiotic. It is supreme. It
cannot last and yet endures. There is a greatness about it which
becomes cowpats and wet grass."

Malcolm the adventurer is master of the pratfall, the comedic *volte-face,* the joke against self. But all for a dual purpose: fun and money.

Given Malcolm's propensity for believing that bigger is better, his ballooning activities went from a $150 trial flight in 1972, to a $120,000 cross-country trip in 1973, to an Atlantic crossing attempt initially budgeted at $750,000 that eventually cost $1.35 million.

But it's all worth it, providing the money comes out of Forbes Inc.'s pretax income as a justified expenditure, and is shown to be valid as a business-promotion expense in the eyes of the Internal Revenue Service.

Malcolm does have fun spending money and indulging his whims. He does it on a scale that is unique for its flamboyance and self-satisfaction. Where other people imagine—in their Walter Mitty moments—owning their own oceangoing luxury yacht with smartly turned-out crew, Malcolm has his. Where others might dream of their private airliners dropping down at their private palace, château, and exotic hideaway, Malcolm has gone that route.

Malcolm enjoys himself with abandon.

And, on rare occasions of self-questioning, when a momentary but quickly dismissed twinge of conscience jabs him, he smiles broadly and forgivingly at his own conspicuous consumption and says in mock horror: "If my father could see me spending like this he'd be spinning in his grave."

2

Cunnieknowe

I am enormously rich, not in the sense that I earn with my pen more than enough in one month to keep me for a year; but because I have a wife and three children worth all the gold in the world. . . .

B. C. Forbes
American magazine, 1920

The third child was Malcolm Stevenson Forbes, born on August 19, 1919. What was his particular heritage? Energy.

Bertie Charles Forbes, founder of *Forbes* magazine, William Randolph Hearst's highest-paid financial writer, stunned friends and colleagues with his prodigious capacity for work.

Though BC had left the New York *American* to launch *Forbes*, William Randolph Hearst had not lost interest in the energetic little Scotsman. Once Hearst saw *Forbes* succeeding, he offered to buy it, to add to the Hearst empire.

BC would not sell. Hearst made a counter-suggestion. If BC wouldn't work for Hearst, wouldn't sell his magazine to him, would he write a syndicated financial column?

BC said he would, which brought the comment from his friend R. W. N. O'Neel, Boston *Herald* financial editor: "I have remarked to my associates many a time that I could not understand where one man got all the time, energy and initiative to do all the magazine work you do, in addition to getting out your own publication . . . now I am amazed to find that your capacity was so far from being exhausted . . . you are taking on a daily column as well. . . ."

Not just journalists, but captains of industry too, were amazed by BC's drive. Just two months before Malcolm was born Percy H.

Johnson of New York's Chemical Bank wrote: "Dear Bert, it was a real pleasure for me to see you Saturday; in fact after I come in contact with you I am sufficiently charged with electricity and enthusiasm to run a full week."

BC had the effect of stimulating other people into activity by getting so much effort out of himself; Malcolm does the same. His momentum, his activity, his humor, his idiosyncrasies and even his idiocies are contagious. It runs in the family.

In 1919, BC was on top of the world. His two-year-old magazine, *Forbes,* had a freebooting, freewheeling character previously unknown to business and financial journalism. The issue of *Forbes* that marked Malcolm's birth—while in no way mentioning it—shows what a good time journalistically its thirty-nine-year-old editor-owner was having: "An awful lot of smoke surrounds the Duke-Whelan Tobacco stocks in Wall Street. When it clears, one or two characters may be found badly tarnished. *Forbes* magazine is to start a little investigating."

Plenty of work, plenty of poker on Friday nights, and the other evenings and weekends with the family. On Sunday there might be a good sermon at the Presbyterian Church, and there was plenty of money in the bank.

The arrival of Malcolm was a happy occasion at a happy time, though there was to be the usual unpleasantness over a Forbes child's christening. Scots Presbyterian BC was not resigned to the fact that two of his three children had been baptized Roman Catholic.

BC's respect for ministers of the Presbyterian calling surpassed his respect even for extremely wealthy and paternalistic self-made men. A son a minister. It was his fondest hope, his secret dream.

Malcolm was to be a Catholic.

BC had known religion would be a problem even before he married. Adelaide was but nineteen, and he at thirty-six had wanted to humor her. But he would never forgive her sister Kitty for the way she spirited his firstborn, Bruce, out of the house to the priest before BC could really do anything about it.

Malcolm Stevenson Forbes. Well, there were plenty of Malcolms in Scotland, and certainly on both the Moir and Forbes sides of BC's particular family. The name Malcolm was familiar enough even in the lineage of the clan chief Lord Forbes.

This son one day would offer to buy the twenty-three-bedroom

Castle Forbes, the clan chief's home. He would deal with the clan chief's son, another Malcolm Forbes, on equal terms.

At that juncture, a half century later, the lord of Forbes Castle, and Malcolm, lord of *Forbes* magazine, would meet head on. They were well matched. "Castle Lord" Forbes wanted "£1 million" (about $2.4 million) for the nineteenth-century red-brick castle. "Magazine Lord" Forbes' advisers told him it wasn't worth one-fifth of that. So Malcolm just boarded *The Capitalist Tool* at Aberdeen airport and was flown back down to London. But in a period when $1 million was his favorite purchase price, Malcolm said somewhat ruefully: "I'd have given him a million bucks for it. Just to have it." And, as he later would remark, "It would have been the one thing I'd spent money on since Dad died that would have stopped him spinning in his grave long enough for him to have a big chuckle. He would have been a proud man to see his son own Castle Forbes in Buchan."

Buchan is not the most beautiful corner of Scotland. It is a hard land that was made productive by men, not nature. Two hundred years of careful farm husbandry has turned the bleak, unproductive, windswept hills of the northeast corner of Scotland into grassland and fields famed for its oats and its cattle—the Black Angus.

This is a rural area, and no rural people are so blighted in spirit that they are without humor. But, because they are dour, the humor is deep. It is the quick play on words, or the slow delivery of the punchline.

In the back room of his uncle's smithy there are cards on the table, and beer or Mr. Dewar's whisky from Perth. The chat is light, and gossip continual. It is 1894 and young Bertie Charles Forbes (the locals pronounce it For-bess) has been allowed to take a hand of Napoleon. "Nap," a fast-moving game played at lightning speed for low stakes—for these are poor people—is under way.

Bertie is fourteen, and because it is his birthday, and tomorrow his last day at the little school of Whitehill, he is being regarded as a man. He is no man to look at. Small for his age, with a peaked, boyish face, he really looks no better and no worse than any of the other nine children of Robert Forbes up at Cunnieknowe, the little stone house on the hill above Federate, the ruins of Robert the Bruce's castle.

In the 1890s the Forbeses of Cunnieknowe were a large family in an age of large families—didn't Queen Victoria herself have nine? For the Forbeses there was Agnes Jean, the oldest child, followed by James, Libbie (likely Isabella), Alex, Willie, Bertie, Anna, Georgina (known mainly as Gina), Wilson and Duncan. Going back on the mother's side to the 1860s, George Moir and his wife, Margaret Caulder, had twelve children alive in 1865. These Moirs, Bertie's great grandparents, had fifty-four grandchildren. It is commentary on the perils and practices of rural life that of those fifty-four children six were illegitimate. There were great aunts like Barbara Moir, who died at the age of ninety-nine, and ancestors who farmed for generations in Haddo.

The village of New Deer boasted little by way of amenities, but Robert Forbes' general store and beer shop was one of those amenities. Robert Forbes, who was not from New Deer, had been visiting when he met and won Agnes Moir, the blacksmith's daughter. His justification for selling beer in the front room of Cunnieknowe, the tiny house with its jaw stuck into the cold northeast winds, was that he was augmenting his income as the village tailor.

If anyone ever said anything favorable about Robert Forbes as tailor or beer dispenser, husband or father, no one bothered to write it down. And it wasn't committed to memory or gossip in the oral tradition that has kept much of the New Deer history alive. BC himself made very few references to his father, and perhaps the nearest he ever got to writing something nice about him was, "My father, a country storekeeper and tailor in Aberdeenshire, managed to get along somehow until the family multiplied much faster than his meager earnings did. Long before the tenth came along, the sledding was painfully hard."

If Bertie For-bess looked like a boy, he played Nap like a man. The stakes were only pennies and ha'pennies, but Bertie had a little pile of coppers to his right. His winnings. His mother watched. One more bairn soon to be off to make his way. To Peterhead, as an apprentice bookkeeper. Bertie, so "bricht and busy," and him with his wild ideas.

He was a worker, this Bertie; maybe he would get somewhere. The world was changing. Queen Victoria was getting old; the nineteenth century was getting old with her. And this small boy, fourteen on the 14th of May, 1894, already had vowed he was going to bring the world to his mother's doorstep.

"Dinnae worry, mam, dinnae worry," he had told her, early in the day. "I'll not shame ye. I'm nae gangling loon."

He was such a hard worker.

The year before, Bertie had been up at 5 A.M. each day to clean the mud off the boots of the fine Englishmen who had come to stay at the admiral's house, just below the Mains of Federate. They'd come for the shooting, but any local would have told them there was precious little to shoot at around New Deer and Maud.

What had he done with those first ten shillings, the amount paid him for the season's work? BC's father had sold him "an old pinchbeck [brass] watch," taking all the money from him. It had been a hard lesson.

Young Bertie was most devoted to the kirk, despite the trouble he was always landing himself in. He loved the sermons and hymns. He liked the communion of the spirit that rose up in the air, the feeling of belonging. He had formed deep friendships, with Jimmy Fowlie and with Wilson, his own next younger brother, and would with Mary Jane Grieg if she'd let him. But Mary Jane Grieg was Gavin Grieg's daughter and Bertie was only one more of those Forbeses from Cunnieknowe.

Agnes Moir Forbes felt pained when Bertie confided about his approaches to Mary Jane Grieg. The big dance was coming up, and he had been taking dancing lessons, with "old Skelly" playing the fiddle.

"Will I tak ye tae the dance, Mary Jane Grieg?" he would ask her at the school. But she would not answer. Finally, on the day before the dance, he stopped her in the school yard, just as she was leaving to cross the road to the schoolmaster's house where all the Griegs lived.

"Mary Jane, is it 'aye' or 'nae'? Do I tak ye tae the dance?"

"It's 'nae,' Patchy For-bess, you will not." And with that slight to his ragged clothes—well or badly patched—she threw up her head and walked across the street, very much the headmaster's daughter, into the gray two-story house that came with her father's job.

Bertie Charles Forbes left New Deer for Peterhead on May 16, 1894, from the little spur line station at Maud, the village where he so regularly went to the kirk. He was off to the unknown—twenty-five miles away.

It was not a total leap into the dark. Older brother Alex, who was to encourage Bertie constantly to get ahead in those Peterhead days, was working already in Peterhead as a clerk.

Peterhead was a shipping and fishing port. The landlady was a drunkard; the lodgers ranged from fishing-boat hands and dock workers to casual laborers. Forty years later Bertie would write that each night he had to go to bed fearing for his life, and was always surprised to wake up alive in the morning.

Headmaster Grieg watched out for job opportunities for all his students. It was Grieg who had learned of the clerical vacancy in a commercial office in Peterhead and recommended young Bertie to try for it.

The small village boy had achieved what was known as the "merit certificate" when he was thirteen, gained the County Council certificate for agriculture, and left school after the eighth grade.

Bertie was to learn bookkeeping. He wrote in the big round hand so much prized in those pre-typewriter days, and so much praised in the lyrics of *H.M.S. Pinafore.*

Whenever he could afford the sixpenny train fare back to New Deer, Bertie would get home at the weekend. One of the duties Bertie had if he went home was to go and visit Gavin Grieg, who would invariably ask Bertie to take his latest article in to Alex Watt at the Buchan *Observer*, published at the Peterhead *Sentinel* newspaper office. Bertie had very little idea of what went on in a newspaper office, but the idea of working in one intrigued him if it had something to do with writing—after all Mr. Grieg was a writer, and had said nice words about Bertie's compositions.

And the word *composition* was to lead Bertie into quite a mix-up as a fourteen-year-old boy.

After working as a bookkeeper for several months, Bertie applied to the Peterhead *Sentinel* for a job.

"I had never been inside a newspaper office before; entirely ignorant of the nature of work," he wrote at age seventeen. "Thought it probably something like clerical work." He was offered a job. "With great gladness in my heart, I signed an agreement to serve an apprenticeship of seven years, starting at 3 shillings [75 cents] a week and advancing by a shilling each year. A rather stiff contract!

"And even worse than it seemed. For I soon discovered that what I had agreed to become was not a reporter, but a compositor." In his innocence, Bertie had thought that being a compositor meant that he would in some way "compose," or write "compositions."

"I soon discovered that what I had agreed to become meant that I was to stand in front of cases of type, day after day, month after month for seven years, doing nothing but pick up one metallic letter at a time, and place it in a 'stick,' the most mechanical of mechanical operations, calling for no originality, no creativity, no writing—I felt as if I had been sentenced to seven years penal servitude."

It was at that point, faced with the prospect of being "second man," when what he most wanted to be was a "foreman," that Bertie displayed the originality and "stick-to-itiveness" that were to mark his rapid progress over the next twenty-five years. It is a prerequisite to working as a newspaper reporter in Britain to master shorthand. That requirement holds as true today as it did eighty years ago in the Peterhead *Sentinel.*

"What I told myself was, 'I'll make them want to make me a reporter.' " He later wrote:

> Shorthand: attended shorthand classes in evening conducted by Mr. T. W. Grant under auspices of Feuars' Mangers. [The Feuars were the town council of Peterhead.] Began in junior class, studied hard, entered senior class same session, and gained third prize—first for 80 words per minute. Value of prize, 1 pound, 5 shillings.

That prize, $6.25, was equal to more than two months' income for Bertie.

It was T. W. Grant, the municipal shorthand teacher, who directed Bertie toward his first reporter's job. There was an advertisement in the Aberdeen paper "calling for a young man, able to write shorthand, to learn reporting." Grant sent BC the advertisement, and Bertie wrote to the paper, the Dundee *Courier.*

"I applied, and a tall, fine looking, beautifully groomed representative came to size me up. What he discovered was a 16-year-old kid, about 4 feet nothing in height, wearing short trousers, and sporting a printer's apron bearing many a scar of war. However he agreed to give me a job—a change in ownership having abrogated my seven year contract."

Alas, a few days later the beautifully groomed young man wrote that the position was not to be filled just then, but that, as he had engaged Bertie, the paper was willing to employ him at what seemed to Bertie to be "the far distant city of Perth." The pay was to be $2.50 a week. "I accepted the job, not without very grave misgivings as to how I was to make out financially. I had saved $4.00, but felt this was not quite enough to insure me against being thrown into the street."

The senior reporter in Perth for the Dundee *Courier and Weekly News* was one William Watson. Watson was at the station to welcome Bertie to Perth. It was practically the only kindly act young Bertie was to experience at the hands of the able, but idle, Watson.

"He greeted me at the station and explained he had been unable to find any habitable place at a figure I could pay; but that he had located a garret in a tenement house where I could perhaps contrive to stay until I found something better."

The two of them carried and dragged his battered trunk across the city until they got to the tenement. Bertie was stunned by his accommodation.

"There was nothing in the garret save one rusty iron bed and two empty boxes. Nothing more! The roof sloped so sharply that I could stand erect only alongside my bed"—and this was a boy of four feet nine. "By climbing upon one of the empty boxes I could pop my head through the skylight; but the only scenery within view was roofs of houses. The landlady kept other boarders; but they dined in the dining room, while I was not permitted to get farther than the kitchen, where I literally fed on scraps that came from the other boarders' table.

"Work! I started at 9 in the morning, and was lucky if once a week I got home before midnight. My superior was very able, but after teaching me the ropes for a few weeks he used to stay at home most of the day, come in after dinner to look over what I had done, and then send me scurrying all over the city to interview people, to report meetings, to do the rounds of the hospitals, police officers, etc., etc. I had won medals as a runner but my legs ached many and many a night. Worst of all, he never spoke one encouraging word to me, but berated me unmercifully several times a week, with or without cause. He made me feel that I might be dismissed any day, notwithstanding all the work I was doing.

"Instead, on my first visit to the head office of the newspaper, I received a joyous surprise. I first discovered that my large, round, easily read schoolboy handwriting had made a hit with the chief subeditor, an old man whose eyesight was poor. While I was 'chinning' with the editor of the *Weekly,* published by the concern, he mentioned a 'great descriptive story' that my boss had written of an epochal long distance swimming feat (it was a famous swim across the river Tay)."

When BC modestly revealed that *he* had written the account of the Tay River swim, that *he* had reported the recent murder trial and that *he* had written the descriptive pieces regarding the visit of Queen Victoria, the Dundee editor told him: "You just put up with all you have to stand for a little while longer, and we'll soon give you a district of your own."

And so at the age of seventeen, having worked as a newspaper reporter for only six months, Bertie Charles Forbes was sent to Brechin as the senior reporter for the district. He had a completely free hand and, as an assistant, cousin Charlie Moir, also age seventeen. His ten shillings a week wage as a "junior" at Perth was doubled to one pound.

To work for the Dundee newspapers was to be caught up in all that was going on in the Empire (India, South Africa and Canada) and all that had gone on in the building of the great American railroads.

In the 1870s, it was Scottish money, much Dundee money among it, that had underwritten the railway expansion of the United States.

Bertie's world was expanding outside the newspaper, too. He played cards at every opportunity, but also had taken up golf. He demonstrated the same determination in chasing the "wee ball" as he exhibited chasing stories. He was good at both.

He began courting. She was a Forbes—one of many Forbeses that were no relation—living a quiet country life in a rural village in Montrose.

Bertie was transferred to Dundee. The light of his life, Miss Forbes, was far away. "She married a fellow nearer at hand—and, doubtless, nearer her heart. Whereupon I did what any self-respecting youth in his 21st year would naturally do. I shook the dust of Scotland off my feet, and sailed for the remotest corner of the world I could think of, South Africa, then in the close of the Boer War, where I figured I could find enough excitement to assuage my black, black woe."

If BC, writing twenty years later in the *American* magazine made light of this, in reality his personal world was every bit as black at that time as he suggested. He took with him to South Africa his shorthand notebook. Pasted inside the front cover was a picture of Andrew Carnegie.

Pasted inside the rear cover was this:

BE SOMETHING

Be something in this living age
And prove your right to be
A light upon some darkened page,
A pilot on some sea.
Find out the place where you may stand,
Beneath some burden low;
Take up the task with willing hand,
Be something, somewhere now!

Be something in this throbbing day
Of busy hands and feet,
A spring besides some dusty way,
A shadow from the heat.
Be found upon the workmen's role;
Go sow, go reap, or plow;
Bent to the task with heart and soul,
Be something, somewhere now!

South Africa in 1901 was like the 1880s in the U.S. wild West with exploiters, entrepreneurs and adventurers. In South Africa expatriates from England and Scotland had followed the missionaries into the native territories. The search for the sources of the Nile and the Niger had attracted great attention. Southern Africa was a strategic station on the sea route to India, an area of cheap raw material, which inspired colonial-minded European nations to seek an ever-greater presence there.

The determination of Britain, under Joseph Chamberlain, to wrest South Africa from the Boers and place it in British hands precipitated the Boer War in 1899. It was at first a popular war against "Johnny Boer," but mounting casualties and an increasing stalemate—mixed with the ability of the daring Boer to take advantage of the countryside as a born guerrilla soldier—made the war unpopular back in Britain.

Not of course that there weren't heroes. And two of the greatest emerging heroes were journalists, Winston Churchill and an imaginative young man named Edgar Wallace.

Bertie always had liked aphorisms. South Africa gave him a new one: "Act in haste, repent at leisure." He had several weeks of enforced leisure in his frantic job searches in the Port Elizabeth area of the then booming—but still at war—South African province.

"I certainly encountered enough difficulties to keep my mind and legs busy. I applied for more than 20 jobs, but could land nothing. The best available was a position as stenographer and typist. I wasn't a typist." That may seem strange, but in 1900 typewriters were a rarity even in the major London newsrooms.

"I promptly went to a typewriting school for two days, and then calmly accepted the position in that capacity with the government railroads.

"Finding that I could take shorthand as fast as he cared to talk, the chief clerk dictated to me his longest communications. Somehow I managed to scramble through, although I did have a cold sweat when I came to the end of the ribbon and couldn't for the life of me discover how to make it crawl the other way. On the pretence that something had gone wrong with the machine, I got another clerk to look it over; he promptly detected the source of the problem, and I discovered how to do the trick."

Months later he landed his first South African newspaper position, and that a good one with the Natal *Mercury*. It was February, 1902. Those seven months of struggle had done nothing to ease young BC's sense of insecurity. His dwindling cash reserves had eaten into his only alternative to job security, enough money to live on. So broke was he that, when his cousin Dora, his only relative in South Africa, was married in Cape Province, the best he could afford was a pair of small decorated tin plaques. Dora hung them on the wall proudly and kept them there for the next fifty years. Indeed, she wrote to him five decades later, "My dear cousin Bertie, they've weathered well. I was amazed that you were able to purchase them at the time. You left the price on them. One shilling and 6 pence."

To which Bertie wrote back, "Cousin Dora, I am indeed surprised, I didn't think at that time in my life I had one shilling and 6 pence left."

Young BC knew the key to his personal success. Once installed at the Natal *Mercury*, pen and shorthand notebook in hand, he quickly reverted to his normal role of superachiever. After only a few weeks he was back into his favorite role, relieving the principal "leader" writer. (In Britain and its colonies the leader is the editorial column. It comes from the phrase "the leading columns.")

When, for example, Cecil Rhodes' will was made public, it was Bertie who wrote in the *Mercury*, "Surely, a nobler document was never penned than that which lays bare the inmost soul of Cecil John Rhodes. . . . Great was he in lifetime; greater still is he in death. He was not perfect; no man born of the earth ever was."

The closing lines of Rhodes' will were on protecting the morals of young men—straight out of the Golden Rule book that Bertie himself lived by: the pure capitalist work ethic. For many, many young men it worked.

It worked for Edgar Wallace, the illegitimate child of a not very successful actress. Wallace had enlisted in the British army medical corps and, while in South Africa, tried his hand first at writing verse and then writing reports for local newspapers. He gradually earned sufficient money to buy himself out of the army, a practice still available in the British military to this day.

Daring journalistic enterprise brought Wallace to the attention of the London *Daily Mail*. Wallace, the *Mail*'s man in South Africa, scooped the world on the Boer War's end.

Wallace had soldier friends on duty at Vereeniging, where the Boers and the British generals were to decide armistice terms. The generals, behaving as they always do, had insisted that no reporters be allowed within a quarter mile of the perimeter of the camp's fence. But the generals had reckoned without Wallace. As his biographer tells it, Wallace arranged a handkerchief code with a friend on guard duty. During the course of the day, the friend would blow his nose with a blue handkerchief (convention moving satisfactorily toward peace) or red (a hitch has occurred) or white (peace is absolutely assured).

All Wallace had to do was watch. The day came when the guardsman pulled out the white handkerchief instead of the blue one. Ignoring military censorship, Wallace immediately cabled the *Daily Mail* in London, and gave the world a major example of how to scoop the opposition.

In 1902 H. Freeman Cohen, an entrepreneurial South African mine promoter, went into the newspaper business. When peace came Freeman Cohen bought the Johannesburg *Standard and Diggers' News*, a practically defunct newspaper, and brought it back to life as the now famous Rand *Daily Mail*.

Wallace, a journalist-hero, was offered the editorship at £2,000 a year (then about $10,000, today probably worth $50,000 to $80,000)—a remarkable jump from the $125 a week that he had been earning as the London *Daily Mail* correspondent.

Wallace recruited Bertie Forbes as the number-two senior reporter.

For Bertie Johannesburg was heady stuff indeed.

Edgar Wallace, with his wide-brimmed hat, his sporty clothes, his yellow gloves and his gold-topped cane, plus his sterling reputation as the world's most enterprising reporter, made quite an impression on the then still very impressionable Bertie. A member of the Japanese royal family made a different type of impression:

In 1903, "I boldly decided to attempt to interview a visiting member of the Japanese royal family. 'Interviewing' in those far off places was hardly known. I finally was told to go to a certain hotel room. When I knocked, a voice called, 'Come in.' But, startled, I drew back on beholding the exalted personage standing stark naked in a wash tub. Bowing low, his highness insisted I enter.

"And I obtained an exclusive story from him, while he, most unconcernedly, finished his bath." As Bertie was to say thirty years later, "the experience caused me to reflect that, after all, there was little difference between the humblest and highest, and that I would never thereafter hesitate to approach anyone, no matter how exalted."

BC had a better than average income, a little of which he spent, a small amount of which he risked at cards, but most of which he saved.

But Edgar Wallace's lifestyle—sustained by his ability to borrow —was troubling the Rand *Daily Mail* management, that is, H. Freeman Cohen. Wallace believed money could always be borrowed. As Wallace's biographer Margaret Lane wrote, "a whispered tip on the gold market, a lucky day at the races, and all could be retrieved. The money would be paid back, and there would be chicken and champagne at the bungalow and a box at the theatre." Worse than that, Wallace was becoming filled with a sense of his own importance:

> Cohen, both as an influential financier and the proprietor of the Rand *Daily Mail*, reserved the right to direct the paper on important matters of policy. It was in the summer of 1903, he found himself in surprising conflict with an obstinate editor. It was on a matter of some importance to Cohen, for he had personally guaranteed £250,000 toward a government loan for the development of certain gold blasting. . . .
> . . . Cohen not unnaturally refused to be argued down; Edgar, with nothing to lose but his opinion of his own infallibility, chose the wrong moment to be obdurate, the quarrel conducted behind closed doors, sent a tremor of rumor and alarm through the whole building. Nobody knew with certainty what was happening, but when Edgar, pale almost to the point of phosphorescence, stalked into the office . . . scrawled "Edgar Wallace: finis!" on his blotting pad, there was no longer any doubt as to who had the final word in the argument.

Instead of allowing Wallace to commit suicide, as he was suggesting he might as he went around the newsroom saying farewell, a few members of the staff—probably Bertie among them—"led him down the dusty ladderway and along the streets to Heath's Hotel, where there was a last lugubrious round of farewell drinks." Several of his employees then took him as far as his home. Surely as teetotal Bertie watched the reeling, stunned Wallace making his way from fame into the oblivion of his little bungalow the lesson was not lost on him.

Even before the Wallace fiasco, Bertie had resolved that Johannesburg, "a mining town which, for all its wealth, had the narrow mentality of a suburban parish," was no place for a twenty-three-year-old journalist who was heading for the top.

"I was now drawing a rather large salary, was allowed to come and go as I pleased, and altogether had a pleasant, easy time. But I said to myself: 'Young fellow, this isn't the right kind of life for a youngster of less than twenty-four. You need to be bumped and buffeted about a whole lot more.' "

So in 1904 he announced his decision to move on again. This time, though, he had a cool head, several thousand dollars, and a plan. His plan simply was first to go home and then on to the United States.

What was it Bertie was seeking? He already knew. The first inklings had come back in Dundee. Business news, international finance, entrepreneurship had attracted Bertie from the first. He was learning how to make money, he was meeting men who knew how to make more.

It had been a long three years. He had started with nothing and once again built himself up to a position of having money in his pocket, his reputation enhanced even further than it had been in his own corner of Scotland.

3

The Immigrant

Dear Mr. Forbes:

Won't you kindly lay out the financial pages exactly as you would have them if you had full authority in the matter and if you want to produce the best financial pages in town? I don't think we have sufficiently important quotations, and I don't think we cover quite enough departments in sufficient detail to make a complete and fully authoritative financial page, and further than that I think we ought to cover prod`ice quite fully in order to make the paper valuable in the country as well as in the city.

There are a great many things in other papers we do not have. Personally, I don't know which of those are valuable or whether all of them are valuable or not. But I know that you can decide all of those matters, and I wish you would kindly lay out two financial pages to be made up mainly of departmental matters of the kind to compel the interest and satisfy the demands of the business community.

Sincerely:
W.R. Hearst
San Simeon

Letter to B. C. Forbes,
Business Editor,
New York *American*
1911

In the middle of August, 1904, Bertie Charles Forbes, late of South Africa and earlier of New Deer, Aberdeenshire, set sail for the United States. First class. One thing Bertie had learned: to be at the top you have to mix with people who are.

The first weekend in New York, Bertie did what any European in the city for the first time does: he spent a lot of time trying not to look impressed. The bustle of the Friday-afternoon arrival, the Saturday filled with shoppers, the traffic, the buildings, the people scurrying to and fro. The majestic townhouses near the business districts, the huge, wide sweep of Fifth Avenue with its marvelous homes. The elegant shops, the obvious wealth, and, for it never escaped his eye, the obvious poverty, too. Always one to enjoy a good sermon, on Sunday he tried a local Presbyterian church.

Full of hope on Monday morning, September 5, 1904, Bertie set off. He sent up his card to editors. Twice he talked to an editor's secretary; otherwise he never got past the front office. The two-year-old Rand *Daily Mail* in far-off South Africa meant nothing to these important New York editors. A list of credentials sent up by a miniature Scotsman in loud clothes, a fellow who said he was twenty-four and looked not a day over eighteen, was a poor risk indeed.

One Scots journalist took him aside long enough to tell him: "For God's sake, mon, get out of those clothes and into something American." Bertie was stunned. From being a fashion plate in South Africa modeled on Edgar Wallace himself, and a sporty-looking character on his trip back home, he had sunk to looking like a visiting foreigner, and with his gold-topped cane, his funny accent, was doing himself more harm than good. On the Friday morning when he next appeared at the front counter of an editorial office, he was wearing a standard businessman's pinstriped trousers and a black morning coat. But so severe had been that initial sartorial shock that twenty years after people had stopped wearing pinstriped trousers and morning coats to the office, Bertie would still be wearing his.

Friday brought no work. September brought no work.

He wrote a long cheerful letter to George Adamson back at the Rand *Daily Mail* in Johannesburg. He was seeing New York and enjoying it but was thinking of not staying on to get a job. Had Adamson anything particularly attractive to offer him?

Bertie couldn't even get into a good poker game. For want of anything better to do some evenings, he was reduced to sitting in the boardinghouse at Bath Beach arduously writing a novel, part adventure story, part love story. It was never completed.

"Hey, young man, do you want to caddy a round?" It was a voice with a Scots burr to it. The club pro made the introductions after Bertie had risen to his feet from his bench outside the Field and

Marine clubhouse. There were several men in plus fours, as Bertie himself was, but far from thinking he was waiting for a game, they thought he was waiting for a caddying job. That was one of the disadvantages of looking so young and being so short.

"Aye, that I do," said Bertie, getting up, "I'll take yours, sir." Enjoying the joke, Bertie willingly shouldered the leather bag of clubs and started off toward the first tee. As the game developed so did the conversation between the caddy and the golfer. They exchanged mutual information about names and birthplaces. Yes, they were fellow Scots. Bertie's tale began to unfold. The golfer became more interested in the tale and less interested in the golf. When Bertie reached the point of explaining he was trying to get a job on one of the leading financial newspapers, the golfer said, "Mr. Forbes, you'll do me the honor of allowing me to send a note to my friend Doddsworth at the *Journal of Commerce*. He's a Scotsman just like ourselves."

The *Journal of Commerce and Commercial Bulletin* of 17 and 19 Beaver Street and 64 New Street, New York, was indeed a leading paper of the day. Bertie could not believe his luck. This was the one chance he needed, the only chance he would ask for. John W. Doddsworth, managing editor, agreed to see Bertie on Monday, October 3, 1904. Bertie, of course, had already tried to get an interview with the editor of the *Journal of Commerce*. This time it was different.

Doddsworth came straight to the point: "Why should I hire a man with absolutely no experience in financial journalism? Why should I hire someone who does not know the difference between Wall Street and Broadway?"

"Because, sir," answered Bertie, "I'll work for nothing."

No editor could refuse such an offer. But Doddsworth said nothing to Bertie except, "Very well, Mr. Forbes, we'll see." Two days later the letter arrived.

Dear Sir:
   Will you kindly report at this office Friday morning with a view of making a trial start. Should this prove satisfactory, we shall be glad to make a permanent engagement with you.
                        Very truly yours, John W. Doddsworth.

By Friday of the following week he was hired. Fifteen dollars a week and a job on the *Journal of Commerce*. A start at long last, but what a start! "I was sentenced to cover the dry-goods market as assistant to the dry-goods editor. Dry-goods! They were well named. I quickly discovered I hated the work, but I found that even dry-goods reporting could be made tolerable by striking out on a new track.

"For illustration: I had to write on raw silk. The custom had been for the newspaper to 'accept' current prices from importers. Importers always named prices well above the actual selling figures. They did this so that they could show customers quotations in the authoritative 'Journal of Commerce,' and then tell the customer that, as a special favor, they would cut the rate substantially.

"I interviewed the leading buyers as well as the sellers, ferreted out the actual prices current, and printed them. This raised a storm. Importers abused me for not having published the figures they gave me, and some even refused to see me again. Protests were made over my head. However, both sellers and buyers began to take an interest such as they never had taken before in these reports; and by-and-by the gentlemen who had quarreled with me eagerly invited me to come to see them regularly, even showing me their books to convince me that they were no longer trying to induce me to publish incorrect quotations."

Bertie was at it again. He'd been allowed to put his foot on the bottom rung of the ladder and he was climbing up faster than a monkey. Always the gambler, Bertie Charles now decided on the very biggest gamble he had taken thus far. He knew that the big financial men of the day were fond of the old Waldorf Astoria— where the Empire State Building now stands. Sometimes they would lunch there, but certainly in an evening that's where they would gather to discuss the affairs of the day over a few drinks. Bertie knew that he looked like one of their "fifteen dollar a week clerks," but he knew too how to gain acceptance of sorts. Still with some money in the bank, and $15 a week in his pocket, he moved from his $10-a-week boarding house in Brooklyn to a room in the Waldorf Astoria that cost him more than he was earning.

Many businessmen used the Waldorf Astoria for an overnight stay if they decided not to go to their homes out in suburban New York, New Jersey or Connecticut. Bertie would spend a lot of time circulating in the evening, linking three things together—that he lived in the Waldorf Astoria, that he was from the *Journal of Commerce,* and that he held a very responsible position. The sort of thrift that had enabled him to save several thousand dollars in South Africa he now employed to help balance his budget: lunch was a ten-cent sandwich. When he was given carfare by the *Journal of Commerce* to travel around the city, he would spend most of his lunch hour walking in order to save that nickel.

In franker moments years later BC acknowledged that the move to the Waldorf did not help as much as he had hoped. But it wasn't a bad thing to have done. And he was developing a technique which was not common in the financial journalism of the day. Instead of concentrating just on business details, he was concentrating, too, on the personalities. His instincts were absolutely correct. People wanted to read about people.

The January 25, 1902, Burns Society dinner, with the McClelland family, John Reed, John Ford and others, was the first time— after being in New York for four months—that Bertie felt "at home." McClelland had invited Bertie to his home, and the company of fellow Scots on Burns night made the welcome complete.

"Six months after landing, my old South Africa paper wrote, asking if I would become their London correspondent, if certain proposed readjustments were carried through. The editor of the 'Journal of Commerce,' curiously enough, happened just then to ask me whether I intended to stay permanently in this country and with them. I blurted out the truth—that I have a letter in my pocket about going to London."

Had it not been for the Burns Society of New York and the McClelland household, there is every likelihood that Bertie would have taken the Rand *Daily Mail* job in London. It was prestigious and it was very well paid. The salary compared very favorably with the $20 a week Bertie was now getting at the *Journal of Commerce.*

Doddsworth, realizing he had a good man, asked what Bertie wanted in order to stay with the paper. BC had no doubts whatsoever. He wanted to be financial editor. Doddsworth offered Bertie the position if first he would serve a period as assistant financial editor. He agreed.

Bertie knew how to get the type of story that other financial journalists were missing. He developed a range of contacts among the biggest names in finance on Wall Street. He persuaded them to see him, assured them that he would not break their confidences, and they in turn were happy to feel that they were playing *éminence grise* to this able newspaperman. It was while he was assistant financial editor that Bertie "pondered how I could do more than the job called for. I decided to supplement my regular work with a daily column of notes, which I headed "Fact and Comment.'"

Bertie Charles had been in the United States for a few years when the editor of the *Commercial and Financial Chronicle* wrote:

> The man who writes our weekly review of the foreign exchange and money market is sick. We understand that you have charge of these markets in the "Journal of Commerce." Could you do this work for us while our man is away? If yes, would you please call to see Mr. Seibert regarding the matter tomorrow? If unable or unwilling, will you be good enough to call up Mr. Seibert on the telephone on receipt of this letter and advise us to the effect?

Was he willing and able? As always.

"Then (in 1911) a curious thing happened," wrote Bertie. "I received a telephone message from the editor-in-chief of another New York morning newspaper. When I called, almost his first remark was: 'We are quite sure you are the man we want because we picked you in two places. We decided that we wanted either the man who was writing the "Journal of Commerce" stuff or the fellow who was writing for the "Chronicle." We discovered he was the same chap.'"

William Randolph Hearst had decided that the New York *American,* his major New York outlet, needed good financial pages. The way to get good financial pages was to find the best man doing the job, and pay him enough to attract him.

On the New York *American,* with his large daily audience, Bertie experienced something he had not known before: power.

A mere paragraph in his column could have the New York Stock Exchange offering its services, or bankers telling him to be careful about flexing his muscle. Leading financiers and businessmen were writing to Bertie daily to offer him counsel and encouragement. They saw him performing a great service, as indeed he was.

For one thing, he was possibly the only person then writing in the popular press to promote the notion that harmony could exist between employer and workers. He had always held that the only form of employer worthy of the name was one who treated his employees fairly. Woe betide any vicious employer who came to

Bertie's notice. He lashed into them unmercifully—as when he heard the tale of railroad employees working seven days a week.

And Bertie was sound. His editorials in the *Commercial and Financial Chronicle* "were as heavy and as solid as the most conservative reader could desire."

One of the pleasures his increased salary allowed him was more frequent poker games. He had moved out of the Waldorf Astoria and back to friendly lodgings in Brooklyn, lodgings where a poker game once or twice weekly was the norm.

He was always an extremely serious gambler. He never played in jest. He played with the same intensity whether the game was half-penny Nap with his mother during a visit to Glasgow, or $5 pots in Brooklyn.

Saturday-night poker sessions in Brooklyn included players such as Mr. Bruce, the neighborhood pharmacist. Frequently enough, Mrs. Bruce would sit in on the games, too. She was a flaming-red-haired Irish beauty. Mr. Bruce was her third husband. She had a quick tongue, a good sense of humor, and something else that had really caught Bertie's eye, a daughter by a previous marriage, Adelaide.

Adelaide had all the beauty of her mother and the freshness of youth. She was a young eighteen, but poised and with a good sense of presence. Bertie, at the age of thirty-four, was, at long last, falling in love again.

Love was not slowing down the writer in him. He had expanded his range of publications. He now was writing for the *Hearst* Magazine. In September, 1914, appeared an article, "The Criminal Railroads," by B. C. Forbes, with a big illustration of Uncle Sam baring the crooked New Haven Railroad under a spotlight highlighting the word "publicity." This was the role of the press, and this was the role of its rapidly rising star, B. C. Forbes: to clean up the worst abuses in the glare of whatever publicity he could generate.

Bertie was considering the possibility of branching out for himself in some way, perhaps by starting his own magazine. There was plenty of money in the bank—he was saving thousands, and investing a little of it very judiciously.

He and Adelaide were married the following year in the sacristy of Our Lady of Angels Church, Bay Ridge, Brooklyn. They could not be married at the main altar because Bertie was not a Catholic.

In the 11 years since he had arrived in the United States, BC had gained a tremendous personal reputation. As an article in *National Magazine* in 1922 later saw it, what BC had done on the New York *American* was to make the "financial pages of the New York American and Hearst papers as much sought as the sports page . . . the magnet attracting real advertisers and readers for those papers." That was a good summary of Bertie's value to Hearst. Forbes was the first popularizer of business. He had a feel for the people who were businessmen. He had an ability to ferret out business news and a facility for turning that dry news into short articles and entertaining epigrams, for producing interviews that showed how the wealthy or the great achieve their wealth and/or their greatness. "He is an ardent enthusiast for justness and fairness. He studies people as he mingles among them and believes in rewarding merit," said *National Magazine*. Steel baron Charles M. Schwab called BC "the great humanizer of business."

If BC's ability to thrust and to cut was ferocious, so was his ability to curry favor and to speak favorably of those successful men he admired. He did more than that. He would send his articles on major business personalities of the day to those personalities when writing a favorable story about them. He had done this when writing for Hearst magazines; he was to do it for his own magazine. Was it unethical? Was he selling out? Was this just a way of ensuring plenty of good, happy advertising for a magazine he might launch? Bertie Forbes' journalistic habits can be judged only in their time.

In the period before and during World War I, it was not unusual or even surprising that Bertie would do as he did. He saw himself as an apologist for big business well run. Did he have qualms about touting the merits of men who were self-made? Not if they stuck to just treatment of their employees.

Bertie Forbes, in 1916, had decided to start a magazine. It would be called *Doers and Doings* and the title would adequately reflect the purpose of such a publication. Its subscribers would be those who wanted to succeed in business, in investment, in life: the salesmen and the junior executives, the young men seeking a way to the top. He would condemn the unworthy, those who did not stick to the Golden Rule. He would willingly expose insider dealing and corruption wherever he found it.

He decided to borrow money in order to have a substantial

amount to fall back on should he need it. The men he touched for loans were all men of business he had written about over the years —men he knew quite well on a personal-acquaintance basis, such as the banker Jacob H. Schiff and the industrialist Henry C. Frick.

BC would tell a story against himself about borrowing money from Frick. The industrialist kept two bank accounts: his business account and a separate account for his charities. On the checks he wrote from that second account was a likeness of a daughter Frick had lost. BC, in 1916, had been to visit Frick at his New York City mansion—which now houses the Frick art collection—seeking Frick's support for the magazine venture. "As soon as the butler closed the door behind me," Forbes related, "I stood on the steps and opened the check. It's hard to tell you how disappointed and chagrined I was to find the check bore a picture of his beloved child. For a moment—fleeting, I assure you—I was tempted to return it then and there. Later on I had a particular happiness in being able to repay the loan—with interest."

Many of the men Bertie borrowed money from for the launching of the magazine were featured in his book *Fifty Men Who Are Making America.* With what degree of independence could Bertie write if they were involved in shady practices or insider dealings?

Bertie had to have enough money to pay wages and printing costs, to advertise and circularize, as well as to keep himself and his family living in the style to which he had become accustomed. His contribution to the magazine was to be his energy—his own savings he regarded as the property of his private world, his home, hearth and family.

The magazine was to be launched as a business proposition, a venture to stand on its own two feet. But the magazine was not going to be called *Doers and Doings,* after all. Bertie was anxious that Walter Drey, the young general manager of *The Magazine of Wall Street,* join him in his venture. Drey was agreeable but only on condition that the magazine carry Forbes' name. Drey knew advertising, and he knew that the Forbes name was BC's biggest asset. He saw the value in cashing in on the fact that for five years Forbes had been the most-read financial writer in the United States.

Bertie agreed to the change. The magazine was about to be born. So was a second son. Duncan arrived in August. The magazine came next, on September 15, 1917.

It was Bertie's boast that, even with a growing family to care for, in order to launch *Forbes* magazine he gave up a salary better than the governor of New York or any member of President Woodrow Wilson's cabinet. The governor of New York at that time was earning $10,000 a year; David F. Houston, Secretary of Agriculture, was receiving $12,000 a year.

Hearst, as was his style, had treated Bertie handsomely in the years immediately preceding his decision to leave the Hearst family. Bertie may have been earning $10,000 a year as early as 1914. In addition to this, Bertie had been writing regularly for other magazines and journals, which means that, in 1976 terms, at the time B. C. Forbes gave up his job to start his magazine he had an income equivalent to a modern spending power of perhaps $100,000 a year. No minor sacrifice.

Forbes magazine applied for entry as second-class mail matter at the post office in New York. "Single copies each priced 15 cents, published every two weeks." With a solid, pillared arch design for its cover, all type and no illustration, *"Forbes* Magazine, devoted to doers and doings," was launched.

4

The Forbeses of *Forbes*

"Don't you sometimes make your character sketches a little bit too favorable?" a very prominent financier once asked me. "Perhaps I do," I replied: "but I have learned by experience this curious fact: often after I have written a long article upon a man's career, including generous references to his philanthropies, it has been followed by some very substantial charitable act on his part. Give a man full credit for being liberally and unselfishly inclined, and the tendency is for him to try to live up to his reputation."

B. C. Forbes
in the first issue of
Forbes magazine
September 15, 1917

Above the title of his first *Forbes* 'Fact and Comment' page BC quoted the Bible: "With all thy getting get understanding." But he attributed it to Robert Burns, as he did a companion quote that had been written by Oliver Goldsmith. BC dropped the second quote in the second issue of *Forbes*, commenting that it was good enough to have been written by Burns.)

Below the "Fact and Comment" title, BC initiated *Forbes* magazine by declaring that "business was originated to produce happiness, not to pile up millions."

BC was soon interspersing the editorials with little lines of wisdom: "Learn today and you'll earn tomorrow. Happily inexpensive joys usually are the best. If you must 'get mad,' get mad at yourself."

If the results were slightly homespun, it was because Bertie was putting out the sort of magazine *he* wanted. He hoped the potential subscribers liked what he liked—because he was writing two-thirds of the early issues himself. It was a level of output he maintained for years.

In addition to three Fact and Comment pages, he wrote a by-lined article, "Keys to Unlock the Door of Success," which began, "Mediocre men wait for opportunity, able men seek opportunity, the strongest men make opportunity," and ended with, "Opportunity can be spelt with four letters. But these letters are not l-u-c-k. They are w-o-r-k."

The first issue of *Forbes* magazine asked:

> Who is America's best employer? Who is the best, the most considerate, the most stimulating employer in the United States? Forbes Magazine is profoundly convinced that the relations between employees and employers are to become the most vital question of all after the war.
>
> As a first step in this movement for the promotion of better understanding and more friendly feeling between employers and their workers, this magazine is offering $1,000 in prizes for the most worth-while answers to the question: "Who Is The Best Employer in America?"

One answer to that question was "B. F. Goodrich Co," written by one of the employees, L. M. Barton, an article which by modern standards would be considered self-serving.

"How Forbes Gets Big Men to Talk"—an article with no byline, but written by BC, was spread over two pages.

The most pungent article in the issue was Bertie's "High-Placed Misfits. George Jay Gould, the Nicholas Romanoff of American Finance. The Tragic Story of How the Gould 'Empire,' the Greatest Patrimony Ever Left a Young American, Has Been Dissipated."

BC castigated George Jay Gould for extravagance and lack of ability: "George Gould betrayed his most fatal weakness—his narrowness of vision, his unreasoning jealousy, his chronic suspicion, his distrust of both subordinates and rivals. He would neither run his properties himself nor give others freedom and authority to do so."

Using two thousand carefully chosen words, B. C. Forbes set the tone of *Forbes* stories for sixty years to come: the sharp attack, supported by some carefully marshaled facts, the quick aside to sketch in an element of the subject's character, the anecdote or piece of physical description to give the reader an insight into the manner or bearing of the subject. The feisty, aggressive, acidic *Forbes* story had come into its own.

No matter what the intervening years were to bring—and some
of them were to bring near disaster—the basic element of the *Forbes*
story at its best was the kind of writing that BC employed in his
Gould piece. What he did with *Forbes* magazine was to take what
previously had been handled in a ponderous manner and make it
intelligible to the ordinary reader. He did with financial news what
Time and *Newsweek* later did with the political news: told the story
through the personalities of the day.

At home in Englewood, as the new magazine was launched, was
BC's one-year-old son, Bruce Charles. And on page 24 of the first
issue of *Forbes* magazine was a short story entitled "The Hero of
Poverty Flats, by Bruce Charles Pere." The editor's note said: "This
story introduces to the public a new writer of fiction." Fiction indeed.
B. C. Forbes' short story, about the hero of Poverty Flats, a maudlin
hero who does well from nothing, filled two more pages of the magazine.

The reader was treated to "Woman in Business, Her Life in
Business and Her Place in the Business. Her Problems, Her Points of
View."

BC didn't miss a trick. The women's section was six pages of the
magazine.

The several pages of the women's section devoted to the trans-
formation wrought in the life of the business girl through the advent
of adding machines, and the need to train women to handle business
machines, surely was not an article to disenchant J. H. Patterson's
National Cash Register Company, or such other potential advertisers
as International Business Machines.

At the back of the book, to which many of the stories had jumped
for more space, BC wrote a "Business, Financial Forecast" which
spread over a further two pages. There was a stock-market "Out-
look" by Clement B. Asbury, with more short comments from several
byline writers. To close that first issue, BC in a burst of patriotism
provided a "Wall Street's Roll of Honor," listing those men of Wall
Street who had gone to war.

BC had a style all his own. Who else would have used the 23rd
Psalm as an editorial? It was given for those who felt they had worries
and was his prescription for "when you feel blue." With it came the
information that "I know quite a few millionaires and multi-mil-
lionaires and I can say with absolute truth that the average multi-

millionaire has more troubles than the average day laborer or salaried employee. Andrew Carnegie once declared: 'Millionaires seldom smile.' "

And, in all innocence, Mrs. Adelaide Forbes was still adjusting to being married to a writer. Not only was she young, she had the habit of telling BC exactly what she thought:

> The reason writers do not strut [said BC], is "because their wives won't let them."
>
> One writer whom I will not name was reading something in the newspaper about a writer one morning when his wife remarked, "I'm so glad I didn't marry a writer." "Thanks," he commented with marked gravity. "I mean—a *real* writer," she corrected herself.

BC was finding it difficult to print, publish and make a profit under wartime conditions. Nonetheless, in the December 8, 1917, advisory to readers about the "Forbes Program for 1918," Bertie wrote that *Forbes* magazine would be used to explain and help in the solution of the big problems of the day, "in a moment more critical perhaps than the history of the world has ever known." The stories would deal with how American business could adapt itself to war conditions, including the mobilization of rails, motor plants as war plants, the textile trade, retail stores and what they sell in wartime, the paint business and camouflage and so on. The articles would further deal with the "rights and duties of labor," looking at the "high price of commodities, the scarcity of foodstuffs, the shortage of labor." Time and again during these years B. C. Forbes returned to the topic of labor:

> Not a few students of sociological phenomenon have already predicted the war after the war—a struggle of the classes. This is a most serious problem, for which we must prepare at once. *Forbes* magazine believes the serious labor troubles can be avoided by promoting understanding between employers and employees. Each side must make concessions, each class must learn to understand the other's viewpoint. All should share their troubles and all must pull together.
>
> Labor must be taught to realize that workmen have duties as well as rights—duties to the nation as a whole and to the welfare of the entire world.

BC was inclined to say only nice things about most people. He mentioned the point himself again editorially:

"You give only one side of the men you write about," I am often told. "At least some of them have another side, a less attractive side; but you rarely touch on that. Why not prepare and publish an honest-to-goodness who's who and what's what, telling the unvarnished truth about the men whose names we often see in the newspapers but about whom we really know very little. These men wield tremendous power, and the public ought to have some unbiased guide as to which of them are worthy of our admiration and which of them ought to be drummed out of their high places."

I confess that my experience is tending, as I grow older, to bring home to me the truth of the urgings that there is "another side" to not a few of our gentlemen, a side to which it might be salutary, in the public interest, to let in the fullest daylight.

Without naming names BC then gave some examples of rich industrial figures and some of the circumstances behind them. He promised to pay more attention to the topic in the future, and to tell more about "what a man is than what he has." He attended to it only fitfully.

Soon BC was off on the sort of national tour he could afford to do for Hearst but could not afford to do as the editor and publisher of *Forbes*. He went West, visiting cities of the West and Southwest, telling their businessmen to be optimistic, to work together and to "sell" their cities to the nation's investors.

As the older generation of self-made men were passing away, BC was increasingly turning his attention to their sons:

Has anyone ever attempted seriously to analyze how successful rich westerners have been, as compared to rich easterners, in bringing up their sons? Well I haven't much specific information, I rather think that fewer western youths are pampered and ruined by being over indulged by their parents. My mind was first directed to the subject when I began gathering information about the career of William H. Crocker, head of the Crocker National Bank of San Francisco, an institution which during the last five or six years has made as much money as all the rest of the national banks of San Francisco combined. Incidentally, this wealthy son of a wealthy father also has a son who is following industriously in his father's footsteps . . . lounge lizards don't fit well into western environment.

BC actually was keeping his eye on the next generation of managers and corporate chiefs. In no instance was this more evident than in the case of the Radio Corporation of America and the Forbes family association with the Sarnoff family.

David Sarnoff was vice president and general manager of the Radio Corporation of America at 266 Broadway, New York. In 1926 he wrote to Forbes:

> Every now and then I notice some very pleasant and helpful thing you have said about me in your interesting daily article in the New York *American.*
>
> Such helpfulness doesn't come to anyone accidentally, according to my observation. It is apparent to me that you have been consciously giving me a lift at every opportunity, and I am sincerely appreciative.
>
> I am aware of the number of papers and cities where your daily article appears and of the strong hold you have upon your audience. I have let other pleasant references to me, in your column, pass without expressing my appreciation, and while I don't know whether the ethical requirement is to say something to the author, or keep quiet, I will feel better myself for having told you that I'm especially grateful for your influence and helpfulness.

At home in Englewood, New Jersey, BC had his own sons to think about.

Malcolm Forbes has to be understood as the son of a self-made Victorian immigrant. That Bertie was self-made, and admired self-made men, governed how he viewed success and achievement, how he viewed the master-worker relationship, and how he saw the opportunities life offered to the ambitious and industrious. If wealth came as a natural by-product of industry, there was no shame in that.

The sons born into the Forbes house on Fountain Road, Englewood, New Jersey, most certainly the first four, were reared in an atmosphere of Victorian Scotland right through the Roaring Twenties.

It was not a house devoid of good times, but it was the house of a Victorian father who expected the household to attend to his needs first, and listen to his words first.

There were Bruce (baptised Catholic), athletic, outgoing and jovial, born in 1916; Duncan (Presbyterian), freckled-faced, tousled-haired, the "engineer and inventor" in the family, likable and quick to like, born in 1918; Malcolm (Catholic), shy, gangling, more serious and less athletically coordinated, bookish, anxious to please and hopeful of attracting the easy attention that came to his elder brothers; Gordon (Presbyterian), a sweet round-faced child, stocky like his father, whereas the others had their mother's thinner frame, born in 1923; and Wallace, the baby, born in 1928. For reasons still in the future, Wallace would be raised a Presbyterian, too.

The house in Englewood, large and comfortable, with Edna to clean, Miss Cordiner to help with Gordon and Wallace, was big enough for everyone without being a mansion. There was plenty of lawn for boys to run wild on—and still leave room for croquet on pleasant spring and summer days.

Cousins came over and there would be impromptu theatricals as the adults—Uncle George and Aunt Aggie, Uncle Wilson and Aunt Mae—with Mom and Dad, sat on the rear steps and watched the shenanigans. They would join in the croquet, or just sit chatting while Uncle Wilson took a long stick and turned over the logs in the charcoal pit ready for the cookout.

BC, proudly displaying his expensive 16-mm movie camera, would capture home scenes in summer, and Bruce's football games in the fall. In 1926, there was a great trip to Scotland for all. Forbes boys later were shipboard terrors. Sent to their cabins for raucous behavior on one ocean voyage, they called for afternoon tea to be delivered to them. When it came, they started throwing everything, bedding and linens, too, out of the portholes.

Another vessel picked up the jetsam and imagined disaster ahead. When the truth came out, the Forbes boys really were punished. And no stewards were to answer the bell.

But, for the most part, the five Forbes boys were normal, and slightly spoiled. The 1920s might be roaring by, but the Forbes family lived a restrained, proper, suburban-town existence. The highlights of those years were Lindbergh's Lone Eagle flight in the *Spirit of St. Louis,* and the afternoons when the huge passenger-carrying dirigibles, uncanny monsters gliding noiselessly overhead, had everyone gazing up in awe. That was adventure. *That* would be fun.

There were Father's own adventures to listen to, his own travels in distant lands. And the ones he wrote about! There was Charles Anceny of the Double-D ranch in California, who had wrestled a cougar with his bare hands. He was in Dad's book *The Men Who Are Making the West.*

Daddy constantly lectured and talked about getting ahead. He would explain how hard work and stick-to-itiveness led to achievement—the attainment of life's desires. He believed it. His conversation, like his magazine, was sprinkled with the "self-help" homilies of what was fast becoming another era.

The boys experienced the simple pleasures and pressures of family life. One pleasure was going by car to meet the 42nd Street ferry—this in the days before the George Washington Bridge. Punishment for bad behavior was not being allowed to meet Daddy at the ferry.

Other than normal quarreling in a house full of boys, the Forbes lads did not do a great deal to incur parental wrath. Occasionally, Adelaide would whack a son with the back of her hairbrush. If that didn't work, she would threaten the disobedient with: "Just wait till your father gets home."

That threat was a real one. Bertie was strict. He was generous; he loved his family and the family scene—wife, sons and relatives gathered around; he was kind. But he did not have the close relationship with his children more common to later generations.

Malcolm explains it: "His time, his upbringing did not equip him for that moment when there was candor in an exchange of opinion with his children, where the thing shifts from being a parent to being a friend."

Bertie had his own way of looking at things. While the mixed baptisms, one for the presbytery, one for Rome, as the boys came along, was something neither church would condone, it kept a tenuous peace in the household. Bruce and Malcolm would have to be up early each Sunday morning for Mass at St. Cecilia's Church. By the time they got home, their father was up and dressed. He loved to listen to the sermons of the Reverend Carl Elmore, the minister of the First Presbyterian Church in Englewood. In fact, Bertie would send copies of Elmore's sermons back to the minister of the "auld kirk" at New Deer, Scotland, with comments attached.

Occasionally, an hour or so after Bruce and Malcolm had arrived back from Mass at St. Cecilia's with their mother, their father would address the assembled boys by saying pointedly: "And now I would like *all* my sons to go to church with *me.*" Those Sundays were the ones Bruce and Malcolm hated most. Double-headers at church were even worse than the family arguments over religion.

Bertie's Victorian scrupulosity showed up on Sundays. The boys were paid a dime each to learn a new hymn—and they didn't get the dime until they could sing the hymn all the way through. The adults, meanwhile, would play cards—BC and Adelaide, and perhaps BC's brother Wilson with his wife, Mae, and his sister Agnes, with her husband, George. The cousins came over, too.

Playing cards meant having a drink, and though Bertie boasted he never took a drink until he was thirty-six, meaning not until he was married, he was drinking socially in the 1920s. He refused to make money from liquor and—perhaps with memories of his own boyhood growing up behind the grocery store–beer shop in a Highland village—in his lifetime *Forbes* never carried liquor advertising. (Even during the Depression, when *Forbes* was down to only six or seven pages of advertising, BC would change the copy on the one-third-page Canada Dry advertisement, from "Mix this with your Scotch" to "Mix this with your drink.")

These were lovely years. Mother, beautiful, warm, with her Irish charm, dressed in an evening gown for a "do" in New York with Daddy, or relaxing in a tailored dress on a chaise in the garden, looked young and pretty alongside the aging—and increasingly heavier—Bertie. The seventeen years' difference in their ages was beginning to show in the sepia-tone photographs. Mother also had her Irish temper and her Roman Catholicism, both frequently erupting.

Romantic by nature, young Malcolm was romantic by pursuit. There were his toy soldiers for mock battles. There were the adventure movies of the silver—and silent—screen: swashbucklers, daredevil pirates, faraway places. The 1920s moved along in a flurry of silly excitement: flagpole sitting, goldfish eating, the Charleston, airplane barnstorming, high-speed auto racing, the merry madness of the times.

Malcolm, certain, slightly stern, the organizer as well as the participant in boyhood plans, was relaxed and ambitious among his peers —and away from his older brothers. He had a quick mind, his father's turns of phrase, and a precocious sense of self that, with his obvious determination, may have been his shield against shyness. He had an obvious liking for the printed word: he enjoyed books, and he enjoyed his home-produced newspapers.

These halcyon days, warm and secure, refreshingly filled with family and friends in a booming, growing, optimistic America, were gone in a day: Black Friday, 1929.

The family on Fountain Road suffered no financial reverses in the 1929 Wall Street crash. Editor Bertie had been warning *Forbes* readers for months to get out of the stock market and had taken his own advice. In fact, not long after the crash, Bertie was back in the market picking up shares at bargain prices.

Bertie was financially safe. *Forbes* magazine was not. The United States, which had feared Bolshevism as World War I ended, again saw seeds of turmoil taking root as the armies of the unemployed accepted unwilling additions to their unsmiling ranks.

Bertie kept a smiling public face but he was living with a grimmer reality; his magazine might not make it. On Fountain Road, the Forbeses were expected to watch their pennies in order to help keep the magazine afloat.

For the Forbes boys—though there were still treats and pleasures—life no longer was the cloudless passage of early childhood. A grim pall hung over all America, and the pleasures of the pre-Crash 1920s took on a special aura.

BC lived the worries of the stock market, Wall Street and the U.S. economy at home as well as at the office. These things were his life. Where once the talk was of success stories all over this young country, now at the dinner table there were many bad stories, accounts of the defamatory letters BC received and a sense of the defeatism felt by many businessmen in those times.

BC had been prosperous, even rich. Now he had an income at a time when many did not, and a sizable income it was. To be employed in the early 1930s was itself a form of prosperity. BC's income came from many people paying a very small amount for a product they didn't want to do without: their newspaper. His Hearst income was as safe as anything could be in those parlous times.

Malcolm, serious and sensitive, felt the stresses of the household as any normal child would. His father was less patient now, more anxious about his *Forbes* magazine, his family's and his nation's future.

On Franklin Delano Roosevelt's inauguration day, recalled Malcolm, "The schools were closed. My father was at work in New York.

Roosevelt had announced the bank holiday, closing all the banks. School was about a half mile from where we lived and a group of us decided to roller skate to the schoolyard.

"I was afraid on roller skates. You don't do anything well that you're afraid of, and I was timid on roller skates, just like ice skates. I was never successful at it because by the time I got interested in it all my contemporaries, or most of them, were good skaters. When you are ten or eleven you don't like to go out and flop down in front of your contemporaries when they can do something well.

"We went off on our skates and as we were going down a ramp I gathered speed and couldn't stop myself. I ran smack into an abutment and broke a tooth.

"When I came home! The despair on my mother's face when she had to take me to the dentist—'here's another bill we don't need.' There was no sympathy for my painful hurt. The break was sharp enough but the nerve was exposed. The real pain came from the expression on Mother's face: 'My God, the banks are closing. We're in the depth of the Depression,' etcetera, 'struggling to make ends meet. And now you have to go to the dentist and here's one more bill to be argued about.' "

Despite inaugural day storms, however, Malcolm, bespectacled and full of nervous energy, already was enjoying his first successes as ninth-grade student council president, advertising manager on the school magazine board of editors, and president of the public-speaking and debating club.

His home newspaper was being printed on the $35 A. B. Dick duplicator he had received as a thirteenth-birthday present. Malcolm was beginning to find a niche.

That same year, 1933, the greatest tragedy of all struck the young family. Malcolm learned of it on his way home from Mass at St. Cecilia's. "Uncle Wilson was waiting for me as I got off the trolley. Duncan was dead."

For Malcolm, with Duncan's death the carefree days of childhood were cruelly, horribly ended. The days of being one of the five Forbeses, pre-Crash days that were themselves becoming almost a fable, now were gone. It was a brutal shock for every member of the family.

Duncan, the freckled-faced kid with the wide eyes, upturned nose, the engineer in the family, and a ringleader in hell raising and practical jokes, was dead at the age of fifteen.

"My mother and father were staying at an upstate New York resort, Yama Farms, with the Alton Joneses. Jones, who ran Cities Service oil company after Henry L. Doherty died of cancer, was probably my father's closest friend in business.

"Bruce had received a rather marvelous present for his seventeenth birthday, a Model A convertible. It was a used car, but a pretty wonderful present. Bruce and Duncan decided to drive up to Yama Farms on the Sunday to see my parents—it was about a hundred miles away—who were coming home later in the day.

"Bruce was driving along Storm King Highway toward a bend. On the far side of that bend a car had pulled over to the side with a flat. Another car had pulled up alongside to be of help but had blocked that side of the road.

"When Bruce came around the corner he had to swerve to avoid the car. Being a light convertible, the Model A turned over. Bruce wasn't hurt—as often happens to somebody behind the steering wheel—but Duncan was thrown out. It had snapped his back and he was killed instantly."

The family was stunned. Bertie held his grief deep inside him and insisted that life go on, and that Duncan be referred to easily and without strain. Adelaide was grieved as a mother and tortured as a Roman Catholic—Duncan had not been baptized in the faith.

Whether Adelaide ever forgave Bruce or not will never be known, but Bruce always felt she never had. That day was a tragedy of profound proportions, and each member of the family could measure only the grief in his or her own heart as a way of understanding the grief in that of the others.

Duncan had been a Presbyterian. Five-year-old Wallace, who would have been raised a Catholic had the strict alternating of faith been continued, was raised Presbyterian to even up the Presbyterian-Catholic mix in the house on Fountain Road.

In an attempt to take everyone's mind off the tragedy, Bertie decided the family would go to Scotland. Soon everyone was saying farewell to friends at the train for Boston, where the family would board the Anchor Line's *Caledonia*. For the boys it would be nine days of deck tennis, quoits, family fun and mayhem until the ship reached Glasgow.

Malcolm, the enterprising reporter-publisher, on the family's return to Englewood described the travels in his latest newspaper, *Family Album,* which he published on the affairs of his family and the *Forbes* magazine employees, the larger "Forbes family": "As we sailed up the Clyde, a river connecting Glasgow with the ocean, we saw the giant Cunarder 534, the largest ship in the world, being built." That ship later would be christened the *Queen Elizabeth.*

In the village of New Deer the Forbes boys were sons of a local celebrity. Bertie had not neglected his village, or his old school. Each year at Christmas he paid for a school party; each summer, for a picnic. This year he was present himself to hand out the prizes after the sack races and three-legged races.

At seventeen, Bruce was happy to throw himself into the races against the local youths and men. Malcolm, the young squire, stood by his father, handing out the florins, shillings and sixpences to the prizewi. mers. BC joined the old ladies for the tea and sandwiches he was paying for. The local newspaper reporter was there to write up the story for newspapers Bertie himself once had written for. And then it was time to sail home.

The gloom of the Depression and the heartache of Duncan's death were not easily forgotten. A year after Duncan's death, Malcolm channeled his efforts, and his sadness, into yet another newspaper, this one named for Duncan: *The City of Dunc Weekly News.* It was a newspaper

> . . . dealing with the happenings of two cities built by Malcolm and Gordon Forbes in the cellar of their home out of cardboard boxes, with cellophane windows and electric lights. In these towns in the evening we play. About 100 Tootsie toy automobiles and about 350 lead men in both towns.

The *Weekly News* masthead showed: Editors-in-chief, M. S. Forbes, G. P. Schultz. That G. P. Schultz was an Eagle Scout with Malcolm, and they both would throw rocks at street lamps on the way home from meetings. Many years later, George Schultz was Secretary of the Treasury under President Lyndon B. Johnson.

In that same issue, Malcolm discussed his autograph collection, and among the list he mentioned the signatures of three presidents: Woodrow Wilson, Calvin Coolidge and Herbert Hoover. By the 1960s, Malcolm had completed his collection of presidential letters and autographs—these are on the walls of *Forbes* magazine's main staircase.

Malcolm's editorial style meanwhile won him first prize in an Englewood school-wide contest on fire prevention. "Hah! The fire was set! Who was careless? Was it a man or a child?" wrote Malcolm, and he continued the theme through to a prizewinning conclusion.

With his school sheet he conducted a poll: best dressed, best dancer, most popular, best looking, most humorous, best mixer, best host, best sport. Malcolm came out "best dressed, the most humorous, and the best host." The elegant, easy-going host of the future already was in the making.

In another issue Malcolm wrote up the student court, called for the impeachment of one of the students, and received a rejoinder from his teacher, who remarked: "Only your last paragraph has the strength of impersonality." The opinionated Malcolm was in the making, too.

Summer came, and in 1934 Malcolm left Englewood Junior High. His news sheet ceased, but only for a week or two. Mr. Frank, the local scoutmaster, asked him to found the *Eagle Scout*, which Malcolm promptly did.

It still was the Depression. Money was tight. As every issue of *Forbes* came out, BC would walk into his Englewood home and say, waving a copy of the magazine, "This has cost me $15,000."

During vacations the growing boys would work at the magazine, at 120 Fifth Avenue. The pay was $10 a week plus $2 for the commutation. "We worked Saturday mornings in those days," said Malcolm. "No worker in America greeted the five-day week with greater joy than I did. It sort of preconditioned me for the four-day week experiment I tried years later at Forbes."

Malcolm worked in a small mail cage with the mail girl, slitting open the envelopes. There might be a $1 bill in an envelope, a response to a special offer, "eight issues for $1." The girl would write down the amount and whether it was cash or a check.

"About 10:30 every morning, my father would come bounding down the hall. He would stop at the mail cage, pull on his cigar, and say: 'How much today?'

"The girl would say $132 or $97 or whatever it was."

" 'Not enough, not enough,' BC would comment and stop off in the men's room. It was a regular ritual. A similar ritual involved his dealings with the accountants when they would start to talk about accounts receivable and bills. 'I don't give a damn about that,' he'd say, 'how much have we got in the bank.' "

No one ever accused BC of being a shrewd businessman. He was a prolific writer, a good copyeditor, a first-class salesman for things he believed in, and a man who wouldn't give in. That's what kept the magazine going.

"There were times when he would have been better off letting the magazine fold," said Malcolm. "But it was his pride, his independence. It made him more than a Hearst columnist; it was his thing in the sun. It was *Forbes* magazine. It was him. He was the only one Hearst ever let continue in private business."

The reality was tough. "I used to watch him pull his coat around on a Friday morning," recalls Gertrude Weiner, his secretary. "He would put a brave face on things and go down to Wall Street to see if he could raise some money to meet the payroll."

Each Friday the employees would wait anxiously to see if he had. Some Fridays he hadn't. He could not drum up promises of advertising from his friends and poker-playing buddies at the big corporations. There was no one who would buy Paramount Securities, the privately issued bonds which had helped BC launch the magazine less than twenty years earlier.

And on those Fridays when payrolls had to be met, and no money had been raised, BC would have to dig deeper into his own pocket to come up with the money. Occasionally his magazine or news-column readers would break the gloom:

ODE TO A FINANCIAL COLUMNIST

Blow ye winds of the morning;
Blow ye winds heigho;
And each succeeding morning
Brings an added woe;
But the stuff that brings
Protruding orbs
Is the stuff you write,
    Rukeyser and Forbes,
Especially Forbes.
And you write and you write
And you write and you write,
All day long and into the night;

And now I'm asking you, honor bright,
What have you written that ever proved right?
    Especially Forbes.

It appears you want to continue under the
capitalistic system with all its gorillaish,
jungleistic, heartless, inhuman methods especially as regards its manner of distributing
annually produced wealth. But it just can't be
done, Mr. Forbes.

Such letters were the price of public fame!

In the fall of 1934, Malcolm was sent to Hackley School, Tarry-town, New York. Bruce already was there. Malcolm did not want to go, and had hoped he would not be sent. In fact, he was somewhat surprised at the decision, and resented it. He was a homebody, close to his mother and not possessed of the easy sportsman outgoingness that enabled Bruce to win friends quickly.

He tried to emulate Bruce, just as he copied—and competed against—his father. But always something of a loner in the crowd— unless he was the prime organizer—Malcolm faced loneliness. He did not like it.

One reason Bertie may have been anxious to see the boys go to Hackley was a breakdown in the harmony at home.

Bertie and Adelaide's problems were several. There was age. Bertie was fifty-five and looking older, stouter; Adelaide was a beautiful thirty-eight, looking younger. Bertie was a man's man, and most enjoyed being among men. His wife, whom he admired immensely and loved in his own way, was relegated to the traditional wifely role: beautiful companion, housekeeper, mother of his boys.

Bertie had never been one for frills for himself. Adelaide loved beautiful things. So they fought over money. Bertie expected to be obeyed. He cast his wife in the role of those Scottish wives of the men he had known growing up. BC and Adelaide did travel together and they did enjoy each other's company. They did not get on well together in the day-by-day household affairs, the giving and taking. Bertie was prepared to give of his money, but not too much of himself.

They fought over religion, over Bertie's endless card playing, over drinking. The undertow of pressures could have been Duncan's death, or a lack of mutual interest after nearly twenty years of married life. For whatever reason, they fought.

Malcolm at Hackley flung himself into work: not the schoolwork but the ephemera—like newspapering. At Hackley, he started, unofficially, *The Underclassmen's Voice*. It did not last long.

Malcolm's next sheet was the Hackley *Eagle*. Soon Malcolm was

> Announcing the discontinuance of the Hackley *Eagle*. . . .
> We admittedly made mistakes, but we will not make the mistake of printing what is not our opinion as we wanted it expressed. No, we can discontinue rather than that. Signed—M. S. Forbes, ex-editor of the Hackley *Eagle*.

The "mistake" behind the folding of the Hackley *Eagle* was an event that must have earned Malcolm some lasting schoolboy immortality in the Hackley annals. The *Eagle* printed columns of schoolboy jokes. Headmaster Gage did not think this joke was funny:

> Did you hear about the absent-minded professor who kissed the trolley and jumped on his wife and went to town?

"I didn't even know it was dirty," said Malcolm. "I just thought it was an absent-minded professor story." Gage had the last word, as Malcolm recalled it:

> The headmaster thought I was getting a sly one in because, of course, the students were convulsed by the libertine joke, so I was called in and told from then on a faculty member had to approve of every word in the paper. So that continued for a couple of issues and then they kept throwing out what seemed to be silly, so one morning I ground out a manifesto saying I was discontinuing the paper because it was impossible to edit an honest paper, and I put that in everybody's mailbox. So the headmaster had a meeting at the school at noon and announced that in all of their history they had never censored free thinking and it was some nasty-minded boy that had done this thing and so on and so on. There was a question whether I should be expelled or not . . .

Bertie wrote to his son, May 1, 1935: "Dear Malc, I have just read 'announcing the discontinuance of the Hackley *Eagle*.' I admire your fearless independence of spirit. Naturally, I'm an ardent believer in the freedom of the press. Love, Daddy."

Bruce graduated from Hackley in 1935. But it was off to Lawrenceville for Malcolm, where his first issue of the Kennedy *Eagle*, named after his shuttered red-brick house at Lawrenceville, got him into nearly as much trouble as his Hackley *Eagle*.

Came a letter from Lawrenceville's official newspaper, *The Lawrence*, signed by its supervisor, W. A. Jameson:

> It has come to my attention that the Kennedy *Eagle* printed this afternoon the all-house football team. They probably do not know that such news is the exclusive right of *The Lawrence* and that in printing it they have been guilty of the gross violation of both newspaper ethics and the school tradition.

But the Kennedy *Eagle* survived that blow and continued, and by the following February, 1936, it had turned a profit of $6.61. Malcolm soon was writing for *The Lawrence* in addition to editing the *Eagle*, and was duplicating his father's early industriousness by writing short stories too. His spelling was atrocious, but the stories weren't bad. The Lawrenceville *Lit* carried Malcolm's "King Neptune versus Castletania." And the story began:

> As the little British freighter *Casteltania* was casually plowing her way through the placid waves of the North Atlantic, homeward bound, her master eyed the falling barometer with a worried appearance. Captain Sundstrom realized his ship was in for a "blow."

Busy writer Malcolm asked his father's secretary, Miss Gertrude Weiner, that she intercede on his behalf for a new typewriter:

> Would you be so kind as to ask Dad if he would get me a new Remington silent portable? While my own typewriter is still in very good shape, its incessant clatter while in operation prevents me from using it as much as I want to and need to for it annoys the other boys who room near me . . . doubtless if you explain this to Dad he isn't liable to refuse my request. Sincerely, Malcolm S. Forbes.

He knew that if Miss Weiner could not catch his father in a benevolent moment no one was likely to.

Malcolm was settling down, studying very hard. He was named

his house chairman of the Republican party for the 1936 elections. With buttons and campaign posters from Landon headquarters, Alfred M. Landon at least swept to success on the Lawrenceville campus, where Malcolm, his campaign manager, carried Landon's campaign by a huge margin.

That year and the next year Malcolm accomplished a very personal achievement, and his father wrote him about it:

> March 17, 1937. Dear Malc, Very hearty congratulations on again winning the *Time* current events prize. My philosophy is that, no matter how much a person may know about ancient history, he is not thoroughly educated unless he keeps abreast of what is happening throughout the world day by day. So, I'm very proud of your achievement. I'll double the prize. And will double any others you may win in similar future contests. We're all looking forward eagerly to having you home on Sunday. With much love, Daddy.

Inevitably, it seems, Malcolm became editor of the yearbook, the *Lawrentian.* In an album there is a photograph of him at work: a rather somber-faced fellow behind his steel-rimmed glasses, with a large mouth.

> Two of the busiest members of the class this past month have been Malcolm Forbes and Wayne Stickel . . . they are determined to break all traditions in recent years by having the year book at the press on the appointed date.

Malcolm was becoming quite serious, and quite the student, though he did not forget to drop his father a birthday line for May 14, 1937:

> "Dear Dad [said the handwritten note]. Many, many happy returns. Not you, however, *but we boys* are the ones who should be felicitated on your birthday—love, Malc.

When Malcolm graduated from Lawrenceville in 1937 he made the flag speech. BC was very impressed. Next day he used the occasion as the subject for his Hearst press daily column: "Today's youth better equipped for life work. Thoroughly trained with commendable grasp of current affairs . . ."

Malcolm blossomed at Lawrenceville owing to that school's particular structure and form of discipline. Lawrenceville knows its job: taking firm but fatherly hold of the sons of wealth and preparing them—often by directing them toward Princeton, next door—for a major role in life.

The Lawrenceville "house" system provides a family atmosphere because the housemaster lives in with his wife and family. After generations of experience, Lawrenceville is prepared for its *in loco parentis* role, and knows that all too often this is the only true family the boy may end up with.

Such was not the case with Malcolm, but at Lawrenceville he could give his energy full play within a disciplined lifestyle that Lawrenceville uses to channel enthusiasm to a useful end. By direction, and by his own natural ambitions and drive, was Malcolm *cum laude* when he graduated in 1937.

Malcolm would be going on to Princeton and was already looking ahead to Harvard Law School—law being a stock-in-trade for ambitious young men with the White House already in their field of vision. Bruce, by this time at the University of Michigan, was not displaying much aptitude for further education. BC was philosophical about it; he did not think all people necessarily were college material, Bruce, apparently, among them.

Bertie, as ever, was busy. He was occupying himself with specialties like *The Salesman's Diary for 1938. Daily Pep Pellets.*

Always the salesman, BC explained for himself why there needed to be such a diary:

> The purposes of this diary are to stimulate salesmen to become more successful. To enrich their feeling of self respect. To enable them to derive joy from their job. To bring home to them the importance of the role they play in creating employment for others in developing national prosperity, in maintaining government.
>
> To inspire courage, energy, resourcefulness.
>
> To offer homely hints on how to win the good-will of prospects and customers, to cultivate effective personality.
>
> Finally, to provide sales managers with an exceptional, fruitful addition to the sales kit—a cheerful daily buck-up "good morning" to their men out on the firing line.

The salesman face to face with the harsh realities of the first Monday of the New Year, January 3, 1938, could open his diary and find:

Pack your sales kit with courage.

If that didn't work, on a Tuesday he read:

Nobody welcomes a jittery, crotchety visitor. Radiate sunshine!

If there were still few sales by Wednesday, the message for that day was:

Concentrate on selling during selling hours. There are none too many of them.

Thursday, with the end of the week in sight:

How much planning for today did you do last night?

By October, 1938, Princetonian Malcolm had launched the *Nassau Sovereign,* "The campus *Fortune.*" It was 35 cents an issue, destined to put the rival Princeton *Tiger* out of business, and to provide an excuse for Malcolm's being the only Princeton frosh with a car on campus. "Cars were forbidden on campus but each publication was allowed one. I bought an old Ford with a station wagon body, 1933 or something. It was used and still more used, but we got a great deal of fun out of it. I got all of my friends to sand the body and shellac it and so forth."

Malcolm was beginning to turn on his powers of promotion. He had sought comments from the New York newspapers. At the première of the *Nassau Sovereign,* October 21, 1938, guests could learn —because they were handed copies of an advertisement appearing in the *Daily Princetonian*—that newspapers such as the New York *Herald Tribune* were lauding the *Sovereign* for its "enterprising topics of interest," and as "the new magazine to swing away from traditional fields in a manner of *Fortune, Life* and *Scribner's.*"

When Malcolm had first approached his father for assistance in starting the *Nassau Sovereign,* Bertie forbade Malcolm to launch the magazine. BC was afraid it would take away from Malcolm's studies.

But Malcolm was developing now a marked trait: he would do what he wanted to do. After all weren't his father's mottoes "They said it couldn't be done . . ." and "Stick-to-itiveness"? He ignored the ban and launched anyway—with such a splash that Bertie had to admit himself won over, and he stepped in with financial assistance.

Malcolm tried poll taking. He persuaded pollster George Gallup, a Princeton resident, to help out with professional advice.

Student-editor Malcolm was advising: "College youth is no longer primarily concerned with humor, sex and beer." Princetonians in those years in Malcolm's polls said they were prepared to abolish slums and poverty even if it meant paying more taxes. The Ivy League students of the late 1930s had their consciences molded by the Depression.

Whether students were less interested in sex, or simply had more interests, is a moot point. Someone typed up the entire tale of the "Harlot of Jerusalem" on one *Nassau Sovereign* letterhead and left it on Malcolm's littered Princeton desk.

Malcolm's own sex life was neither precocious nor stunted. In those pre-promiscuity days of yore, many young men did without, despite the tales of derring-do, and "darling, do!" they brought back to campus after a weekend. Malcolm was otherwise occupied. The $5 a week his father allotted didn't go far enough and he was periodically begging for more.

Bruce was about to join his father in business, but by going to Detroit to set up a *Forbes* advertising office in the motor city. Automobile manufacturers were the nation's number-one advertisers.

Malcolm's Princeton room—a photograph shows him thin-faced, serious, about to finish off some copy in his typewriter—was fashionably untidy. His wall carried a large poster bearing a photograph of Bertie and the legend "This famous American says it first."

Malcolm was doing some serious thinking. The *Sovereign* had interrupted his studies. He still wanted to pursue a political career; he would have to come up with some sort of power base. By the time he graduated in 1941 he had decided—with Dad's help—to buy a weekly newspaper in Lancaster, Ohio, a state that had produced more presidents than any but Virginia.

The Fairfield *Times* was Malcolm's initial career venture. He was nearly twenty-two and was filled with ambition. With this newspaper—one that served the mainly rural area around the town—and a new urban shopper, the Lancaster *Tribune,* he was starting to build a base. Perhaps this could be built into a chain of newspapers to provide the financial independence to pursue a political career.

But, though Bertie had been able to start a magazine with a war raging in Europe in 1917, Malcolm was not able to make a success of a newspaper with a war raging in Europe in 1941.

Not that he didn't try. All his money was going out in bills and staff. He was paying himself no salary, living in a single room, and eating in a restaurant free of charge in exchange for printing the restaurant's menus without cost.

Always the realist, soon Malcolm realized there had to be an honorable way out of his plight. Pearl Harbor provided it. He would enlist. But, with his eyesight, no one would take him. The marines and navy quickly said "No," even though they were impressed by his leadership abilities.

Rejected, but not dejected, Malcolm heard about some new-fangled invention called the contact lens. He went to Chicago and had them fitted. The army doctors never even noticed them, or didn't care, and Malcolm was accepted into the U.S. Infantry, eyesight normal.

Three more characteristics that later were to mark Malcolm's rapid progress once he became owner of *Forbes* were brought into play. He would ruthlessly cut his losses once he had decided *for himself:* hence the rapid exit from Lancaster. He would not take "no" for an answer, and that was how he got into the army. Nor would he take advice—or even listen to it—unless it coincided with a decision he had already made. "No," he would not go for a commission; "no" he would not stay out of uniform.

The independence that Bertie had hoped would take root in his sons flowered in Malcolm almost into defiance.

In khaki, in 1942, Corporal Forbes, publisher of the *Times* and *Tribune,* started writing on Army life: "One Fellow's Viewpoint." But it wasn't long before, in 1943, he was writing: *"Times-Tribune* plans to suspend for the duration." Not far from his photograph in full battle rig, gun, tin helmet, and all, the end of the *Times-Tribune* was spelled out:

> Machine and labor shortage influenced move. Publisher expresses hope he may return here, from army service after war. Upon completion of this issue the *Times-Tribune* plant will be dismantled and the machinery and equipment disposed of, it was announced today by Malcolm S. Forbes, publisher. "Increased costs of operation, shortage of labor, lack of adequate replacement parts for the machinery and the general uncertainties of wartime publication, make it imperative that we suspend for the duration of the war. . . ."

"Definite arrangements have been made to satisfy unexpired subscriptions," the newly promoted Sergeant Forbes concluded. He would be going overseas shortly.

Malcolm's Catholicism had long been on the wane. At Lawrenceville he would go to Mass only when his mother came to visit. Finally, when at Princeton, he told her he was no longer a practicing Catholic and did not intend to be so again. In an unusual step, both for its display of integrity and as an indication of how much he wanted to square things away, he went to the Roman Catholic chaplain and formally renounced his religion, asking that his records show no religion at all. Malcolm "didn't want to be buried under false colors."

Malcolm had another problem, not on his mind or soul, but on his heart. He was in love. She was from Lancaster.

It was a family rule that any prospective daughter-in-law of BC's had to undertake the rigors of going on vacation with the family. First BC wrote to Malcolm:

> Dear Son: Think not only twice, but half-a-dozen times and more before you take the most fateful plunge of your life.
>
> It is, of course, perfectly natural for any and every young man to want to get married.
>
> But I regard your case as similar to Bruce's. I urged him, when he broached the subject to me, to wait until he had cleared his feet financially, until he could start without a lot of debt around his neck. Had I known all that I do now about the extent of his debts, I would have been much more emphatic in my advice.
>
> From what you have told me about your financial situation, and about how little you have been able to take from your business to live

on, this would not seem an ideal time for you to reach out for very heavy added financial burdens. . . .

Mother is fond of relating that you told her once, when she was all arrayed in her bestest one night, that you would want your wife to wear evening dress all the time! By waiting until you become more soundly established, you would at least be able to do much more in that direction than you could possibly do by plunging headlong into matrimony now.

However, I would not presume to give the historic advice once offered a man who asked about the advisability of getting married: "DON'T!"

After all, as I have tried to impress upon you and all your brothers, each of you, each of us, has to lead his own life.

Malcolm pressed his case. In 1943, the young lady accompanied the Forbeses on a vacation to Maine. True love fizzled out and Malcolm went back to army camp.

Malcolm's was not the only love to fizzle out that year. On September 20, 1943, Adelaide left Bertie. The following day she filed suit for separate maintenance. BC was really hurt. The *New York Times* played the story at the top of an inside page:

JERSEY CITY, Sept. 22—Bertie C. Forbes, editor of Forbes financial magazine and a financial columnist for the Hearst newspapers, was named defendant today in a suit for separate maintenance filed by his wife, Mrs. Adelaide Forbes, in Chancery Court here.

Charging cruelty and stating that he had an income of $50,000 a year and financial holdings totalling $500,000, Mrs. Forbes asked custody of Wallace, 15 years old, the youngest of their four sons, and counsel fees.

The plaintiff, in a 13-page affidavit supplementing the petition, cites instances of alleged drunkenness and brutality and characterized her husband as a "bully, egotist, tyrant and boor."

In recent years his drinking habits became chronic and she had been forced to act as his "man servant, tying his shoe laces, buttoning his shirt, drawing his bath and opening the door of his car," the affidavit alleges. On one occasion in 1934 he prevented her from visiting her mother who was in danger of death, the plaintiff relates.

The couple were married in 1915 and have made their home in Englewood. Recently, Mrs. Forbes says she was "forced to leave their home" and take residence in the Plaza Hotel in the city.

BC quickly damped down Adelaide's outburst by agreeing through counsel to provide $100 a week maintenance, provide for Wallace and pay $1500 counsel fees. When the *Times* reported the settlement it omitted the word "boor."

As with most separations and divorces, the public statements hid more than they revealed. The religious differences were at the bottom of it, gnawing away at Adelaide, who, when she filed her affidavit, dug up incidents stretching back nearly fifteen years.

As BC explained it in a letter to his sister:

Adelaide suddenly went berserk one night. She had become so enamoured of a supposedly extremely pious Catholic woman that all of us had been greatly disturbed. This woman, from what I could gather, convinced Ad that to live with a Protestant was to live in "sin."

Outside of warning Ad against making a public fool of herself, I let her have her own way when she was misled into taking the matter to court and making a lot of diabolically false statements about me. As a matter of fact, although newspapers all over the country printed stuff about it, I didn't and haven't suffered one iota in reputation, since everybody who knows me knew better than to believe any of the lies told.

It was soon brought home to her, after she left, that she had made a tragic mistake. But it will do her good to lie for awhile in the bed she made for herself. If I take her back, she'll have to come back in a very different frame of mind. Everybody familiar with our life blamed me for having spoiled her "beyond a' recognition." And I now realize that I did.

It may be that time will heal my wounds, and that I'll forgive by and by.

5

Malcolm and BC

MY FUNERAL

I do not want any of my busy business friends to be invited to take time off to attend.

The only ones I'd like to be there are the immediate members of my Family and office associates, particularly *all* of the Members of the FORBES Magazine Veterans' Club.

No flowers! Instead, anyone desiring to send flowers is requested to send a check to the Englewood Hospital.

If possible, I'd like the Rev. Carl Elmore to conduct a very brief Funeral Service.

I request that all who attend my burial be invited to luncheon (or other meal) at the Knickerbocker Country Club.

And, most especially, that the occasion be absolutely without sorrowing, since I ardently desire that:

> "There may be no mourning at the bar
> When I put out to sea."

The good Lord has been infinitely merciful to me, a most unworthy but most grateful sinner.

B. C. FORBES

Affluence is a tide; it ebbs and flows. The seas of affluence that washed over Wall Street and its investors in the late twenties had receded now to reveal only the bare rocks: poverty, hardship, despair.

BC had done well in anticipating the crash of 1929. He hadn't seen the second crash, of 1931, and was badly hit in his own investments.

The collapse of the stock market had already been too much for Walter Drey. The two men who had started the magazine together, BC and Walter, had watched it grow together. But the quiet Walter had been deeply into the stock market when the crash came. He was wiped out financially. The shock of seeing his life's savings disappear had brought on a nervous breakdown. The association ended, and Walter Drey's name, as business manager and vice-president of *Forbes,* disappeared from the corporate masthead. Drey did make a comeback; he eventually launched Drey's Listing Service, a mailing list for magazines and newspapers and direct mail advertisers.

"Scotch week" became a necessity. It was BC's device for keeping going. One week each month no one got paid. But, as the Depression took its heaviest toll, having a job at all was a near miracle, and the employees were glad of theirs.

In the nation at large, shock gave way to bitterness. Letters arrived which said:

> Well, B.C., I've lost faith entirely after you and Brisbane who (I thought like the fool I am) were not hypocrites . . . have the courage of your convictions and demand shylock Hearst take back some of your wages and if you are really sincere you could turn the swag in rakeoffs on speeches at meetings in Chambers of Commerce, robbery and free advertising for such damnable rascals as Sloan, Wiggin, Mitchell, Ford, Mellon, Edison and Rockefeller and Alladin Hoover . . .

The criticism was bitter more often than not:

> As far as I am concerned *Forbes* is no more than the Securities Industries "Tout Sheet"—whether the economy goes up or down—likewise the Dow Jones average—the main thing is to keep the inventories turning over. *Forbes* is more influential in starting the turnover—with the concurrent enrichment of the touts—than it is in providing any meaningful help for a *small* investor (that's me) . . . I like Mr. Forbes' editorials but he is limited by his uppercrust idealism. Yours is a rich man's magazine—with the rich man's outlook and symptomology as well as his own special set of psychoses. In short, sir, your magazine ain't for me.

The editor of *Forbes* fought the despair of the times with the only weapons he had, optimism and aphorisms: "A prophecy: 1933 will be better than 1932; the shortest days are over. The darkest days also, probably; currency inflation brings damnation; where do we go from here? Forward. Income tax is becoming a misnomer."

How did BC see the middle years of the Depression?

I have four sons, two of them approaching the age when they must go out and face the earning of a living.

President Roosevelt's recently announced ambition to have the government guarantee "the security of the home, the security of livelihood and the security of social insurance" causes me to wonder if the prospect of so much sheltering, so much safeguarding, so much financial protection, so much paternalism will cause them to discount, disregard, despise my teachings.

I have tried to impress upon them that they must fit themselves to make their own way in the world, that they must develop self-reliance, that they must cultivate a spirit of manly independence, that they must be prepared to *earn* every penny coming to them, that they must expect nothing for nothing in this world.

To achieve this, I have emphasized that they must be studious and industrious, that they must exercise rational frugality and self-denial until they have accumulated a competency, that they must aspire not only to take care of themselves and their dependents, but to acquire means to aid generously those who are in need.

I have warned them against extravagance, ostentation, thriftlessness, thoughtlessness, in order that they may escape the hardships and humiliations which befall so many in old age, explaining that it is infinitely better to be able to bestow charity than to be compelled to accept it.

Don't let any professor convince you, I tell them, that the world owes you a living. Get it firmly into your head that it is up to you to fit yourself to earn a living and that you will encounter plenty of competition. Don't hesitate to sacrifice in the fore part of your life if you hope to fare well in the latter part of your life. Rainy days will come. Make diligent provision for them.

I tell them that, going forth in this spirit, eager to put more into the world than they hope to take out of it, and possessing unshakable faith in the eternal laws of justice and righteousness, they will find life joyous, they will accept difficulties as a challenge to their manhood, that, doing the right thing, they will never be tempted to give way to despair, but will find their own life increasing in happiness and service with the passing years.

Above all, that they must not be drones, loafers, leaners; that they must exert themselves to the utmost to be useful; that through self-discipline and self-denial they may reasonably hope to earn the means to practice generosity and unselfishness.

Forbes magazine struggled. The circulation was about sixty thousand and the advertising pages were few—six or seven pages in some issues. It took BC's personal ability to get those advertising pages filled. It was a treadmill. Though employees were living with Scotch week, elsewhere in New York—at Hearst, for example—people were paid every week, "but not much," as one old Hearst employee recalled.

There's little doubt that there was no established editorial direction. BC was bewildered by what was going on. There was a succession of managing editors until finally in 1936 Harwood Merrill arrived and stayed four years. The magazine was moving away from being a financial and stock-market magazine and "taking on a more industrial bent," said Robert Flaherty, who studied the magazine's history for the fiftieth-anniversary issue. Merrill was determined to make a go of things and the magazine became heavy with management "how to" stories. One day Merrill asked circulation director Richard Kline whether it would be easier to change *Forbes* into a strictly American management-type magazine or to start a new magazine. Kline said, "It would be easier to start a new one—and damned if he didn't" *(Modern Industry,* later absorbed by *Dun's Review).*

By 1936 BC was insisting that "recovery is certain." But the Trenton (Missouri) *Missourian* was not impressed. Editorially it replied:

> Persons who have taken sympathetic interest in the naive B. C. Forbes, little brother of the rich who discourses with ponderous solemnity on finance and economics, will be glad to see that the creeping horrors which were about to overcome him on the terrible state of the Union have given way to a blithesome gladness.

Not that Bertie was losing his own sense of humor. When one letter writer told BC that he and a few others gathered together to discuss his columns, he replied, "Your fortnightly meetings of 15 citizens of Plainview recalled to my mind that Biblical passage: 'Where two or three are gathered in my name, there am I gathered in the midst of them.'

The Depression—and the thirties—drew to a close. Gradually,

after several false starts, the national economy picked up. There were jobs, there was war demand—war erupted in Europe in 1939.

In 1940 BC accepted the nomination to the Englewood Board of Education and was a short-term cause célèbre. He attempted to have banned the teaching manuals of one Professor Rugg. The story made the front page of the New York *Herald Tribune*. Professor Harold Rugg of Teachers College, Columbia University, had developed what today would be called a "social studies course." BC reflected the opinion of many other Americans when he wrote to the president of the Englewood Board of Education that "after thorough study, I am profoundly convinced that the Rugg teachings are un-American, unpatriotic, unfit for the young minds for whom we are educationally responsible."

Changes on the board, new members, a lack of decisions, an apology by BC to a teacher who felt slighted, and the whole affair just fizzled out.

In 1941 Malcolm went into newspapering in Ohio, and by 1942 was trying desperately to get out of it. BC watched these fledgling attempts somewhat resignedly. The year 1943 brought its double blow: Adelaide walking out; Hearst canceling BC's syndicated column after twenty-three years. BC had never had a contract with Hearst. After leaving the New York *American* in 1917 to found *Forbes*, BC had just freelanced until approached by Hearst himself.

Now Hearst was cutting back and BC wasn't cheap. The abrupt end broke BC's heart, but heartbreak always stung him to action. With Ben Javits, brother of the present U.S. Senator Jacob Javits, BC started the Investors League, a Washington-oriented lobby to look after the interests of the small investors. It survived until the 1970s —twenty-odd years after BC's death.

Bertie's real 1943 heartbreak was Adelaide's departure from Fountain Road. Among her less-articulated complaints were her suspicions regarding Bertie's relationship with Gertrude Weiner, his lifelong secretary, who had started with *Forbes* as a sixteen-year-old typist in 1919. With his Scots brogue and fussy ways, BC until then hadn't kept a secretary long, and Gertrude was asked to substitute in an "emergency." The emergency lasted until the day BC died.

Gertrude and BC made an odd couple. Backstairs gossip at *Forbes* long assumed a relationship more than platonic. But the gossip failed to take into account the basic makeup of both Gertrude and Bertie Charles.

In the days when typewriters were gaining popularity, the typewriter manufacturers competed with one another by running secretarial schools. Train a girl on a Royal and she would stick with it during her secretarial career. Most such schools charged $50 for a ten-week course. Gertrude's family was broke. But her father promised that they would pay the $50 once Gertrude got a job.

With her typing and shorthand skills acquired, Gertrude was referred by the school—which also acted as a job-placement agency for companies who bought its typewriters—to a downtown office. On the subway, reading through the classifieds as she traveled to her interview, Gertrude saw a job advertised at *Forbes*.

She got off the subway at the nearest stop and successfully applied. By the time she retired, the entire history of *Forbes* and three generations of the Forbes family entwined her life. In 1973 she simply walked in to Malcolm one morning and, after more than a half century with *Forbes*, said it was time to leave. In her Palm Springs home she prefers now to think only of the good times—the harsh memories have been allowed to drift away into oblivion.

What brought BC and Gertrude together as platonic companions? Gertrude's early poverty matched BC's own. Her hard-up Brooklyn Jewish family had a tradition when company came, "FHB" (family hold back), to make sure the visitors could be fed. Gertrude, as a young teenager, once was rushed off to the hospital with suspected tuberculosis. It turned out to be malnutrition. She had been holding back too often.

When this poor working girl applied, and when BC saw her willingness and ability to work, he had a fellow spirit. She developed into his assistant and, as the years rolled on, his companion for company's sake. "Oh, I had to fight him off once or twice," she admitted, "but that's not unusual in a business office." And that was as far as it went—even though, in BC's later years, BC would ask Gertrude to go along on his return visits to Scotland. Her cabin was "always at the other end of the ship. Just so people wouldn't talk. The first time he asked me to accompany him (after Adelaide had left) he said he would not take me if my parents objected. They trusted him; I trusted him. We were right."

In Scotland BC's strict and eagle-eyed Scots Presbyterian sisters wondered about it too, but they saw soon enough that Gertrude was secretary and friend, and that was all. Who else would have played gin rummy in his office until ten o'clock at night when he didn't want to go home? Who else would have put up with his irritable ways and yet constantly, unwillingly, forgiven him? With BC Gertrude saw broader horizons than she otherwise would have done. She earned them; she gave her life to him and the magazine. "He turned down all my boy friends. Always had something to say about them."

But he did more than that. Though he was cheap, and inarticulate when it came to praise or thanks, he cared and she knew it. Every Christmas he sent notes saying how important she was, and how much he relied on her, and how she was worth much more and that when business improved she would get it. He was good with words, but slow on delivery. The first thing his sons did when BC died was raise Gertrude's salary.

BC wasn't just tight with Gertrude, however; he was tight with all the employees. Recalled one of them: "BC was amazed when he found out I was getting married. He wondered how I could do it on how little he was paying me."

Gertrude and BC had one thing in common which helped them understand each other; both came of parents who had battled hard for a living. It was enough. The working partnership that saw them develop as a team did the rest.

"Woman," BC would snap around 2 P.M., with his daily column due, "I'm a writer. I cannae just sit down and do it, it has to come fra within." But he would sit down and do it and his column would be ready by 3 P.M. Then he would get his revenge. He loved to tell bawdy jokes. Gertrude hated to listen to them and would walk out. He would call her in to dictate a letter, and slip in the first line of the joke. She'd leave. They'd try the letter again later, and he'd slip in the second line. It might take all day, or two days, to get the letter dictated, but Bertie would finally get the joke told. And Gertrude would provide no reaction whatsoever to BC's gales of laughter.

Even Adelaide eventually got over her suspicions. Occasionally, long after BC and Adelaide had separated, Adelaide and Gertrude would lunch. They had much to commiserate with each other over, with a demanding man who thought first of his work, and secondly of himself.

By the end of 1943 BC sat down to reflect on his life, his family, his magazine. He began to get his affairs in order, and the affairs of his sons:

Dear Malc.

. . . As I recall, you sent me a list of your debts long time ago. If you are not sure just what is your most pressing obligation, I'd be glad to have you send me an up-to-date compilation, and then, together, we could decide what would be the best thing to do at this time. . . .

Bertie was concerned about the rationings and shortages in wartorn Europe affecting his family and friends there. There were brother Alex's wife, and his own brothers and sisters. Just seven of the ten Forbeses children from Cunnieknowe now survived. And early in 1944 BC was ordering Macy's to "send things which in your experience has taught you would be most acceptable to the recipients . . ."

That year BC celebrated "50 years of hard work." He was sixty-four; a half century had gone by since the short, skinny, ill-educated, ill-equipped young "Patchy" For-bess had boarded the train at Maud Junction for Peterhead.

By 1944 the Forbes sons were scattered. Bruce was doing war work with the Bendix Corporation. He was married, but there were no grandchildren yet. Malcolm was a staff sergeant "itching to get into action." Gordon was in the Middle East in the American Field Service alongside the Eighth Army, and Wallace was still at home— but headed for Lawrenceville in September.

The following year, two weeks before the Battle of the Bulge, Malcolm would fall, one leg badly shattered by German machine-gun fire.

As a soldier Malcolm was conscientious, and responsive to the need to give orders and to obey them. He was a loner according to one machine-gun squad member: "He spent most of his free time reading. He didn't spend a great deal of time socializing with the rest of us." With Malcolm's different social and education background, it perhaps was not surprising that Malcolm found little in common, except soldiering, with the rest of his buddies.

Army buddy George Kinzel explained one marked Malcolm ability: "Whenever something needed to be explained, the officers always asked Malcolm to do it. He could take the most complicated things and explain them in a simple way so everyone could understand." That was a valuable gift indeed for the leader of a machine-gun squad.

Staff Sergeant Malcolm S. Forbes left for Europe in September, 1944. True to form, he started a troopship newspaper and, as ship's reporter, soon was writing a column, "Dog Face Barks," in *The Daily Duffle Bag,* for his fellow comrades in arms in "The Railsplitters," the 84th Infantry.

In addition to whatever news Malcolm could scrounge from the ship's radio operator, the *Duffle Bag* ran a selection of jokes that would have given Headmaster Gage conniptions had they appeared on the pages of the Hackley *Eagle* of ill-repute:

> Irma Trud was a good girl.
> Irma Trud was a bad girl (no period)

Only weeks later the next headlines concerning Malcolm were printed in the United States:

> Malcolm Forbes wounded fighting inside Germany. Sergeant Forbes, publisher's son, hurt in Germany. Sergeant Forbes, according to notification received by his father, was wounded at Aachen, is now confined at a Paris hospital. None of the details have been received, Mr. Forbes said today.

The details were: "FCC, Femur, left. Spastic condition." It was uncertain whether he would have to lose the leg—the decision would be made in the United States. As soon as he could be moved Malcolm was flown to Butler General Hospital, Deshon, Pennsylvania. He wrote on arrival to his Army buddy Sergeant John Bresky.

> Dear John, Since that night I have been waiting until I could write to thank you one hell of a lot for your aid that night. I guess I acted awful but John, I sure hope to hell I never have to go through such agony again in a hurry. But you, Sigle, Puckett, Wachter, Dvojsack sure were buddies when a fellow really needed some. And I'll never forget it.
>   Lying here a helpless pincushion, hour after hour, day in day out, I think constantly about you all and sure hope that all is well with ye old 7th and 8th squads. Johny, I ain't "a praying man" but I do ask God to keep you all in one piece until it's over.

The letter came back: "Returned. Deceased."

Malcolm was in a body cast. The doctors had patched together the leg. Bertie immediately contacted business friends with plants or factories in that area, asking them to have people call in on Malcolm to cheer him up. Charles Hook of the American Foundry Company, whose own son, a tank officer, lay seriously wounded in Nichols General Hospital, Louisville, Kentucky, contacted one of his managers near Deshon and the man would stop by to see Malcolm. Hook said he understood what it meant to "have friends take an interest in these boys."

Bertie hurried down to Deshon. Miss Weiner made the trip with him. It was with some trepidation that they went in to see the badly injured Malcolm. Body cast or not, he was propped up on pillows, copies of *Forbes* magazine strewn on the bed around him. He was busy with paste pot, scissors, sheets of cardboard, redesigning the *Forbes* format.

"We might have known," commented Gertrude Weiner. "It was an incredible sight. But then, Malcolm is incredible."

He wanted most to talk to his father about some new ideas for the magazine. Advertising was down from the previous year, Bertie reported, but they were surviving. By February, 1945, Malcolm was hobbling around with sticks, and by the time notification of his Bronze Star came through, he was writing for *Forbes*.

He was smartly clothed:

Dear Malc. You can take this to Rogers Peet as authority to order and charge to me a complete civie outfit. Namely: one pair of shoes, one pair of socks, one suit of underwear, one suit up to $55, the most I ever paid for a suit, one shirt. Daddy.

The announcement of the Bronze Star—accompanied by a photograph that could have been a duplicate of his father's Hearst column photo twenty years earlier—stated:

Meritorious service in connection with military operations against the enemy in Germany, November 26, 1944. While making an independent reconnaissance for his section, staff sergeant Forbes discovered a wide and unprotected gap on the right flank of his battalion which he promptly reported to his Battalion Commander who immediately took corrective measures. The initiative, resourcefulness under live action displayed by Sergeant Forbes prevented possible encirclement of the battalion and reflected high credit upon himself and the armed forces of the United States.

He was also awarded the Purple Heart.

The April 15, 1945, issue of *Forbes* announced a new series: "A Soldier Speaks: What GI's are expecting after victory." It was offered "in the belief that it is of vital importance for our businessmen and others to know what our fighting men are thinking." Malcolm was all set to tell them.

Postwar! Time to look ahead. BC had an aversion to spending money on his business surroundings, but he agreed to having the "girls' rest room" refurbished ("we made a big hit with that") and was considering doing something to the entrance, "though I am not very fussy myself about these things." (Malcolm, wrote BC, was urging an improvement because he regarded the offices as "not spruce or swanky enough.")

Sometimes Malcolm was sitting in now in BC's big club poker games.

> Had one of my de-luxe poker parties at the Metropolitan Club last night —it was an extremely nice party—Malc was there and at one time losing about $100 (of course, I was staking him) but ended up winning about $40. Everyone won but me! However, it was worth it, from a business angle.

By early 1946, with BC taking off by plane for Scotland, Malcolm was taking off on a more romantic journey. He was courting Roberta Remsen Laidlaw, a pretty twenty-two-year-old Englewood girl.

In social terms Malcolm was doing well for himself. The Laidlaws owned a company with investment-banking traditions covering a century with commodity dealings on Broad Street, in New York's financial district, before that. The first Laidlaw in the firm of what became Laidlaw and Co. (and today is Laidlaw & Coggeshall) was Henry Bell Laidlaw in 1854. His father had been a professor of English at Edinburgh University.

In personal terms, Malcolm was more than lucky in love. He

found a wife whose upbringing and character are such that she was prepared to serve the best interests of the family and her husband's career. Hers was not an unusual sacrifice. Roberta's mother, a somewhat autocratic and socially correct woman, who viewed BC with some alarm—especially at the wedding when he went home and changed into his kilt and returned with his bagpipes—had brought up her daughters to be helpmates.

Roberta, the youngest of the five daughters of Robert Remsen Laidlaw and Isabella Carter Onderdonk Laidlaw, was named Roberta, the story is told, because father Robert always had hoped for a son to carry on his name. To Malcolm, Roberta became Bertie.

Malcolm, long of no fixed religion, became an Episcopalian and took an active role in his church for a period. But his ever-busy mind, goaded on by his ever-present ambition, was more concerned with getting *Forbes* mentioned in the best places—those high-circulation newspapers and magazines read by the advertisers and advertising agencies. In 1946, *Advertising Age* was reporting:

> Over at *Forbes* these days things are buzzing. There is a revitalized zip and snap that have been absent some months. In the past four months circulation has jumped 26,000 giving this veteran among business magazines its record high of 90,000 subscribers. And Malcolm S. Forbes, son of the magazine's founder—and only 26—says that by October the magazine will reach 100,000 business and executive subscribers.

Malcolm knew the magazine had to attract advertising and subscriptions. Being talked about was essential to both.

Businessmen around the country—and many newspapers—were talking anxiously about *Forbes* after Malcolm, who now was sharing the "Fact and Comment" pages with his father, told the National Association of Manufacturers to "drop dead." Once the uproar had died down, Malcolm spent a day with the NAM organization and wrote about what a splendid job they were doing.

Malcolm knew what a tough job lay ahead for *Forbes*.

Malcolm pushed for *Forbes* to hire people in the editorial department to get away from the dependency on submitted articles. Said Malcolm: "My father was a tremendous editor in the literal sense. He could take a piece and get the junk off it and make it say the same thing better in fewer words. He was a tremendous writer, but he was not an editor in the sense we think of one today—and he was still writing his daily column, six days a week—so, on the whole, we missed.

"When we emerged after the war, we had nothing to emerge with editorially. We tried to make gradual changes, but by 1947 we were still doing pretty much the same as we always had—scissors and paste. I don't take credit for having inaugurated a new era, but I did inaugurate in the new era that we had to have our own people.

BC continued to "rule *Forbes* with an iron pen" as Malcolm put it, but "the competition was dominating a field we had had to ourselves during the twenties."

What hope had *Forbes* magazine of growing in circulation? If it could appeal to the new wave of potential investors—the returning GIs now settling down to colleges and careers on the GI Bill, the emerging middle class, however defined—the subscriptions could grow. If it developed an editorial content that aided those neophytes in the stock market, *Forbes* magazine could be their investing tool.

BC had long had a service whereby readers paid a few dollars and obtained lists of whatever stocks the *Forbes* columnists were mentioning—in advance of the magazine's hitting the street. It was a bit sordid, and not particularly remunerative. Malcolm's idea was a separate service, Investors Advisory Institute (IAI), promoted directly to the *Forbes* magazine mailing list—the subscribers themselves. It went like wildfire at $35 a year. (By 1950 IAI was turning in $51,000 a year in after-tax profit. Twenty years later, just as the stock market began to slide, Malcolm peremptorily killed IAI, retaining only a profitable Special Situations Service at $125 a year. Malcolm's timing on starting IAI was excellent. Younger brother Wallace, who ran IAI during the sixties, commented on Malcolm's guillotine of IAI in 1970: "In retrospect his timing was excellent again.")

If Malcolm was teaching his father some new tricks, BC was teaching Malcolm some old ones, at the poker table. BC's poker playing was legendary in corporate business circles. Only once did

BC find the stakes too high—in Hollywood, where they played "wild games." Poker—and gambling at cards generally—was good business and good fun. Bert's close friends would always be sending along little notes:

> Last evening I was reading your October 15 magazine and discovered the public statement that you like me and the taxi starter at the 42nd St. ferry. If you really like me I attribute it to the generosity which I have exhibited at some little private gathering you have had and I suggest you bring the taxi starter to the next one.

His pal William Irving was not to be outdone:

> I feel very much flattered to have my name appear over your initials as one of the men you particularly like. I presume part of this effect comes about because I'm so soft in a poker game.

Perhaps the best outside description is that by Arthur "Red" Motley, who for years was editor of *Parade:*

> I still laugh over the BIG poker game I got into with B. C. Forbes. . . . I was making $7,500 and everybody else in the game including Forbes was rich. Grant, VP in charge of sales at General Motors, was in the $400,000 to $500,000 bracket. John Chick, head of Cadillac was in the $300,000 bracket, etc, etc. After they took the limit off, I went to the bathroom. Old Man Forbes who was Scotch and never played a customers' game—always out for blood—knew what the score was and he came in to comfort me with the thought that rich as these guys were, they didn't know how to play poker. He was right. I won $67, but I never went back. It was too rich for Motley.

BC would cover Malcolm's debts at the card table, and allow Malcolm half his winnings. (There was a card game at which BC couldn't touch Malcolm, however: bridge. Malcolm's bridge game is sufficiently good, and consistent, that his hands regularly are quoted and played in newspaper bridge columns.)

BC was talking to Adelaide again, meeting her for lunch occasionally, visiting her when she was in the hospital with complaints ranging from shingles to pleurisy.

Malcolm Stevenson Forbes, Jr.—Steve—the first Forbes and Laidlaw grandson, arrived July 18, 1947, just as IAI was getting under way. Second son, Robert, would arrive just as Malcolm's next venture was launched: a new type of magazine to be called *Nation's Heritage*. It would carry no advertising, be huge and beautiful, the sort of thing people would want on their coffee tables, or be able to give as gifts. Corporations could buy subscriptions for local libraries so that everyone could benefit from the information and beauty of the *Nation's Heritage* even though individual copies of the magazine were to cost $35 and an annual subscription $150.

In 1945 an ambitious young Princetonian named Robert K. Heimann had approached Malcolm to ask if Malcolm would give permission for the *Nassau Sovereign* to be revived. Malcolm was delighted to agree, and even more pleased with Heimann's abilities as editor. With *Nation's Heritage* in mind for a mid-1947 launching, Malcolm brought Heimann in as its editor.

Looking at *Nation's Heritage* today one is reminded of a mammoth collection of huge Christmas cards—twelve by fifteen inches—magnificently bound. It was launched with flair in the Empire room of the Waldorf Astoria.

Years later BC publicly summed up the *Nation's Heritage* saga in the New York *Herald Tribune*: "It was Malc's brainchild, the most beautiful magazine in history. But banker Winthrop Aldrich put his finger on it when he said as he bought his subscription for $150, 'glad the Chase National Bank isn't financing it.' " Gordon's comment to his father also summed it up: "It certainly was a worthy, if a bit impractical, undertaking."

The bills that remained to be mopped up, for the expensive inks and costly coated papers, the master craftsman bindings and the high-priced packaging, ended up on BC's desk.

Malcolm was already into new fields. By knocking on doors all over Bernardsville, the New Jersey township where he lived, he had been elected to the Bernardsville Borough Council. With his customary leapfrog reasoning, he figured that, if one jump could take him to the borough council, why not a second jump, based on doorbell ringing, into the state senate?

Malcolm also was busily promoting *Forbes*. He did a mailing to corporate executives of his father's testimony before the 1947 Taft Committee on the Economy. Senator Robert Taft was so impressed by young Malcolm he offered him a place on his staff. Malcolm said he preferred to stay with his father's magazine. To mark *Forbes'* thirtieth year there was to be a huge gala dinner—BC called it "the monster November 5 party"—to include those top fifty American businessmen chosen by *Forbes* readers as the fifty foremost leaders of U.S. business.

When President Harry Truman later used the occasion in an attack on anti-New Dealers, he quoted to the audience from the advance publicity the fact that the combined annual income for those men was $7,500,000 a year—an average of $150,000. "The sponsors looked around for a speaker who could talk the language of those who make $150,000 a year. They didn't ask me."

"Wrong," replied BC editorially. "The truth is that the President of the United States was the first person asked to make the address on that occasion . . . it is charitable to conclude that President Truman didn't know the facts."

As Malcolm was beginning to get into his political stride, his father was starting to reminisce more and more about "the good old days." In 1948 he again went to Scotland. By the following year he was arranging his affairs for the disposition of the business after his death. "I am delighted to tell you," he wrote Wally, "the business will be left to you and my other sons absolutely free and clear, that there will not be one bond or share outstanding, owned by an outsider. You and your brothers will inherit the business without a penny of debt —except, of course, current bills. I am most grateful to the Good Lord to have been able to achieve this."

In 1948 Malcolm sat down to prepare for the annually worst copy of *Forbes* magazine—the thin, unattractive January 1 issue— and decided it was worthwhile trying to grade the various corporations much as does a school report card. "You know them, Dad," he told BC. "You go through them and give them an A, B, C or D— whatever they deserve." From those humble beginnings grew the *Forbes* January 1 issue, today a two-hundred page compendium rating the top seven hundred U.S. corporations for profitability, sales, return on equity and much else. It is fat with advertising—better than $2 million worth.

In a 1949 note to son Wallace, Bertie wrote: "Business prospects for 1950 are fairly good. Looks as if the magazine will do somewhat, but not greatly better, than in 1949. IAI continues to be our star money maker. Thank Heavens we have finally liquidated *Nation's Heritage*'s terrific obligations."

Bertie said he intended to distribute more *Forbes* stock to his sons to mark his seventieth birthday the next year, and celebrate with another trip "home," to New Deer. There, in 1950, the children of Whitehill School reciprocated BC's 40 years of generosity to the school—the gifts that each year had paid for the Christmas party—with an ebony cane, "suitably engraved." Back in the United States, BC started lunching more regularly, and found it was a good way to do business. At a particularly successful luncheon for Cleo F. Craig, the new president of American Telephone and Telegraph, BC regaled AT&T top executives with personal stories and accounts of Thomas A. Edison and Theodore N. Vail—who actually built up the company—as well as long-time but long-gone AT&T president Walter S. Clifford. As lunch ended Craig called BC aside and said: "Anything that this company can do for you and your organization, please let me know and we will be more than delighted to do it."

Of Malcolm eyeing the state senate, BC wrote: "I feel he has enough responsibilities running this organization without having to devote time and energy to running for political office." But, if anything, the award by General Eisenhower of the Freedom Foundation gold medal to Malcolm for *Nation's Heritage* had only heightened Malcolm's political ambitions. The *Forbes* treasury had benefited to the sum of $1500 from the Freedom Foundation, and it also benefited from all the favorable publicity.

In the election on April 18, 1951, Malcolm took New Jersey's Somerset County and was elected state senator. He received this telegram: "Congratulations on your first big step toward becoming a major part of the 'nation's heritage' stop. The Forbes family." BC had privately commented during the campaign that despite Malcolm's bucking the Republican machine he would not be surprised to see him win. "If he does, well and good. If he doesn't, well and good."

Malcolm was now beginning to apply his talent for promotion both to the magazine and to his own political future. *Forbes* magazine sponsored a television show—a panel discussion and nationwide survey featuring leaders of big business and "an important address by Governor Alfred E. Driscoll." *Forbes* took big advertisements in all the newspapers of the New York metropolitan area. At the same time, Malcolm was busily writing to Mrs. Dwight D. Eisenhower urging her to urge Ike to run. Mrs. Eisenhower wrote back to Malcolm: "Regarding your hopes that my husband will feel a political duty in 1952, the general constantly reaffirms his desire as rapidly and completely as possible to accomplish his mission as Supreme Allied Commander in Europe."

That story was soon to make the national and international news wires. It was a good scoop and Malcolm had it. He did not let go of his momentum. Instead, he formed the New Jersey Ike-Nixon clubs and flew to Paris to petition Eisenhower personally to accept the Republican nomination for the presidency.

In addition to catching national headlines both for himself and the magazine, Malcolm was scaring the pants off the New Jersey Republican old guard. All New Jersey politicians and most New Jersey state employees have free rail passes. Immediately on election as state senator, Malcolm sent in his rail pass and introduced a bill to ban all free state passes. The politicians defeated him on that one. The GOP-dominated New Jersey state senate made all its decisions in caucus, and Malcolm said that was undemocratic and pressed them publicly and privately to the point where all future bills would be allowed onto the senate floor, so that all senators could vote on them rather than a gag's being imposed by the caucus.

The Newark *Star-Ledger*, in January, 1952, said that

> Senator Malcolm Forbes, who began his legislative career with bills for bingo and against free state railroad passes, claims he's going to "lie low" for awhile in creating sensations, yet he is the only legislator who hires a full time publicity agent to promote his views. Forbes, New York publisher who launched the New Jersey Eisenhower for President boom tells this one on himself: A leading industrialist wrote Forbes he "ought to be in a mental institution for supporting Ike." Forbes wrote back: "I've already been in one." He explained that with other state legislators he had recently inspected Trenton State Hospital.

Malcolm did not endear himself to the state political fathers by saying on a radio show that "a few old goats with a monopoly on office run politics in New Jersey."

An item in the Newark *Star-Ledger* ably summed up Malcolm's approach to statewide politicking:

> The Republican old guardsmen would be willing to go on a march to the White House in support of a movement to have young Mr. Forbes given the post of American minister to Tibet or a still more hidden country if one could be found. Anything, in fact, to get him as far away as possible from New Jersey.

When Nixon appeared in New Jersey in October, 1952, the Union County Republican Club presented him with a kennel for his dog Checkers. (But, throughout Ike's entire campaign, Malcolm was invited by the state speakers' bureau to make only one speech for Eisenhower. Despite all his efforts, and the fact that he had given $2500 to Atlantic County alone, Malcolm remained ignored by the old guard—though not by President Eisenhower.)

Malcolm could not handle both magazine and politics—and politics was winning out. By 1953 the magazine was lackluster once again.

Late in 1952—once the thirty-fifth-anniversary party was out of the way—BC announced his plans to bring Bruce out of Detroit. "We here see relatively little of Malcolm, he is busier than a beaver 'politicking' and is receiving an extraordinary amount of newspaper publicity. (Malcolm was looking even further ahead.) "He feels his chances of being nominated and elected governor are bright—all political candidates are eternally hopeful!"

BC had watched Malcolm throughout 1952 and commented that though he was "at home very, very little, he seems to revel in it. He is quite optimistic over his chances of becoming governor. But his is an expensive venture!"

Malcolm was already receiving letters saying, "If you can manage to stay the way you are, as you move up through the governorship and the presidency, it would be one of the greatest things that ever happened to this country."

Malcolm wrote the foreword to the *Political Almanac* issued by Dr. George Gallup and the American Institute of Public Opinion. At that time Malcolm said that the most significant fact of the times "isn't the relative number of Democrats or Republicans, but the vast steady growth of those people who call themselves independents."

It was the independents Malcolm was after; he understood them. Malcolm was having more fun than he'd ever had in his life. In addition to announcing that he himself was considering running for governor, Malcolm opened the New Jersey Republicans for Eisenhower office at 40 West State Street, Trenton.

At first, wrote a local newspaper, "If any politician was standing near the headquarters in the next few weeks they must have come along after sundown." On January 7, General Eisenhower's candidacy became a reality. A handful more of the adventurous professionals began dropping in on Forbes. The campaign still wasn't made of solid stuff . . . until the morning after Eisenhower won the New Hampshire primary.

"Then," wrote Bruce Biossat, Newspaper Enterprise staff correspondent, "professionals suddenly found it fashionable to be caught loitering in the vicinity of 40 West State Street. The amateurs exulted."

Malcolm, always good with a quick turn of phrase, developed another one: "If you can spare one of the Truman fifty-cent dollars after paying your taxes this week, send it or as many as you can afford to Ike headquarters." By March, the state Republican organization had taken over the Eisenhower for President drive and the amateur Eisenhower clubs were eased off to one side. Malcolm already had spent several thousand dollars of his own (and his father's) money promoting the local Ike clubs. Those clubs were receiving nothing from the state GOP organization or from the national organization. But, as a Trenton *Times* editorial so aptly remarked, "Malcolm Forbes seems destined to be a factor in politics in New Jersey either with or without the blessing of the Republican party leaders."

Malcolm Forbes predicted that Ike would take the New Jersey primary by 150,000. On April 16, 1952, the Associated Press reported Ike's victory by a 150,000-vote margin. Despite the fact that Malcolm was not invited to a select New Jersey Republican meeting with General Eisenhower at Columbia University, he had made a name for himself.

Some Republican backers around the state were watching him. Wrote Mrs. Evelyn Baltz: "You are wealthy in the number of friends you have made. That confidence remains and we hope someday to have the opportunity of applying it to your personal advantage. Your ability, sincerity, honesty and devotion to the work at hand should lead to bigger and better things. I sincerely hope so."

When Malcolm wrote back to Mrs. Baltz, he said he would put her letter in his scrapbook so that "when I am old and grey and try to prove to my grandchildren that I was a fine fellow I can have this letter to help do it." The letter is in Malcolm's scrapbook. But his grandchildren are not yet old enough to understand.

In 1953, Malcolm declared himself for the gubernatorial candidacy, without the support of the Republican state machine.

Not in a long time had any U.S. state witnessed such a campaign. Malcolm would turn up on time at political rallies; he would ring doorbells, talk to old ladies, stand at factory gates, and tell people exactly what he thought he should say rather than what they wanted to hear: "Corny appeals based purely on party loyalty, regardless of party record in office, do not win votes. The old-time party politicians may sneer as they will, because independent voters can deliver no patronage nor win an election on an independent ticket; but those pros are learning the hard way that party organizations can't win an election unless they prove their case beyond the confines of those who vote blindly the straight ticket."

Malcolm understood the political middle, those uncommitted Americans who could be persuaded. He knew them as a politician, and he knew them as a writer–reporter–magazine editor. But he still lost the election.

In 1953 Malcolm had taken time out to sail his forty-two-foot yacht, *Wings,* on a daring first: to Labrador. He ran into foul weather and the yacht was for a while reported missing. Six-year-old Steve and editor Robert Heimann were both along for the trip.

Unvanquished, Malcolm headed out again a few months later.

He made Nova Scotia and was on the way back when foul weather forced him and Steve and Heimann to send out an S.O.S. They were picked up by the Coast Guard. Steve's comment was: "Daddy's no longer a captain. He lost his ship." But *Wings* was recovered, up to her gunwales in water. Malcolm sold the boat. He was neither bloodied nor bowed. He simply was determined that his next yacht would be big enough to ride out a storm.

The stock market in 1953 turned down, and a downturn in income affected IAI—down $40,000 a month. Bruce, now ensconced in New York, was running the business and having sessions with advertising-agency executives, a mission his father had regarded as something that had needed to be done for quite a long time. BC could feel himself slowing down. He was getting to the office only two or three days a week now, and was bothered by numbness in his right arm. It had been a complaint that affected his father prior to his death and had shown up in brother Wilson, too.

Having settled into a routine of visiting Scotland every second year, BC nonetheless decided not to wait until 1954 for yet one more trip. He left for Scotland (after first establishing a Forbes pension plan). Did he know it would be his last trip?

On a cold December Sunday in 1953 he stood in the auld kirk at Maud. There were few faces from his childhood now in the congregation. Bertie stood close to the baptismal font, which he had just presented to the church. He had provided a small endowment fund. But no eyes were on the font. Those in the church were not listening to the minister. They were looking at Bertie.

John Webster, whose wife was Gavin Grieg's granddaughter, said: "It was obvious to all of us, and to the old man himself, that this was his final visit. A lifetime of generous service to the villagers, to the people he'd grown up with, and to their children, was coming to an end. There were tears in BC's eyes and in the eyes of everyone in the church. No one needed to say anything."

Bertie sailed for home. In 1954, like an old firehorse rallying at the smell of smoke, he launched into a series of vigorous editorials, political editorials, attacking Senator Joseph McCarthy—the era of McCarthyism had gripped the United States. On April 21, 1954, BC

posted a notice regarding the *Forbes* family picnic, "family" meaning the staff of *Forbes* magazine as well as his own family:

> Toward the end of next month, May, I will celebrate the completion of
> sixty years' work. I am planning to invite you all to a picnic at my home,
> in Englewood. There will be drawings for six prizes of sixty dollars each.
> Good luck to you! I hope everyone will enjoy a pleasant day.

. . . and it was signed in a big round hand of curling *b*'s, rolling
s's, and a well-flaunted *F* for Forbes.

Two weeks later, at the end of the afternoon, BC was working
away in his *Forbes* magazine office, at 80 Fifth Avenue. Gertrude
Weiner had left for the day to attend an evening meeting of the
Seraphics, a professional association of executive secretaries.

Each evening, after business had ended and the employees had
left for home, the elevator operator, Andy Grammick, was sure to
check that all the lights were off in *Forbes* magazine. BC would give
him a small tip once a week for doing so. On that evening, May 5,
1954, when Andy popped his head around the door to look into BC's
lighted office, he saw the old man sprawled on the floor, dead.

Bertie Charles Forbes, nine days short of his seventy-fourth
birthday, died as he'd lived: pen in hand.

6

Malcolm and Bruce

BC Forbes left each of his sons $15,000 from insurance policies, and as promised a debt-free magazine. The ownership was divided into nearly one-third each for Bruce and Malcolm, one-third between Gordon and Wallace, with a few shares for Gertrude Weiner, who earlier had bought some for herself. BC had valiantly hoped that perhaps Gertrude could break any voting deadlocks that might develop between the sons.

Of one thing he could be sure, looking out from wherever Scots journalists go, he couldn't have left control of *Forbes* to two more disparate individuals than Malcolm and Bruce. They were destined to endure an uneasy partnership.

One long-time Forbes watcher felt that BC did not really trust either of his sons to run the magazine, and doubted Bruce's ability to do so. "After Malcolm started IAI he had reason to treat Malc with more respect, but it was obvious that Malcolm might be good at ideas, but lousy at executing them. During the years Malcolm toiled alongside Bruce he would go up to the Racquet and Tennis Club for hours, apparently just talking to people there, for something to do. He wasn't just bored; he was lost. He was a fixture there. The trouble with the Forbeses was no taste, or poor taste. They ran pages and pages of tributes after the old man's death. The old man may have lacked judgement in some things—he has to be judged according to his time—but he did have a sense of propriety. Not Malcolm."

Bruce was candid, easygoing and gregarious. He had done a great deal for *Forbes* in Detroit, where his golf game and broad, smiling face were major assets.

His friendships with people like Semon "Bunky" Knudsen (then general manager of General Motors' Chevrolet division), with Governor Thomas E. Dewey and with David Mahoney, then of Colgate Palmolive (later chairman of Norton Simon) were good fun, and good for business. His crowning achievement was a social one when he became commodore of the Key Largo Anglers Club, and was inducted by former president Herbert Hoover.

With his second wife, Ruth, Bruce had moved to New York at BC's behest once BC realized that he was slowing down and that Malcolm had interests and ambitions aside from the magazine.

Malcolm was more eager, more ambitious, more the loner. He was still attracted and distracted in a variety of directions, feeling that there was much he could accomplish across a range of pursuits. He owed the magazine his living, but, from the early 1950s on, his heart was in politics. When his father died, he was in the midst of planning a trip to Europe, a trip that was to be a respite from politics. He delayed the voyage until the fall.

What Malcolm lacked in his rarely contained fountain of bubbling enthusiasms was the sort of judgment that would prevent him from overplaying his hand. As a basic idea man, his plans were sound. But he would not listen to advice, and was unwilling to take the counsel of others. Those others included his brother Bruce.

By going his own route in New Jersey Republican politics, Malcolm had seen his efforts defeat the machine, end the state GOP caucus system, promote the presidential nomination of General Dwight D. Eisenhower, and enhance his chances for election as governor of New Jersey. When his father died, Malcolm was only thirty-four. He was young and very ambitious. He had a flair for the grand gesture which worked well in politics, and a turn of phrase that did him yeoman service on the speaker's platform. "I never know what I'm going to say until I get on the platform," he told Joe Kerrigan, reporter for the Plainfield *Courier-News,* during one political battle.

If Malcolm was single-minded, it was to the point of selfishness once his goal was set. No challenge was too great to meet, no obstacle too severe to be overcome. This single-mindedness when he wants something may strike others as incredible. When Malcolm was in uniform BC was always trying to persuade him to apply for a commission: "I have been for your becoming an officer all along," he wrote to his sergeant son. "I still feel the same way. When I think of your education . . ."

But Malcolm had no intention of taking a commission. He believed that having "enlisted man" on his political campaign literature once the war was ended would be far more attractive to the electorate than boasting about a commission.

Malcolm was sacrificing everything for success: family, business and interests. Those are the normal sacrifices in political life. And the family still is expected to honor its role as an "asset."

Roberta, resigned, and equally hardworking during the campaign, developed more than a clockwork smile; she was able to be interested in the people in the supermarkets. Her obvious concern for home and children struck a responsive chord among the onlookers, and she occasionally would rise to the political occasion with a quip herself. When Christopher was born, Roberta commented, "His father will have to wait twenty-one years for this vote."

Newark *News* reporter Edith Hutchinson saw Roberta as a "naturally shy person" whose "most difficult achievement" was to adjust to meeting hundreds of new people daily during the campaigning.

But, noted Ms. Hutchinson, Roberta tackled it nonetheless with "the determination of her Scottish ancestors . . . Mrs. Forbes also has an English Dutch strain, cropping out in her blue eyes, fair hair and rosy complexion."

Roberta did not really want to be interviewed, and spoke only reluctantly of her World War II work after Shipley School and Bryn Mawr, when she worked for the New York Information Center of Anti-Aircraft Artillery, plotting planes approaching the New York area.

Though she had known some of the Forbes boys in Englewood, she said, she didn't meet Malcolm until 1946, by which time she was studying at the New York School of Interior Decoration. "I didn't finish the course," she told the Newark *News* with a smile, "because I got married."

She turned the conversation to the children and home life. That was where her interest was, and was to remain during the next twenty years until the children went away to school. "It will be a long time before I have time for hobbies or clubs," she said in the early 1950s. She was right.

Malcolm was involved enough for both of them. He believed that "it's the people who don't come to political rallies who control the results." Ringing doorbells and getting out among the crowds was his recipe. Sticking to his guns over difficult, and unpopular, issues, Malcolm proved to be an able and honest politician—rare enough in any state, an endangered species in New Jersey. Malcolm was good at politics because he understood the independent American. He understood that American as a potential *Forbes* subscriber, too.

Here was Malcolm at his peak—politicking for things he believed in on behalf of people he liked. The best of him showed through—he wanted people to know he couldn't be bought. He was taking a good reading of the U.S. pulse—supported by his own feel for the "liberal" mood of the country. Only a decade or so earlier his Princeton contemporaries voted 87 percent that slum clearance was in the public interest, 64 percent of them favoring it even if it meant higher taxes. The young state senator knew that Americans, most of them, were prepared to go part way down the path of paying for a just and equitable society.

Malcolm was a politician of his time, and he was a good politician —on the move rather than on the make. But, just at the time Malcolm was building his political base, his father died. BC had complained periodically about Malcolm's tending to politics and not to the shop. Often enough he would stop by the editor's desk and ask, at 11 A.M.: "Is Malcolm in yet?" During Malcolm's politically active years, editor Byron "Dave" Mack would reply: "Not yet."

With BC gone, there was only Bruce to make demands on Malcolm. On BC's death, Bruce had become president, Malcolm the publisher and editor-in-chief. It was a sensible arrangement, and there was a brief tussle as to who would occupy BC's desk. Bruce won.

The rivalry stemmed from the conundrum as to who, really, was boss. The answer was: neither. The editorial side was Malcolm's general concern; advertising and circulation were Bruce's. Malcolm believed himself a better businessman than Bruce while strongly believing that Bruce probably was the best advertising man *Forbes* could have. Bruce, meanwhile, had to take a stronger role on the editorial side because Malcolm was too busy with his political ambitions to give the magazine the attention it needed and deserved.

Where Bruce and Malcolm agreed, the magazine flourished.

In 1954, only three weeks after BC's death, one of the *Forbes* readers summed up his own views of what was happening to the magazine:

> *Forbes* started getting silly and smart-alecky the day Malcolm joined the business. It began to get hopeless as a source of information the day it started its sillier investment advisory service. It became a vicious organ of political propaganda the day Malcolm went into politics. Enough is enough. Please cancel.

But this was offset by the other type of letter:

> This is not written for publication. I just want you to know my reaction to your column having succeeded your dad in this department . . . I consider your column one of the most refreshing items in *Forbes* magazine.

Malcolm's interests were threefold: traveling, politicking, and writing "Fact and Comment." His travels in 1954 took him on the *Île de France* to Europe, where he met Premier Mendès-France and Chancellor Konrad Adenauer. His politicking, arranged by Douglas Dillon, included campaigning for U.S. Senator Clifford P. Case.

In 1955 he was off to Europe again, this time on a junket connected with the listing of Simca, the French automobile company, on the New York Stock Exchange. Malcolm almost didn't make the plane home. Sampling a slice of Paris night life not easily duplicated in the United States, Malcolm had lingered through the wee hours. At Orly airport everyone else was aboard the plane and fastened in when a breathless, red-faced Malcolm turned up in the nick of time on the pillion seat behind a French motorcycle gendarme.

Back home, Gertrude was dismayed when Bruce and Malcolm

decided that *Forbes* ought to have a company yacht for entertaining top executives and potential advertisers on the Hudson River at lunch and on weekends.

"Why would executives come and dine on your yacht?" asked Gertrude, visions of BC's hard-earned money going down the drain, and the magazine following close behind. "They've got their own yachts." But the sons insisted—with their shareholdings that wasn't difficult—and Gertrude later admitted, "They were absolutely right. It worked, but I didn't think it would."

The two brothers had the best interest of the magazine at heart, but they were differing personalities with different operating techniques. The major intrusion into the peace was Malcolm's devoting increasing energy to politics—drawing his energetic contribution away from *Forbes*. Malcolm might believe himself the better man for handling editorial and business matters, but it was Bruce who had to step into the breach:

"We agreed [said Malcolm] that the advertising potential always lay in the corporate end—the broader business end. The financial advertising had been important when we were primarily a financial magazine. But we veered away from being principally a financial magazine, transforming *Forbes* into a broader business magazine. It began when we changed our editorial content. Bruce got out and developed a corporate advertising program of our own, *Forbes* had never had that. He spread the word that *Forbes* was something different than it had been and did it very effectively. *Very* effectively. He'd had no editorial responsibility after Dad's death, but Bruce had to move into that area when I moved into politics, when I was not doing my job there."

In retrospect, Malcolm admits that the magazine would have moved ahead much more quickly when he was editor-in-chief had he not thrown himself into the political arena. "I just didn't put the time into *Forbes* that I should have."

Bruce and Malcolm understood magazines instinctively. They had grown up in the business; they knew it philosophically, and they knew it as professionals. Their question: How to make *Forbes* grow? The key, improved editorial content, had been turned when Malcolm persuaded his father to start hiring *Forbes'* own people instead of buying outside articles.

After *Nation's Heritage* folded in 1949, Robert K. Heimann, who had edited it, became *Forbes'* managing editor. It was Heimann (after all, he had recreated Malcolm's *Nassau Sovereign,* a Malcolm S. Forbes "original," out of admiration for the product) who began to flesh out the new *Forbes* editorial skeleton. There were to be more corporate stories, snappily written, designed to catch the eye of the would-be investor. The corporate chiefs would be looked at in a more critical fashion, and that would appeal to the businessman reader. This was a variation on an old theme—BC's thrust, parry and praise during *Forbes'* earlier heyday.

Turning a magazine around is a long job. Bob Heimann followed Malcolm's editorial lead, and then—as Bruce moved into the editorial side, and Heimann moved out to American Brands, where he later became president—Byron "Dave" Mack took over.

If there was friction, if Bruce thought he was carrying most of the burden while Malcolm fought for his state senate seat (which he held on to by less than 400 votes) in 1954, the brothers were nonetheless in general agreement about *Forbes'* potential.

The circulation figures began to tell the story.

A magazine (or newspaper) is dependent for its profits on the loyalty, buying habits, income bracket and interest of its readers. This is not because magazines make that much money from subscriptions (few do, once distribution and printing costs are deducted), but because they can make a great deal of money from advertising. Advertisers want specific audiences easily reached in large numbers.

The readers want their interests met, and to be informed, educated and entertained in varying doses. Promotion can get a reader to take an initial trial subscription, but only the editorial content can keep the reader coming back for more. If the readers keep coming back in increasing numbers, the circulation grows. Once the circulation starts to reach certain proportions, and once the readers can be classified in various income groups, job roles and buying habits, then the advertiser can be wooed. And if the advertiser finds the medium delivers at the price ($8,000 black-and-white, $15,000 full-color page in *Forbes*), he is going to keep coming back for more.

Dave Mack, editor, brought in researchers: the facts and figures appearing in the *Forbes* stories began to be thoroughly checked out. More certain of the facts and figures, the writers could be bolder in their assessments. *Forbes* circulation figures began to swell.

Even while the magazine was creating its own success story, it was not the success story Malcolm wanted for himself. He wanted political success, first the governorship, then a crack at the White House (that had been Woodrow Wilson's path). Other young first- and second-generation Americans felt the same way—though John F. Kennedy was going the congressional route.

Malcolm and Roberta's fifth and last child, Moira, born in 1955, brought the quip from the Bernardsville (New Jersey) *News* that "as Forbes has caught up to Peter Hans Frelinghuysen who has five children . . . one reflects on the ways of young men in politics and concludes that added to other blessings . . . the more children the more votes."

Malcolm received applause for his statesmanlike stand on the location of a much-needed reservoir that brought him into disfavor with his own constituency, the newspapers stating: "We are pleased to give credit where credit is due. Forbes in this very difficult matter has proved himself a capable, and what is more important, an honest representative." Another newspaper declared: "It's open season on Senator Forbes with no limit on how many shots you can take."

Malcolm pressed his 1956–57 candidacy, first for the GOP nomination, and, having gained that, for the governorship.

These political years Malcolm was beginning to lose what *Time* magazine had said in the early 1950s was his "lean and Lincoln-esque" appearance. He was broadening out, developing a round face and the traces of a flabby chin. The high cheekbones, the angled, vulpine face with its gleeful smile, now had softer contours.

Politics requires more than an impromptu and off-the-cuff response to the gut feeling. Malcolm had gone far without necessarily caring to lay a solid groundwork. He had pulled off with zest and jest what many politicians could achieve only by slowly building up the party organization. Malcolm did have the party organization with him for his 1957 gubernatorial bid—but he still relied heavily on his own campaign style as the prime vote getter.

Malcolm's political style later provided his campaign manager, Raymond H. Bateman, with enough material for a *New York Times* article: "How to Lose an Election."

Malcolm's own comment: "I was nosed out by a landslide."

Of all Malcolm's highjinks, the one Bateman shuddered over most was the moment when Malcolm rolled up his trousers, took off his shoes and socks, and waded into a lake to woo swimsuited potential voters. "He looked like a clam digger," said Bateman. "That photograph must have appeared in every newspaper in the state. There's no way of knowing how many votes it cost him—but it did cost him votes."

Nor did Malcolm win many votes from the New Jersey National Guard. When Governor Meyner was invited to inspect a Guard contingent, he did it with the cursory attention to detail expected of that form of inspection. Malcolm inspected thoroughly—as only a machine-gun staff sergeant could.

One of Meyner's neatest tricks was the television appeal in which he was on the air immediately before Malcolm's TV pitch. Meyner made his presentation to the audience, then the screen showed the U.S. flag and the national anthem was played. Not surprisingly, many late-night (for those years) viewers thought the evening's television was over—and turned off the set before Malcolm's presentation came on.

Some of Malcolm's aides were urging their candidate to make mention that Meyner once had been a Roman Catholic. "He was brought up Catholic, you ought to use that," they told him. Malcolm later said laughing that he played the whole thing "self-righteously, telling his aides, who did not know that he too was raised Catholic, 'Oh, I wouldn't dream of such a tactic.'"

He tried many other tactics, including the unflagging statewide campaign that brought in Vice President Richard Nixon as a booster. Nixon, when he returned to Washington, was asked what he thought of his trip to New Jersey. Replied the Vice President: "I met a lot of wealthy people there."

Though Malcolm had received the New Jersey GOP nomination by a large plurality, New Jersey voters were not in a Republican frame of mind in 1957. Malcolm was defeated in his gubernatorial bid even though he received more votes than any previous Republican governor or candidate. That was success in defeat, but Malcolm saw only the defeat. Within months he had resigned from the state senate and quit politics.

Malcolm had pursued political prominence, a place in the national sun. Politics had consumed him—and taken away from his business and family life. Two unsuccessful gubernatorial bids had shown him the political route to glory was longer, and harder, than he had imagined. He would have to find success some other way.

The individual who had the greatest effect on Malcolm at this period was Charles W. Engelhard, a near neighbor and fellow Princetonian. Engelhard, head of Engelhard Mining and Chemicals, was truly wealthy. This dealer in precious metals, a multimillionaire, had financial power far beyond the normal political power of office.

Engelhard, according to *Forbes* executive editor James Cook, who wrote the first in-depth article on him, was the model for James Bond's Auric Goldfinger. Engelhard certainly took to calling a stewardess on his private gold-colored airliner, Pussy Galore.

During Malcolm's state senator days, Malcolm and Engelhard had campaigned against each other. It had been friendly.

But when Malcolm, his political ambitions in ruins, was casting about for some path to follow, consciously or subconsciously he used Engelhard as a model.

Malcolm couldn't get the fame; he'd go for the fortune.

There was only one place he would make his fortune. Malcolm had publicly stated that if he was elected governor of New Jersey he would resign from *Forbes*. So now he had to return—yet again—to the magazine his father had founded.

By the end of 1958, four years after BC's death, with Dave Mack as editor, and James W. Michaels managing editor, *Forbes* was blossoming not just for its editorial content but as a very profitable business. In meetings with direct mail users, circulation director Richard Kline, who had been with *Forbes* since 1936, was telling an enviable story of *Forbes* editorial, advertising and circulation growth. Kline explained that the reason businessmen and investors bought *Forbes* was that it was the only magazine that actually looked at how well or poorly a company was doing from a dollars-and-cents point of view. "It's the only magazine that talks about business in the language of business—mainly money—the very language top management uses when it looks at itself."

Kline said that by asking hard questions of more than 600 U.S. corporations a year *Forbes* circulation had doubled between 1954 and 1958—to the then current 265,000.

The industrial expansion that took place after World War II had brought about a big increase in the number of investors and executives, and a high-income-tax economy. With the shrinking value of the dollar, executives were interested in investing in common stocks for the tremendous tax advantages of capital gains.

The *Forbes* "book"—as magazines are known in the trade—was serving at least two readerships: business executives looking to stock options in the companies they worked for, who valued *Forbes'* outside assessment of those companies; and the ordinary investor who needed a journal that easily explained corporate finance and individual corporate worth. And, if all this was done in a feisty and fearless sort of way, with large dollops of entertainment, so much the better.

For the small investor there were specific stock suggestions by the growing number of signed columnists in the back of the book—men like Lucien O. Hooper, Heinz H. Biel, Sidney B. Lurie, and Elmer M. Shankland, some stockbrokers, and a businessman.

The *Forbes* reader was getting stock-advice columns at bargain prices, and so was the magazine. Columnists wrote for $40 per column, but gained immensely in their stockbroking business from the publicity they received from the rapidly increasing *Forbes* circulation.

In such side business projects as the Forbes Investment Portfolio, the emphasis was changing too. In 1952 the *Forbes Study in Growth Stocks Survey* had the headline "Retire in Comfort with These Growth Stocks," and by 1957 it was "Best Growth Stocks Now to Build Your Family Fortune."

Malcolm's own fortunes were mixed. He was throwing himself as enthusiastically as he could into the magazine. But he knew that his style called for a fast individual race; riding teamed in harness was irritating, even galling. He was still a young man, still dissatisfied, still burning with ambition, but lacking an avenue of his own. Since his college years he had pinned everything on his political ambitions. And those were gone.

Malcolm, the solitary figure who took lunch alone at Schrafft's across Fifth Avenue from *Forbes,* buried his head in a book and his dreams in hard work. He lingered for hours at his New York club. He was entering the middle years when all ambitious men's lives are touched with that "quiet desperation." He was unhappy, uncomfortable and unchallenged—other than by the normal demands of getting out a twice-monthly magazine. And for a man with his energies that was not sufficient. He was a man with "a destiny, but no destination." He also regretted, in retrospect, that politics had allowed him to delegate the "Fact and Comment" columns to editor Jim Michaels, written over Malcolm's signature. It was quite a reversal from a half-century before: B. C. Forbes had written columns over Edgar Wallace's signature.

Malcolm saw himself as a failure. He had not experienced a true personal business success since the *Nassau Sovereign* at Princeton. His political hopes lay in ruins. He could turn his energies only to the editorial content of *Forbes,* pushing its material to an even snappier tone than previously. Which way led to fortune and excitement?

The Forbes brothers in the early 1960s decided to buy the handsome Macmillan building, at 60 Fifth Avenue, on the corner down the block from their rented offices at No. 80. The eight-story structure, built in 1925, would house *Forbes* magazine on the first four floors, with the top floors rented out. The brothers also bought the adjoining townhouse on West 12th Street as an office, corporate dining room and attractive *pied-à-terre.*

In the office, Malcolm did not get along with editor Dave Mack. Mack quit. Malcolm, who long had wanted Michaels in the job, appointed him editor. The two of them, both abrasive and direct when necessary, began to hone the *Forbes* needle—its investigative reporting—to a sharper point.

On the general business side, though the days were receding when *Forbes* would do almost anything for a dollar, there were still plenty of modest income producers in the stockroom. Down the mail chute would go promotional mailings urging those on the *Forbes* subscription list to buy anything from the collected wisdom of BC's books to the Forbes Stock Market Course. That course, written decades earlier and needing only periodic updating, still regularly pulls in $200,000 to $300,000 a year.

Stockroom shelves carried such pearls as "Guideposts to Wall Street" and "America's Twelve Master Salesmen" by B. C. Forbes, "How to Meet Management's New Challenge" by the editor of *Forbes* (BC). *Forbes* could supply "Opportunities Unlimited," "Forbes Market Research Studies," "The Forbes Investor," and a barrage of printed advice in the business and investment field.

Early in 1964, *Forbes*—Malcolm and Bruce—began to think in terms of more outspoken, attention-getting advertising. There was some question as to the limits of "good taste."

But another 1964 development, far more serious, clouded everyone's days. Bruce developed cancer. The end came very quickly. On June 2, 1964, Bruce died. He was forty-eight.

Malcolm, the third son, had i-n-h-e-r-i-t-e-d *Forbes* magazine.

7

Malcolm, Michaels and the Magazine

I was very disappointed, you might even say depressed, by the Prince Rainier story. It made no point, helped people not at all in their business investments. Had it at least made fun of him, pudgy as he has become, it might have been amusing.

Memo from Michaels to the *Forbes*
European Bureau, London

Having succeeded to complete control, Malcolm exploded into an orgy of enthusiasm, energy, ambition, imagination, daring and expenditure. He was soon to approve the highly controversial "Capitalist Tool" advertising campaign, and a $1 million renovation on the *Forbes* building and the townhouse.

Bruce's widow, Ruth, distressed when she saw Malcolm being credited in the papers with spending so much money, feared for the security of the 30 percent ownership in Forbes Inc. that Bruce had left. Malcolm offered to buy her out, and she decided to sell. But how to establish a fair price for the 30 percent? Ruth talked to Bruce's friends, former Governor Tom Dewey and Norton Simon executive David Mahoney. A price was agreed on—Malcolm became a 60 percent owner of the business.

But he was not satisfied with that; he wanted total ownership. He badgered his two other brothers until they too agreed to sell out. "Minority stockholders have very few rights" was Wallace's wry comment. Gertrude held on to her few shares until Malcolm, often in public asides, finally wore her down. After a *Forbes* party, when

Malcolm again referred to Gertrude's being the only other stockholder, in such a way as to indicate he was hoping the situation would not long continue, Gertrude felt "if he wants them that badly he can have them." She too sold out. *Forbes* and Forbes Inc. were Malcolm's —all Malcolm's.

Malcolm did want it *all* that badly. He wanted to turn *Forbes* into the best-known, most-profitable business "book" in the United States. *Fortune* and *Business Week* possessed huge staffs and advertising budgets in the millions of dollars. What *Forbes* had was Michaels and Malcolm's daring.

The first major ploy was a massive advertising campaign to get *Forbes* talked about. The magazine's slogan would be *"Forbes:* Capitalist Tool." The idea was that *Forbes* had to get the readership—and advertising—away from its competitors.

"A capitalist tool: something businessmen use to find out how other businesses are run." Editor Michaels had his own slogan to describe the gutsy *Forbes* story: "Not what *happens,* but what it *means." Forbes* was there to interpret what was going on in the corporate world, in individual corporations, in politics and society and come up with stories that made entertaining good sense to managers and investors.

The year after he took over, Malcolm and his family sailed on his yacht, the *Highlander,* through the Great Lakes, stopping in at Cleveland and Detroit, the children, kilted, piping the guests on and off the yacht.

What Malcolm was doing was skillful enough—all of *Forbes'* contacts in the Cleveland and Detroit regions were Bruce's. With Bruce gone, Malcolm had to establish his own relationships. Local papers now were quoting "Malcolm Forbes' view of Cleveland: 'Citizen Vitality . . . Booming Business.'"

As *Highlander* made its way through northern waters, there was a Forbes story everywhere the yacht docked. The one in the Cleveland *Press* stated: "Nice work for kids if Dad owns a yacht." The four boys were pictured practicing on their bagpipes prior to lunch.

Forbes' Emma Stock, director of communications, was behind much of the successful sales promotion. But it was Malcolm's own availability, and flair for publicity, that were doing the bulk of the headline-grabbing work, such as: "Forbes Tells How to Publish a

Successful Business Magazine," by James Gavin, Chicago *Tribune.*

Malcolm told the Chicago *Tribune* of *Forbes'* circulation jump, from 70,000 to 410,000; added that he had never wanted to work for his father; that his youngsters saw very little of him while he was politicking "except for picture-posing sessions to indicate a togetherness we really didn't have." He was telling more about himself than the newspaper readers realized.

Nor was Malcolm beyond taking a crack at old friends. "How much longer can we afford to sit by and watch Labor Secretary Schultz trying to make the shipping strike go away by shutting his eyes to it?" he asked.

Forbes magazine geared up its publicity program, the promotion department putting out press releases on upcoming articles. Heavily touted were snappy comments from Malcolm's "Fact and Comment" which he was now writing.

By the mid-1960s *Forbes* was finding greater success for itself.

Forbes ran newspaper and magazine advertisements showing a large sow: Capitalist Pig.

The legend read, in part:

> You want to know what inflation is? Buy some pork. The price is up 30%. It's in a league with Black Sea Caviar. . . .

And, if nothing else, the *New York Times* and *Wall Street Journal* readers would be led into an entertaining description of *Forbes* and some current stories it was carrying. In the third quarter of 1966, when *Forbes* circulation passed that of *Fortune,* the punchy advertising copy read:

> A capitalist tool: something businessmen use to get ideas for new markets. Could this be why *Forbes* now has 35,667 more U.S. subscriptions than *Fortune?*

Perhaps the most talked-about photograph and caption *Forbes* used in an ad showed a beggar sleeping on a sidewalk, apparently in India.

"Hey, mister," ran the copy, "want to buy a Cadillac?" Malcolm does not like to talk about that one.

At that time, if Malcolm had to make a choice between catching headlines or being accused of questionable taste, he took the headlines. As his father once told Gertrude Weiner: "Robbie Burns said, 'It's better to be talked about than ignored.'"

Forbes certainly was being talked about. The magazine captured twenty-seven awards for its 1966 advertising campaign, a campaign rivaled only by that period's equally clever Volkswagen advertising.

If nothing else, left to his own devices, Malcolm developed the Midas touch where free publicity was concerned. By saying what he wanted to say, and by doing what he wanted to do, he caught attention, headlines and good story copy. He works while he eats.

Business over lunch at the Forbes townhouse is a strange affair. Its end is obvious—but its means sometimes are a little bizarre. Chairmen, presidents and chief executive officers of the largest corporations are invited to lunch. A couple of Forbes editors, with Malcolm, perhaps publisher James Dunn, and Malcolm's son Steve, will make up a party of seven or eight.

The limousines arrive. Usually they pull up on West 12th Street. Malcolm is on hand, official greeter.

The slow sidewalk procession, simultaneous introductions, and then in through the revolving glass doors. For first-timers the effect is quite stunning, the Fabergés, the black and white marble; the Russian Imperial flag; a picture of the DC-9.

As Malcolm leads the visitors up the marble stairs toward the mezzanine and *Forbes* research department, he points out the *Forbes* collection of presidential letters and photographs: Bruce with Herbert Hoover; Malcolm receiving the Freedom Foundation medal from Dwight D. Eisenhower. There is a tale behind a Richard M. Nixon framed piece, which shows Nixon with Malcolm campaigning in New Jersey during Malcolm's bid for the governorship.

When Nixon first was President, that picture came down from its first-floor landing to the lower level, where it could command more attention. But as Nixon's star dimmed, once his reputation tarnished, then became grimy, the picture moved up the building, one flight at a time, until it reached the third-floor staircase wall— safely out of sight.

The townhouse sitting room, expensively furnished and decorated in yellows and light tones, once had few paintings, the most noticeable of which was a Howard Chandler Christie nude. Her derrière could not fail to raise at least an eyebrow as the unsuspecting visitors were ushered in. In the 1970s, given the extent of Forbes' oil painting acquisitions, there is little wall space at any Forbes establishment not covered, cheek by jowl in some cases, with paintings.

The little sunlit sitting room alone bears enough oils to provide a decent-sized afternoon's showing. And the once lone and luminescent derrière now competes with soldiers, landscapes and sporting prints. Elsewhere are the Toulouse-Lautrec, the Polisseu, and the Paul Cadmus oils—the latter considered pornographic shockers in the 1930s, with their scenes of rape, tramps, tarts and the demi-monde of Babylon-on-the-Hudson.

The townhouse steward serves drinks.

If the luncheon guests are from a liquor firm, then their liquor is prominently displayed on the drink cart. But the drinks are served in such huge and heavy glasses that the guests have great difficulty in setting them down noiselessly on the glass-topped tables. After the first embarrassing "thunk," the guests tend to nurse their drinks in their laps until lunch is announced.

Conversations at these townhouse lunches are guaranteed as "off the record." Confidences are exchanged, or competitors blasted, or a maker of women's foundation garments will confess that by the time the U.S. housewife comes to his company's product "she has given up hope."

If the guests are dull—and corporate chairmen rarely are dazzling wits or men capable of gifted small talk—Malcolm can become quite aggressive. He will criticize a story Steve has written, or throw an unanswerable question to one of the editors. He will cut off one of the guests in midsentence to make his point.

For *Forbes* editors these can be uncomfortable sessions.

Malcolm sometimes overdoes his hospitality. The wine goblets don't help: they are inverted stags' heads made by Tiffany's and engraved with the names of the visiting chief executives. Wine is served in them, but maneuvering the goblet, with its spiky antlers capable of doing an accidental cornea transplant during the chicken livers and spinach, is a delicate task.

Lunch done, the editorial staff depart hastily before the gentle squeeze is applied. Over coffee, Malcolm brings up the matter of advertising, and *Forbes* as a medium. Much business is done. And soon the executives are escorted on a brief tour of the wine cellar.

The chief executive is shown where his goblet will be kept, available for him whenever he wants to stop by for a drink, or is invited back to lunch.

New York magazine added its closing note on a townhouse lunch:

> Being feted on a recent occasion were two marketing executives whose advertising had been missing from *Forbes* magazine for a year. The host ventured the hope that it would return, mentioning that his magazine has a higher percentage of readers in the top brackets—"the head knockers," Forbes calls them—than either *Business Week* or *Fortune.* As he concluded his pitch, he said, "And now, gentlemen, you're deductible."

Executives exeunt. Malcolm tells his secretary he is "in conference" to all callers, and goes for a nap. Making sure he gets plenty of sleep is characteristic of the man: "Seven hours of sleep is to me one of life's unadulterated delights."

Another delight was that by 1967 *Forbes* publisher James Dunn could boast a Simmons Study showing *Forbes* led all magazines in those figures big-money advertisers go for:

Adults with $50,000 or more life insurance.
Adults taking domestic air trips for business.
Adults belonging to business clubs.
Adults owning $50,000 or more in stocks and/or bonds.
Adults visiting Bermuda or the Caribbean.
Adults owning one or more cars bought new.
Adults who are members of country clubs with golf courses.
Adults who are Bourbon users.
Adults who are club officers or committee members.
Adults who are Bell Telephone Credit Card holders.

On the lighter side, *Forbes* has the largest concentration of:

Men who most often used Colgate's toothpaste in past month.
Adults who bought golf balls in the past year.
Adults who bought tennis balls in the past year.

Malcolm could boast of something else, as well, a good rapport with readers. If he was being outrageous, or hilarious, he still knew and knows his audience. He almost knew when he wrote the following that a reader would reply:

When I have a drink—never more than one at a time (have you ever tried drinking from two glasses at the same time?)—the sharper I get.

My wife spells "sharper" d-u-l-l-e-r. She never was a good speller.

The reader did:

Sir: Strange thing—your wife spells just like mine (*Fact & Comment,* Feb. 1).

—Norman E. Halbrooks
Tyler, Texas

And Malcolm knew that not because he wanted a reply, but because his instincts are good. He does understand the free-enterprising and capitalist American, the investor and the executive. He knows what turns Americans on:

Trees sent Joyce Kilmer, but nothing quite sends most Americans like the smell of a new car interior and the soul-satisfying sound of shutting a new car door. There are few among us who don't find that sound as exciting as any bar of music. There are few of us who do not put a new chariot's aroma on a par with the perfume of the loveliest blooms. It's a deep yearning for both of these that, at this time of year, drives so many to the nearest automobile showroom. Call it what you want, or call for the psychiatrist, but it's a powerful fact of American life.

He knows what turns them off, and sometimes is outrageous for the sake of it. More often than not the readership indulges him when he calls the Teamsters "loveable lovers of this land," or when he referred to Chicago's late Mayor Richard Daley as a "unique antique." After all, who else is writing aphorisms today, or beginning editorials with "Who'd have thunk it" and ending them with "Seems crazy to me"?

Whether he is holding forth from a platform, or being opinionated in print about Scotch, Malcolm is entertaining the readership: Promotion jaunts included moderating a panel of big names of the annual coal convention. His views on Scotch were in "Fact and Comment":

According to *Forbes* there ain't no bad Scotches. The main virtue of "premium brands" is their price! The whole bit about "better" Scotches is all a snare and a delusion. In fact, the best-selling light Scotches sell for more, while the stuff in the bottle actually costs less to make than most lower-priced blends.

It is sad indeed what life does to one's cherished illusions.

But I refuse to get too upset. I can't do much about that Romanov-Saltykov bit, but I'm going to go right on drinking my J&B. I don't care if it costs me more and the distiller less than some other brand. I know darned well I *like* it better.

Status symbol or no, to me it *tastes* better.

Even the distillers are not going to persuade me otherwise.

This factual stuff can be carried too far.

While Malcolm was out promoting and doing a good job as public-relations man himself for *Forbes,* Michaels was castigating p.r. men generally in the magazine's "Sidelines" column:

American corporations spend tens of millions of dollars a year on public relations and not a little of the money is wasted; in fact, the PR men some companies employ do them more harm than good.

We know because we have to deal with dozens of PR men in the course of putting out each issue of *Forbes.*

Don't get us wrong. This is not a blanket indictment. . . .

Let's talk about another press agent we *like.* This is a man who works for a big manufacturer of heavy equipment. It's an old corporation with a fine reputation; but it hasn't been doing too well of late. We called to ask him to arrange an interview with the president. A couple of hours later, he called back and said: "At first, my boss didn't want to sit still for an interview because, as you know, we have been having problems. I've convinced him that he'd better; you're obviously going to run a story about us whether he talks or not. So send your man out here. We'll open every closet door for him. All we ask is this: Have your man hear us out on our comeback program."

Our story was critical, naturally, but it was criticism tempered by a recital of what the company was doing about its problems. . . .

Unfortunately there are also the big shots: "I know your publisher well." (He met him once.) Or, "Your editor is an old friend of mine." (They talked on the telephone a few times.) Not many PR men have many editors or writers in their pockets, and it's a good idea to distrust one who says he does.

Malcolm could write about a visit somewhere and see his story reprinted in newspapers throughout the country. One such 1966 cameo concerned Malcolms' trip to what he described as his "first Commie country":

> One night in Split I was a guest at dinner in a small Yugoslavian-patronized restaurant, when what to my wondering eyes should appear, but a couple of Greenwich Village Dears.
>
> Typical of the phonies who have so long overrun the Village, they made their grand entrance garbed in Garbled Peasant—sandaled, dirty feet, her toenails in peeling red; his hair tangled shoulder length, hers with a sugarbowl cut; she in a quasi-bare-topped dirndlly hopsack, he in carefully sullied Bavarian Lederhosen held up by window-sash cord and topped by a dirty red T-shirt. Obviously, much thought had gone into this costuming so they would be in what they felt was appropriate Balkan Left gear.
>
> Conversation at every table ceased.
>
> The couple was the cynosure of all eyes.
>
> Everyone else in the restaurant of course, being Yugoslavian and out for dinner, was in his Sunday best. Suits. Ties. About as bourgeois-looking as a group gathered for a Sunday social in Anyville, Idaho.
>
> Apparently the Villagers' shock at seeing me equaled my own at seeing them.
>
> As they clattered by the table, she glared at me and turned to him, "Kerist, did we come all the way to Split to see one of those damn Brooks Brothers dummies?"

Criticized, Malcolm is unabashed. In 1949 he had taken two pages in *Advertising Age*. Those two pages were completely blank with the exception of eight words in small type in the lower corner of the right-hand page. The words: "Agency clashes with client. See story page 28." Malcolm was demanding more white space around the ads, but *Forbes'* advertising agency, Albert Frank–Gunther Law, Inc. couldn't see much sense in buying full pages and leaving them practically nude. All this had prompted the *Direct Mail Advertising Journal* to comment: "All this, we assume, was concocted to gain cheap publicity. *Forbes* will have the honor of wearing the crown for using the most white space until somebody tops them."

Malcolm ran an editorial reminiscent of his 1949 *Advertising Age* gimmick.

The editorial subtitle was:

(An editorial saying all that can be said about the perception, imagination and achievement of the Secretary of State in furthering the interests and ideals of the United States throughout the world.)

What followed was two blank pages. Reader response was mixed: forty-eight letters against the editorial, sixty-four in favor.

The art of promotion that P. T. Barnum well understood was to find endless variations on the few same old tricks. And, as any conjurer or stage magician would admit, there are few different tricks, one generation to the next. But the effort is worth it if there's applause.

Fan mail boosts the batteries. Helen Gurley Brown, editor of *Cosmopolitan,* dropped Malcolm a postcard:

> Saturday morning I was reading your editorial pages at breakfast. I think they are simply wonderful and everyone writing editorials should be such a good, clear and easy-to-understand writer.

To which Malcolm replied:

> What a thoughtful, inspiring note. . . . I read it at our regular Monday morning sales conference and it gave all present a lift.
>
> Usually when we get a pat on the back it is from a non-expert in the business of writing who is simply pleased once in a while with a specific comment, but to have such words from such an immensely successful "pro" is mighty good for morale.

Again, in business, editorial writing, promotion and publicity, just as in politics, Malcolm was encouraged to feel that by following his nose and notions he was doing what was best.

He was unfettered and unchecked by father or brother. He was responsive to the limits imposed on him by the needs to attract advertisers and maintain the magazine renewal rate while attracting new readership. But it was at this time, in the mid-1960s, that Malcolm began to respond primarily to a constituency of one: himself.

His formula was working. Why should he hold back? Success was coming. He was making money; he already was a millionaire. And what further proof did he need than the success of the 1967 *Forbes* fiftieth-anniversary party. It was a bash to end all bashes, a publicity stunt to rival Caesar's silver-caged circuses.

Unlike Caesar's circuses, staged entirely on debt, Malcolm's gala celebration in huge tents on his New Jersey estate was paid for in advance by the guests. Only the top officers of the major corporations were invited, and then only if the corporation took at least one page of advertising in the *Forbes* fiftieth-anniversary special issue. That made it a minimum $8,000-a-plate dinner.

Hubert H. Humphrey was the celebratory speaker. Malcolm's neighbor Charles Engelhard wanted Hubert to stay at his place. Malcolm let it be known that unless the Vice President stayed at the Forbes' home, Timberfield, he would not get to speak at the banquet.

HHH, "the only vice president here," in his own words, stayed at Timberfield.

Mrs. Helen Meyner, wife of former New Jersey governor Robert Meyner, who had defeated Malcolm in 1957, wrote the evening up for the Newark *Star-Ledger* this way:

> Talk about parties!
>
> In this affluent decade of gala and lavish social occasions, the din-ner-dance hosted by Mr. and Mrs. Malcolm S. Forbes Saturday night at their home in Far Hills was a party to end all parties.
>
> Fabulous is hardly a strong enough word—but that's what it was.
>
> President of *Forbes* Magazine, a former New Jersey state senator and Republican candidate for governor in 1957, Malcolm Forbes held the elaborate black-tie get-together (that's hardly the word either) to mark the 50th anniversary of *Forbes* Magazine—and no golden anni-versary celebration ever had it so good.
>
> Guest of honor Vice President Hubert H. Humphrey was a major attraction and the list of dignitaries included chairmen of the board and presidents of most of America's top industrial and business corporations who gathered from all over the country. . . .
>
> Although the arrival time of the more than 750 guests was stag-gered—invitations read 7:30, 8 and 8:30 P.M.—traffic was bumper to bumper as chauffeured limousines and private cars inched slowly up the sweeping driveway leading to Timberfield, the family estate.
>
> Acres of grassy fields had been turned into a gigantic parking lot. There were police and vice presidential Secret Service men who checked names off the guest list.
>
> Inside the handsome white house, the guests lined up to greet the vice president, their host and hostess and then wandered to the garden with the enormous party tents expertly decorated like a rural Scotch castle, with lots of candles and yards of plaid in the green, blue and red —the colors of the Forbes family tartan. There were tables set up for

six and ten, an orchestra section and a sizeable dance floor.

Floral arrangements of yellow, orange, white and rust chrysanthemums were used as center pieces and to complement yellow table cloths and pumpkin colored napkins. A sumptuous dinner of lobster cocktail, filet of beef and grape sherbet was served with white and red wine and fine French champagne.

An elaborate menu, program and guest list embellished in gold with the Forbes family seal had been put at each place and there were gifts for everyone.

Gentlemen received "The Forbes Scrapbook of Thoughts on the Business of Life"—an encyclopedia of famous quotations bound in maroon and engraved in gold.

For the ladies there were silver bowls from Tiffany's engraved with their names and wedding date.

My husband and I shared a politically non-partisan table with Vice President Humphrey, our host, former Gov. and Mrs. Alfred Driscoll and former New Jersey State Sen. William Ozzard and Mrs. Ozzard.

I was seated between Gov. Driscoll and the Vice President who was obviously enjoying every moment of the spectacular occasion.

"When Malcolm first invited me," he said, "he told me this would be a small party for his family and just a few of his friends, but look at this."

"I'm glad to know a man with so many friends! Have you ever seen so many chairmen and presidents? I'll bet I'm the only Vice President here."

A man of obvious energy and enthusiasm, Vice President Humphrey talked about the busy day he had spent in New Jersey.

"But I'm not tired yet," he continued, "and when this party is over I'm going to New York to meet my wife who's flying in from Europe.

"This official life has been great for Muriel. She's really blossomed and she did a terrific job in Europe on her own."

While the Vice President made some last minute additions to his speech, I complimented our host on the magnificent decor.

"The construction for the wooden flooring under the dinner tent began well over a month ago," explained Malcolm Forbes.

"This place has been in an uproar for weeks. Hurricane Doria gave us quite a scare," he continued. "Last night as I sat in our house working over the seating arrangements for tonight, my wife Bertie opened the window and there was a terrible gale. I thought—oh boy—this is it. All those tents blown sky high. All those people coming—but luckily Doria changed her mind."

Parties aside, Malcolm does not always please. When *Forbes* sent out one renewal notice, part of the promotion stated:

> You may have . . . the astute stock selections made by our highly skilled security analysts.

A *Forbes* subscriber penciled a ring around the remark and placed a large question mark alongside. His letter said:

> You may discontinue my subscription at expiration date. You have a sprightly, well-written magazine, but I no longer feel it carries benefits for me.
>
> If I were petty, which I hope I am not, I could fault at least one instance of non-credibility . . . [on the part of one of the columnists who] . . . rather pointedly recommended General Public Utilities as a "good buy" . . . on the strength of this I bought a few shares (not an odd lot by any means) . . . at my age of 74 I may not be around when this stock gets to the point where it can be profitably sold.

Forbes is not always right. In the 1950s it decided that a small corporation with the unlikely name of Haloid wouldn't go anywhere. That company later became known as Xerox. *Forbes* is daring.

Harold "Hal" Lavine, now columnist–editorial writer on the Arizona *Republic,* wrote a cover story showing how the Mafia washed its money clean "in the snows of the Alps"—meaning the Swiss banks. James Flanigan's story on Litton's "shattered image" seriously affected Litton Industries' credibility on Wall Street. That's what the *Forbes* readers put their money down for, candid assessment.

The effect on the internal structure or the public image of a major U.S. corporation as a result of a *Forbes* story can be quite startling. Directors of corporate public relations have been fired from their jobs as a result of a *Forbes* interview castigating the corporate chairman or assigning blame for a drop in the corporation's current earnings. Often enough, however, the chairman's or president's ire is aroused not by reference to the poor bottom line of the corporation, but by reference to the chairman's waistline or his hairline.

Editor Michaels pushes his writers all the way out to the end of the limb on corporate stories. That makes working for *Forbes* one of the toughest tricks in U.S. journalism. Sometimes the magazine doesn't quite pull it off: in 1970 Kinney National Service, Inc. sued

Forbes for $55 million—$50 million compensatory, and $5 million punitive. Six months later the magazine printed a clarification. The *Wall Street Journal* told the story:

> *Forbes* Magazine is running a correction to settle a $55 million libel suit by Kinney National Service Inc.
>
> The suit arose over an article in *Forbes'* June 1 issue. The article, "Market Mystery," analyzed Kinney's methods of accounting and capitalization. An accompanying article aired rumors linking Kinney with the Mafia.

To the editors and writers of *Forbes,* the stories are worth the risk—no other magazine or newspaper in the country so boldly holds the corporations accountable to the investors.

Forbes magazine does not do all these things without attracting a great deal of external criticism and occasional flashes of internal criticism. Can *Forbes* magazine, or Malcolm Forbes, or the writers be bought? No. Or bought off? No. Can a good story be eased into *Forbes* magazine or a bad story be kept out? No. Are there pressures or preferences that influence how a story might be played? Yes. Malcolm has his friends. Yes. Jim Michaels, who hates to drive a car, detests the highway and trucking lobby—and is a great railroad supporter.

Forbes writers at one time used to complain that an unfavorable story could never be written about National Cash Register because NCR had never withheld advertising during the Depression. True or not, the first major *Forbes* putdown of NCR did not appear until the 1970s.

Most *Forbes* writers do not know that equally significant advertising roles in *Forbes'* struggling history were played by Metropolitan Life and Cities Service, both of which have received periodic panning over the years.

When Metropolitan Life was the subject of a downbeat story in *Forbes,* one reader replied:

> Sir: The next time you have vinegar instead of fruit juice for breakfast ("What's With the Metropolitan?", *Forbes,* Dec. 1, p. 17)—don't write anything until later in the day.
>
> —Timothy J. O'Leary
> Glen Cove, N.Y.

Individual writers, or issue editors, have specific complaints regarding specific stories—a downbeat story on Chase Manhattan Bank was modified by Malcolm to be less severe. Malcolm justified his pencil work as editor-in-chief with the explanation that because he was closer to the top executives he knew better than the writer exactly what was going on.

That is something his brother Bruce also would have done, but Bruce once told editor Michaels, "You have to find out for yourself," when he was privy to good inside information the editorial department needed.

In the 1960s, when Malcolm was more likely to be around 60 Fifth Avenue than in Tangier or Tahiti, he was often inclined to insert his editor-in-chief's pencil.

On that rare occasion when Malcolm contacted a *Forbes* writer without going through editor Michaels, or arbitrarily made a change, the relationship between owner and editor was aired.

Michaels, who at less than five feet five was on a par with BC, would likely snap: "That fucking Malcolm." Down would go his cigar in the ashtray, his lips would tighten and his eyes would glint through his glasses.

He would grab in frustration at the one or two remaining strands of hair on his otherwise bald dome, and with the other hand snatch up the story copy or the offending note. By this time he was already out of his seat. Thin and lithe, in good shape at fifty-plus, he'd hurl an obscenity at whoever brought him the news, cuss his way out of his corner office, and flat-foot noiselessly along the thick-carpeted, dark-paneled halls until his red-and-white striped shirt disappeared into Malcolm's office in the adjoining townhouse.

After that, whatever owners say to editors, and editors say to owners, they say only to each other.

Malcolm does want it known, however, that he played a major part in establishing the tone and vitality of *Forbes* editorially, as associate publisher and, later, as editor-in-chief. But neither Malcolm nor other Forbeses of *Forbes* come through unscathed in the judgment of employees, past and present.

One writer summed up the Forbes employee-employer relationship saying: "They were ill-advised as to how successful they were. And not knowing, kept going until they stumbled over success. They all have been cheapskates toward everyone but themselves." Another writer, still at *Forbes*, describes Malcolm with a classic complaint of many who know him: "It's difficult trying to communicate with him. He does not listen. He jumps on a word in a sentence and never hears what the rest of the sentence is."

Former *Forbes* Washington bureau chief James Srodes, now covering Washington for the London Sunday *Telegraph* and the Rand *Daily Mail*, said not long after he left: "Malcolm actually listened to something I had to say on two separate occasions. He heard me all the way through."

Malcolm's short attention span is one of his trademarks. He wants to be doing everything at once, but once started on something, he already is looking for the next thing. "It makes him seem scatterbrained at times," said a slightly exasperated senior editor from the front corridor.

Malcolm is extremely demanding. Family, editors, ranch hands all agree that Malcolm commands, demands and gets. "He gets just that bit more out of you than you really want to give—you're already working hard and willingly," says one long-time *Forbes* employee. Then with a smile he added: "He's a great productivity booster."

His father, tight with money for employees, made a big play out of small gifts. As one older staffer recalled, "BC loved gratitude." He expected the help to be bowled over by the Christmas bonuses or the gifts of heather he brought back from Scotland. "It was an act of bestowal rather than simple gift giving."

Said the same writer: "Bruce was slightly more generous. He had a mediocre mind but really lovely personal qualities: generosity, friendliness, caring for people—he cared about the clerks." Malcolm and Michaels both referred to these qualities of Bruce's in their final editorial tributes to him.

Under Malcolm, commented the staffer, "it was back to the old 'faithful retainer' concept. Even under Bruce anyone who quit was regarded as a traitor to the family. It was—and still is—patriarchal. The kicks are supposed to come from living on the other side of the keyhole. The Forbeses, hobnobbing as often as they could with 'the great and near great' began to feel they were great. Frankly I was always appalled by their notion of who actually was 'great.' "

For the writers, working at *Forbes* is like working in the boss's den—a sort of "Upstairs, Downstairs" rendered horizontal. Malcolm is approachable and no snob. He is cordial; it is possible to argue with him a short part of the way. Then he stops listening and says what will be done. He is, first and finally, the boss.

One *Forbes* columnist has said that "Malcolm would cut off your balls while looking you straight in the eyes." One oil company executive came to a *Forbes* townhouse lunch because "I just wanted to meet this guy who doesn't give a shit about what anyone says or thinks." Malcolm wants things his own way.

A *Forbes* writer who assessed RCA's precarious situation in the computer field, used the word "disastrous." Malcolm had it modified to "interesting." A year later, RCA took a $400 million write-off and crawled away from its licking in computers.

Such an incident is the exception, but they do occur. When an issue editor objected to Malcolm's using the word "brilliant" to describe the editor of *Cycle* magazine, Malcolm took umbrage. He told Tom Stevenson, who was issue editor: "It's not because I own the magazine. We aren't childish around here. But I am editor-in-chief. I always go in to see Jim Michaels because he also is a very talented, brilliant editor." Malcolm, like his father, is fulsome in his praise.

When Malcolm wrote a flattering "Fact and Comment" about James Moran, "Flintkote's astute and carefully able new CEO [chief executive officer]," the column was circulated among the editorial staff with one wag's addition, "Because, perhaps, he has 10 pages of ads in 1972."

Malcolm, in turn, regards his columns as his privilege. He likes to hand out bouquets. In July, 1966, he admitted it:

> It was some 25 years ago that my father first wrote on these Fact and Comment pages a little feature entitled, "Men I Particularly Like," listing two or three every once in a while.
>
> I will never forget this feature because it led to my first "serious" run-in with my employer. When I saw the first proof of this projected feature, I told him I thought it was the corniest, most unprofessional sort of editorial comment to appear in a national management magazine.
>
> Dad's initial reaction was one of patience . . . "always happy and pleased to have the view of associates on my views," and so forth. As my protests persisted, he began to react with less of the politeness of an employer and with more of the finality of a father.
>
> "Son, you were fortunate enough to have a father who could pay

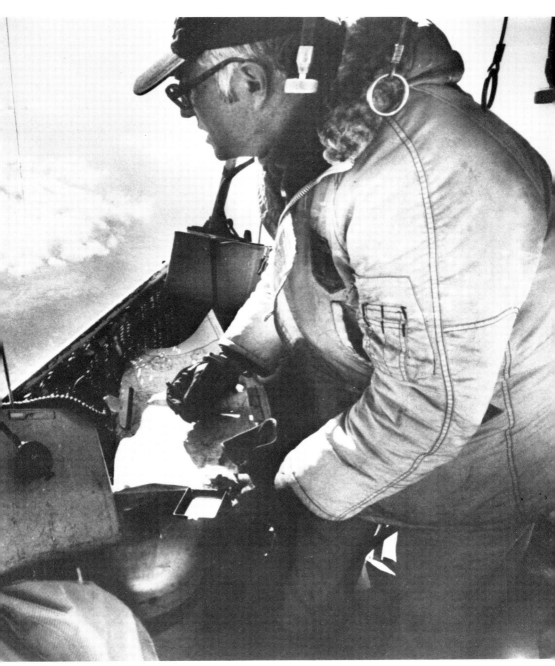

Malcolm airborne. *(UPI)*

Like father...B. C. Forbes. (*San Francisco Examiner*)

Like son...Malcolm S. Forbes. (*Derry Moore, UPI*)

"My headmaster led me to believe I could write," said B. C. Forbes of his headmaster, Gavin Grieg.

Cunnieknowe, BC's birthplace in Scotland. Ten children, all living in the little granite house. The front room was a grocery store and beer shop. (*Arthur Jones*)

Natal *Mercury.* BC's first employment overseas, in South Africa, at the height of the Boer War, 1901.

BC at thirty-eight as the *National Magazine* readers saw him, already Hearst's leading financial columnist and a magazine owner.

BC with his wife, Adelaide, on tour in the 1930s. (*San Francisco Examiner*)

Gertrude Weiner, BC's secretary, treasurer, and gin rummy buddy. (*Arthur Jones*)

Malcolm, the budding politician, at thirty-eight. (*Wide World*)

Roberta Forbes, the candidate's wife. (*Wide World*)

They like Ike. The Forbes boys meet the president. (*Wide World*)

The candidate as maharajah... (*Wide World*)

...and the *Highlander* fit for a prince. (*Wide World*)

The young family. (*Wide World*)

Clan Forbes. (*Wide World*)

How to lose an election. (*Wide World*)

Promoting—his candidacy, 1957. With Vice President Richard Nixon in Washington. (*Wide World*)

Promoting—his magazine, 1966. With Wisconsin restaurateur in Milwaukee. (*Milwaukee Sentinel*)

Motorcycles... *(Yale Joel)*

... Balloons ... *(Yale Joel)*

... Tanks. *(Stan Ritova)*

On Laucala, his Fijian island, with Fiji's Prime Minister Ratu Sir Kamasese Mara *(left)* and deputy Prime Minister. *(Stan Ritova)*

Moroccan interlude. Robert Forbes bussing the Comtesse de Breteuil on the marmac at Marrakech after a lunchtime visit to the Comtesse's magnificent home, Villa Taylor. (*Arthur Jones*)

Malcolm's Tool. (*Yale Joel*)

Robert Forbes at the Tangier palace with Robert Gerofi, supervisor of Malcolm's Moroccan interests. (*Arthur Jones*)

Family entertains in France... *(Yale Joel)*

...relaxes in Tahiti. *(Yale Joel)*

Merry Christmas
and
Happy New Year
Malcolm and Roberta Forbes
Timmy Moira Bobby
Kip Astrid Roberta Bina Steve
Charlotte   Catherine Sabina
                              Nov. 8, 1976

1976   Far Hills, New Jersey

The family Christmas card. Each year Roberta writes more than 1000 by hand.

for you to have a better education than he had, but perhaps there's a wee bit you have left to learn.

"I'm a few decades older than you. I have known a lot of men in business. There *are* men I particularly like. One of the pleasures of being the *owner* as well as the editor is that I can say what I damn please —whether or not some smart young fellow thinks it's corny or not."

End of conversation.

This episode came back to my mind the other day when I sat down to write in a warm way the regard that *Forbes* and the Forbeses have long had for that unique human being, Red (Arthur H.) Motley, publisher of *Parade* magazine.

He has undoubtedly inspired more salesmen to exceed their capability than the most extravagant bonus plan ever devised. His exuberance is contagious; his wit is such that while splitting your sides, the point penetrates the mind and remains. He gladdens the heart, and not just the hand.

In rummaging around for a way to say what I wanted to about Red, that long-ago argument with Dad about "Men I Particularly Like" came to mind.

Forbes writers craft stories well knowing that publication could mean a loss of advertising to *Forbes*. Some corporations have pulled six or eight pages of advertising as an expression of displeasure over how they have been handled. Eight pages of pulled advertising, worth anywhere from $65,000 to $120,000 a year, is a relatively small price to pay to maintain one's influence. No magazine could sustain ten times that amount of pulled pages.

In no other magazine in the corporate field can writers range so far and wide, or exercise such freedom of expression in nailing down their personal view of an individual, a corporate entity or a particular trend. *Forbes* is authoritative because its writers are able to write with authority and tell it as they see it. They just have to be right. That's what Michaels wants; that's what Malcolm wants.

Forbes magazine truly is an anachronism—a national magazine owned lock, stock and masthead by one person. *Forbes* magazine is the last bastion of national, personal journalism on a grand scale.

Often enough—though libel lawyer Tennyson Schad works his way through *Forbes'* most sensitive stories prior to publication— what protects *Forbes* from libel suits is not what is *not* said, but how what is said *is* said. Michaels understands that.

The Luce-like editor, Michaels, is a former United Press Delhi bureau chief. His greatest scoop was being first with the news of Gandhi's assassination.

Michaels generally presides over a bloody ritual every two weeks: the *Forbes* story meeting. It takes place in the conference room, oils of BC, Bruce and Malcolm hanging on the paneled walls to witness the Grand Guignol. Sixteen reporters, writers, researchers and editors take their places in the white armchairs around the huge table. A black bull is in the center of the table along with a model of the yacht *Highlander II.* Lest anyone forget, photographs of the possessions—the Forbes air force (aircraft and balloons), the Forbes navy (powered and sail), and the regal real estate—proclaim their worth from the walls.

Each senior editor and associate editor of *Forbes* is expected to take a turn being editor of one or several issues of the magazine each year. Most of them dread it and would rather be writing. But everyone in the upper echelon—the front corridor—has to take a turn in putting out the book.

No matter what a staffer's title on the magazine masthead, when he (and rarely, she) is not the issue editor, he (and sometimes, she) is a writer. The only exceptions are Michaels and Executive Editor Dero Saunders. (Saunders, a man of quiet quality, sees the magazine through to production, and eliminates grammatical eccentricities in the writer's copy.)

Story meetings set the scene for the upcoming issues. Writers are expected to turn up with ideas—and at least two of those ideas apiece have to withstand the onslaught of editor, issue editor and peer group.

Michaels usually attends, Malcolm never. The issue editor presides, slowly working his questions around the table, asking for story ideas. Sensible writers have left their egos in their desk drawers; really smart ones have come prepared. As contributions to the next issue are requested, sloppy ideas are unmercifully hacked to pieces. Michaels' strength as an editor includes his sharp eye for a strong idea buried in the dross.

In his fifteen years as *Forbes* editor, Michaels has become something of an editor maker. When the tart-tongued $100,000-a-year editor last year plucked *New York* executive editor Sheldon Zalaznick out of that chair and plopped him into a managing editor's chair at *Forbes,* Michaels was not limited in his choices.

Zalaznick had been at *Forbes* before he went to *New York.* Carol Levy, *Dun's Review* managing editor, went there from *Forbes,* as did Ray Brady, the managing editor she succeeded.

Institutional Investor managing editor Wayne Welch joined his present employers from the Michaels ménage; Kenneth Schwartz, Opinion Research's *Public Opinion Index* editorial director, was *Forbes'* last special reports editor.

Frank Lalli, executive editor at *New West, New York*'s California-based sister magazine, was a top *Forbes* writer until wooed west earlier this year.

What does Michaels offer so that after a few years at *Forbes* people feel they can leave and take on their own editor's chair?

"High standards," says *New West*'s Lalli. "Michaels sets very high standards for writers. Few editors today know how to make demands on writers. The result is that the writer, not the editor, controls the story. Whether the writers believe it or not, that's bad for the writers."

"Michaels teaches tight writing," said Opinion Research's Ken Schwartz. Schwartz gave a clue, too, to the price—and pain—involved. "You get the ability to find fault with your own story. You know Michaels will discover its weaknesses if you don't. You wake up suddenly, four in the morning, and *know* there's something wrong with it, even without knowing what it is. Then you go and find the fault, and find the story in the last paragraph. That means spending the rest of the weekend rewriting it."

Michaels makes demands. *Dun's Review*'s Levy, a *Forbes* researcher in the 1960s, confronted Michaels with a stack of research notes for a good story. Michaels told her to write it. She protested she was only a researcher. Michaels insisted: "Just write it like you'd tell it." Levy broke into tears. Michaels still insisted.

And, admits Levy, "I wrote it. Jim was the first person to show me I had capabilities."

Wayne Welch was at *Forbes* when Michaels instituted the still-functioning issue-editor system.

"I was issue editor and I was in trouble," recalls the *Institutional Investor* managing editor. "There were empty pages. The top three or four writers had each turned in three or four stories. The rest had turned in only one or two.

"I went to Michaels and told him I was going to assign stories to those who had turned in only one or two pieces. Michaels told me to give the assignments to those who had turned in three or four stories for that issue."

Welch told Michaels: "That's not fair." Michaels replied: "Do you want to be fair, or do you want to get out of trouble? When you're in trouble you lean on your strongest people."

Michaels' "strongest" people operated, at least in the late 1960s and early 1970s, in an editorial-management style best described as "middle period Hollywood"—the star system.

Michaels likes an applicant's résumé. Executive editor Dero Saunders, an ex-*Fortune* writer who exercises a subtle hand on many *Forbes* staff members' during their initial few months, does a preliminary screening. The approved applicant meets Michaels. Michaels offers the job. The candidate, grilled, wonders if he can handle it. Michaels snaps, "Do you want it or not?" The applicant says yes. Smiles all round.

The beginner shows promise. Michaels shows the beginner how to strengthen the sting in a story's tail ("Never forget that a touch of nastiness can liven even the dullest subject"). Michaels rewrites. The newcomer's ego usually ends up on the cutting-room floor.

The writer turns in a really good piece. Michaels exults. The guy who last week was a $16,000-a-year reporter now is an $18,000-a-year staff writer.

Michaels pushes the writer further out along the limb, stretching him, testing him ("I like that last piece, but weren't you a bit bland?"). The ingénue tries harder, turns in more stories. The pace quickens.

The starlet, now heading toward in-house stardom, visions of sugarplum bureaus dancing in his head, pushes harder. Michaels responds in kind: "You force me to do it: you're not officially due for a salary review until July or whenever . . . but your stuff is getting so hot you force my hand. I'm putting you in for a $2,500 salary increase effective April 1 . . . make me do it again."

Naturally, the $22,000-a-year staff writer, who April 1 will be a $24,500-a-year associate editor, wants Michaels to do it again. Already the Michaels dynamic is working. The pressure for turning out good stories is shifting from Michaels-the-overseer to the eager and anxious-to-please writer. The discipline is self-imposed now, and a guilt complex accompanies it when a story fails to meet expectations, or fails to meet a deadline.

The writer who starts to slide down the productivity ladder, from ill health, booze or flagging energy, quickly hits Michaels' "shit list." Few manage to unstick themselves.

Not all newcomers make the star track. If they can't produce, they're expected to realize it and look elsewhere. If they can't get the message, they're canned. (The same goes for the pros who can't sustain their productivity levels.)

But it's not always their fault if they can't get the message. Michaels is abrasive, abrupt—sometimes unfair. The novice writer, looking for an explanation of what's wrong, instead gets the illuminating remark: "It's shitty, that's what's wrong." That's Michaels' problem: he is able to communicate with some writers and not with others, and that means he's lost some good people for the wrong reasons.

One ex-Forbesian, David Pauly, now at *Newsweek*, after watching people having their psyches whipsawed, dubbed the *Forbes* editor "the great humanitarian." Bruised psyches are part of the price.

Michaels doesn't care how hard he drives people. "Jim's first loyalty is to the magazine," said one, "and that means to himself."

The now $30,000-a-year associate editor, writing skills sharpened, now may be ready to be turned into an editor. What takes place is not a bad definition of what an editor is. There are two stages.

As Michaels explains it, says Lalli, an editor is a writer who can't get to all the stories he wants to write. The editor "splits himself in seven; seven writers are surrogates working on seven stories the editor wants."

The second stage of editorship is something that happens between an editor and a writer. The editor recognizes a story he wants, recognizes it as one he would do himself. But he succeeds as an editor when he encourages the writer in such a way that the story finally is better than the editor himself could have written it.

"That's the reward," says Lalli, speaking from his own experience.

How did Michaels get his experience?

He learned about life the hard way and the easy way. The hard part was the Depression in Buffalo, New York, and taking his turn in the box office of his father's Palace Theater, known in town as the Palace Burlesque.

Michaels, a skeptic barely a column-rule width from cynicism, cuts savagely through people's illusions. There are few illusions backstage in a theater; those are saved for the audience out front. And there are few illusions left when *Forbes* rips into public-relations puffery, con artists, the pompous, or, as Michaels would call them, "the pricks." Stripping corporate emperors—and princes—of their clothes is all in a *Forbes* staffer's day's work. Or else.

Memos demand: "Cut through the p.r. bullshit." Or they socratically ask: "What's the story *really* telling the readers?" Lalli says Michaels "sees *all* of life's ironies. That's some burden."

When Michaels saw the movie *The Sting,* he spat out the criticism: "They made the Depression seem fun. It wasn't. Like hell it was."

When the London *Times* editorially worried about the ability of the United States to give President Richard Nixon a fair trial, Michaels scrawled the comment: "Unctuous bullshit." When a Philadelphian wrote to Michaels and appended after his signature "Ph.D.", Michaels wrote back and signed his letter: "James W. Michaels, B.A."

That B.A. was from Harvard in the Michaels progression—the easy part—from Buffalo to boarding school to Ivy League.

After Harvard, with World War II under way, Michaels volunteered for American Field Service ambulance work alongside the British Army in India. Wooed by the British to accept a commission, Michaels instead let the U.S. embassy persuade him to join the U.S. Information Service. War ended, in 1946 Michaels joined United Press in Calcutta.

He joined *Forbes* in 1954 and soon was managing editor. In those days *Forbes* was a revolving door. By 1961 he was editor sending memos such as this one:

I recently wrote Jim Flanigan a Michaels-composed editor's prayer: Dear Lord, give us the courage to pick living targets, not dead ones, and the judgment to pick the right targets. This is by way of saying your Canada piece [growing economic nationalism] looks better all the time;

or an article we did on Lockheed when it was at the peak, saying they were, maybe, stretched too thin.

These are the hard pieces. People say we're full of crap. Our competitors run counter articles. The editor glares at the writer with that you-put-your-foot-in-it-this-time look. But these pieces keep the readers awake and renewing.

Keeping the readers happy *is* a major part of the editor's job. The editor has to give the readers what *they* want before he can give them all that *he* wants. Michaels does both. He has to have a team of good, reliable writers: then he leans on them—and keeps his fingers crossed. Another memo:

> Half fearfully, half hopefully, I went through *Time, Newsweek, The Economist,* to see whether they had any inkling of the workers' control thing in their Denmark coverage. Not a line. Not a glimmer. Not a smell.
>
> Now I hope you know what a good editor you have. Editors are by nature a timid lot. We like to be first, but not very first. You know the old news agency joke. The cable comes: "Your assassination DeGaulle exclusive congratulations." And then, "Assassination still exclusive." And, finally, "DeGaulle assassination still exclusive, how come?"
>
> The point is you finally convinced me you had caught something which the politically-oriented press had not. So I went with it. It's you and me and *Forbes* against everybody else. I'm arrogant enough to be willing: our planes to China and our Canadian nationalism were out ahead, but right, and so were some of our skeptical company stories. I know it's sometimes profitable to be out of step.
>
> But I say: I went with it because I have confidence in you—not of course until after I've sneered questions and doubted and tried to discourage. But I did go with it, which is more than most editors would.

Editors may want to keep the readers happy, but rarely are they as certain or cocksure as they seem:

"I did go with it," wrote Michaels, "which is more than most editors would." Most *Forbes* writers, past and present, know that to be correct.

Generally *Forbes'* staffers cover the beat. But other sources are called upon—Basil Caplan was *Forbes'* London-based stringer before there was a bureau. *Forbes*—overseas or in the United States—is staff written. Only a very small percentage of outside stories make it onto

Forbes pages; the rates are not that high and the stories are not easy.

Forbes writers are expected not to become specialists; they are to be able generalists who never get clubby about one particular topic, or chummy with a particular company's executives. Not surprisingly, some *Forbes* editors do acquire a great deal of specialized knowledge along the way—but their breadth is broad indeed, and the magazine reflects that breadth.

Executive editor Jim Cook can go from a story about the future of coal to an extensive in-depth review of whether in fact the multinational oil corporations really jacked up the post-OPEC-embargo price of oil. Dero Saunders can switch from seeing the entire magazine through production to turning out a cover story on the future of the lumber-owning corporations. Robert Flaherty can shift from a sophisticated examination of ITT to a short, sharp personality profile. Steven Quickel, delicately analyzing McDonnell Douglas, may next be doing an autopsy on a great corporate failure.

Current European chief Geoffrey Smith—the man who started the *Forbes* "Numbers Game" section (an entertaining insight into what accountants do with corporate earnings figures) applies the same disdain to other aspects of the game. Bill Reddig, like Smith ex-*Newsweek*, showed that topflight sportsmen are simply businessmen with popular entertainment appeal.

Howard Rudnitsky, a one-time *Forbes* statistician turned senior editor, who reads annual reports, balance sheets and six-point footnotes as other people relax with a bedside *Esquire* (he also reads bedside *Esquire*), is diabolical once he is on the scent, and intransigent once he has hooked his calculator into the corporation of his choice.

For many—if not most—*Forbes* staffers, five or so years is enough. At that point the stories can seem to repeat themselves. It's primarily a challenge for young seasoned bloods good at the craft. Those who last five years often are looking for the next challenge.

In the late 1960s and early 1970s many of the corporate executives *Forbes* writers were interviewing were making small fortunes from stock options—or at least they had been in the 1960s. Reasoned the *Forbes* writers, remembering Malcolm's pledge to make them the best-paid writers in New York, why not stock options in *Forbes*? They did not know the extent of Malcolm's determination to make it all his. To stock options Malcolm said: "No way." By way of explanation to those who didn't fully understand, Hal Lavine growled: "Malcolm is like the boy who invited everyone to his birthday party then ate the cake himself."

Malcolm wants it all, and a favorable press, too. He was really stunned by a *Wall Street Journal* piece that described his lavish lifestyle—after all, just nine months earlier he had described the *WSJ* in "Fact and Comment" as "that extraordinary and invaluable national business daily," and had praised "its usual comprehensiveness." Malcolm's reaction to the *WSJ* piece was the same as his father's reaction to the *New York Times* story about his separation from Adelaide: He was mortified.

One *Forbes* reader read the *Journal* story and wrote:

> I do hope you will take a few minutes in your busy schedule to read what I have to say.
>
> In the . . . Wall Street Journal there was an article entitled, "How Suite It Is." It was rather interesting and thought provoking yet quite sad. Sad because while millions of people starve money laden Americans live their lavish life.
>
> The description of your lavish office is somewhat revolting. From the red-carpeted private elevator all the way to the wine goblet of sterling silver, each inscribed with the name of a major corporation's president, who alone may sip from it on his visit to you. Is all this image-making necessary? I leave that for you to decide.
>
> I will close this short note by stating that my subscription to *Forbes* Magazine expires next month and I do not intend to renew. You may feel that one less subscription can't hurt. True. But look at it another way Mr. Forbes, that's one less wine goblet.

Malcolm always acknowledges letters. Stung by this one, and by the *Journal* story, Malcolm replied:

> Thank you for your letter and your candid comments. I would have felt as you had after reading that snide, malicious and totally exaggerated account.
>
> The Wall Street Journal is a principal competitor of *Forbes* for the advertising dollars of American corporations with messages for American businessmen.

He didn't send a carbon copy to the *Wall Street Journal*.

8

The Not-So-Eccentric Eccentric

There are few intangibles . . . that Malcolm Forbes enjoys grappling
with with quite as much energy, it would seem, than the art of legiti-
mate tax deduction—particularly if related to business, his lifestyle,
entertaining, travel, and the Forbes mystique.

Patrick O'Higgins
Town and Country
November, 1976

Forbes Inc.'s revenues probably exceed $50 million but the amount
budgeted for Federal Income Taxes in 1972, according to one internal
document, was a mere $8,000.

Chris Welles
More magazine
April, 1977

Malcolm Forbes is no snob. Once, caught off guard during an interview with the *Guardian* of London, he was asked what sort of millionaire he was. It was an honest response when he replied: "A
pleasant one, I hope." A pleasant imp who never really grew up?

Chris Welles, writing in *Auction* magazine, said Malcolm has a
"childlike enthusiasm about his acquisitions." He could have added
that Malcolm, in making his wants known, can behave like a spoiled
brat.

A visitor to Trinchera ranch remarked to Malcolm he should do
some selective tree felling. Malcolm said he wanted the trees left
alone. When the visitor pushed the point a little further, explaining
that tree felling could be good for the forests, Malcolm snapped the

conversation to a close: "It's my ranch, I'll do what I want."

He does. Though he now allows tree felling.

As for Malcolm's following his gut instincts and yen for excitement, one long-time family friend summed up the opinions of other Malcolm watchers with the remark: "There's *nothing* Malcolm wouldn't try once *he* had decided he wants to try it."

He can be abrasive, or he can charm the birds out of the trees, with quips that come out entertainingly if he keeps them short, and garbled if he keeps on going. But, when dealing with the media, he can smile and calculate the effect simultaneously. His image, and that of his family, are paramount. With the success of the 1960s have come not just wealth, but the commanding need for sober respectability.

Fortunately, however, Malcolm can't help trying to maximize the moment, and remains humorous and human as he follows his instincts. The only time he is really on the defensive is when someone talks about his money or his taxes. When it comes to trying for tax deductions, he is alongside the English milords in the state of the art. He is their equal in his reticence to talk how much he's worth—but their superior when it comes to making money and getting tax deductions.

And one thing simply leads to another.

Malcolm enjoys eating and drinking. He likes good wine and good booze and a steady flow of both. Having learned to host the business lunch in the townhouse and trips up the Hudson on his yacht, the *Highlander*, Malcolm also began in the 1960s his "Non-Critics Critique" of places in New York to eat.

Periodically in the magazine he reviewed a few fancy restaurants: "This is the best buy in steak and service that you'll find anywhere. I didn't say the best steak. I didn't say the best service. I said the best *buy*."

Malcolm followed his thumbnail reviews by launching the *Forbes Restaurant Guide*, a $36-a-year service offering four selections a week. The recommendations would not be on the basis of food alone. For the busy businessman, Malcolm reasoned, reservations being honored, prompt service, pleasant surroundings and low noise level, *as well as* good food at a decent price, were the important mix for people doing business while they dined.

The free-spending *Forbes* editors, led by Forbes himself, were a marked contrast in restaurant style to the magazine's founder, BC. He would meticulously go over the bill, calling the manager over for the slightest discrepancy. Mrs. Adelaide Forbes at first would suffer in silence at this performance, particularly because her husband was a cheap tipper. "But later," she told a friend, "I came to admire him for it"—though not for his tipping. The story is that the family used to slip back to the table to add some money to the amount BC had left by his plate.

Forbes editors could spend $75 for lunch for two and know the *Restaurant Guide* was claiming it as an expense. The reviews were as lively as *Forbes* stories or Malcolm's editorial comments:

> There are those who insist that Luchow's isn't what it used to be. It's not hard to understand why . . . cocktails are to be recommended as a means of whiling away the time during occasional glimpses of your passing waiter . . . service is practically non-existent and if noise really does cause loss of hearing . . . Luchow's is *the* place to go deaf.

One review brought a $2 million libel suit. Malcolm handled it with ease. When the writer said, "Malcolm, I've been writing too long to make any excuses about writing it that way" (the soup was called "dish water"), Malcolm replied, "And I've been editing far too long to make excuses about letting it slip past. Don't worry about it." Forbes won the suit.

While the *Guide* was flourishing, it—like everything else Malcolm got into—captured the print media attention. "Where a Bromo isn't the Dessert" was the title of Dennis Duggan's article in *Newsday*.

> Malcolm S. Forbes thinks all too many restaurants are far more interested in their customer's wallet than his stomach and that while a spoonful of Bromo can quell an upset stomach, nothing can ease the ache of an empty wallet.
>
> That's why the 50-year-old publisher of *Forbes* magazine, a prosperous 53-year-old business publication, recently began publishing a weekly restaurant guide which is a welcome relief from the gratuitous, not to say outright phony restaurant "plugs" run by most publications.
>
> He doesn't deny reports that he tried to acquire the prestigious and wealthy *Gourmet* magazine or that he made passes at *Holiday* magazine.

When the *Wall Street Journal* ran an article on food critics, a disgruntled Hal Lavine was quoted as saying of Malcolm's *Guide:* "It's ruined me at my favorite restaurant. To me, it's a four-star place, but the guide gave it only two stars because Malcolm claims they spilled soup on him."

When the *Guide* folded, after two years of fabulous lunches and dinners for writers who added inches to their waistlines learning the difference between *mouton cadet* and *Médoc* at the company's expense, one newsletter stated: "Taste for high living behind unsuccessful restaurant guide. . . ."

It was the *Gallagher Report* that referred to Malcolm's real-estate ambitions as an "international land grab." The columnist Suzy delighted New York *Daily News* readers in July, 1970, with:

> That prodigious spender, Malcolm Forbes, hasn't let up on his buying spree. No sooner had he got back the use of the Forbes Plane, Capitalist Tool,—by posting an $80,000 bond until the dope smuggling charge (brought against the plane's cook), for which it was impounded by U.S. customs officials in July,—is settled, than he was off on the road (or through the skies) to Morocco to shop for a palace.
>
> It took fast-moving Malcolm no time at all to find one to his liking. He closed the deal on the spot. The palace will be sumptuously furnished and used to entertain important folk near and dear to Forbes' business magazine. Avidly concerned with creature comforts, Malcolm intends to fly the new chef from the Forbes' private New York townhouse to Morocco in the Tool to gratify culinary needs en route (and after arrival) in case the Moroccan cuisine proves too, well, you know, too icky for Western tummies.
>
> On the way back home, Forbes, stopping over in the south of France for a glimpse of the local real estate, spied another shack suitable for business entertaining—a cozy little 47-room villa of which Forbes, Inc., is now the proud possessor. . . .
>
> One sad note attributed to the recession: Forbes has decreed that the daily supply of fresh flowers for the yacht be discontinued and only one wine be served with meals until things pick up. (Sigh, sigh.)

One 1971 invitation was a first for Malcolm, the first time he had been invited to a king's birthday party. (Previously his best was an invitation to the christening of the Crown Prince of Greece.) As the new owner of the Palais de Mendoub, the former governor's palace in Tangier, Malcolm Forbes was one of the more recent foreigners to buy a place in Morocco. That was one reason why he had been invited to the informal celebration the following day marking the forty-second birthday of Morocco's King Hassan II. The other reason was that Malcolm and the king already had met.

Malcolm personally is well suited to entertaining Arabs. In the Islamic tradition hospitality is one of the two major marks of individual worth. Public oratory is the other.

Malcolm possesses a very Arabian characteristic: Arabs in no way agonize about making, having or spending money. Westerners, many of them, have mixed emotions about consorting openly with Mammon. But this white-Anglo-Saxon-Protestant diffidence had not infected Malcolm. He enjoys earning it. He loves having it. And he luxuriates in spending it, doing all three things without a touch of self-consciousness or a twinge of conscience.

In true Arab tradition Malcolm had arrived at his first meeting with the king bearing a gift, a 750-cc. Honda motorcycle. Much to the dismay of the security men, Hassan immediately tried out the bike along the palace drive.

The king ordered the palace gates open and was roaring off down the road to the nearby village before his security men realized what was happening. They were still organizing themselves into pursuit cars and shouting at one another in their walkie-talkies when the king swung his new yellow-and-black bike back in through the palace gates.

He had enjoyed the bike, and Malcolm. Hence the invitation.

There would be dozens of well-knowns and lesser-knowns at the birthday party. The King had even invited his jeweler, Pierre Chaumet, from Paris' Place Vendôme.

Sunday, July 10, 1971, was one more Moroccan day of clear skies promising much heat if one moved too far inland from the sea breezes. Palais de Mendoub, built to take advantage of the prevailing Mediterranean winds, needs no air conditioning. Those same winds can rise to a fury carrying sand and dust into every corner of the clothing, car, palace or eye. Two hundred miles southwest, on the Atlantic coast, the king's summer palace—one of his many palaces, four of them with professional golf courses—similarly was cooled.

The wind carried mutterings of unrest and dissatisfaction which the king and his courtiers knew about, but which they had chosen to ignore. Ill omens were being collected from conversations that arose among groups of men in a eucalyptus grove outside Rabat, where 1200 military cadets from the training camp at Ahermoumou, and their leaders, were spending the night.

These young Moroccans, future noncommissioned officers in the royal army, were armed with automatic weapons. Many had been told that their king, His Imperial Highness Moulay el-Hassan ben Mohammed el-Alaoui, was being held captive by subversive foreigners and conspiratorial Moroccans. The cadets' job, their duty, was to rescue Hassan.

What a simple scheme, to lead the cadets into believing they were rescuing the king when, in fact, they were about to assist in a *coup d'état* aimed at removing Hassan and replacing the monarchy with a people's republic.

Other cadets, mainly those who would be sent to capture key radio stations and government buildings, were being told they were part of a great and honorable people's revolution, that the country was being bled dry by a luxury-loving elite with Hassan at its head.

On July 9, 1971, as the cadets in truck convoys had made their way across several provinces to the eucalyptus grove, the king was not being held captive. He was relaxing with friends. It was his forty-second birthday and the following day, a Sunday, hundreds of people would be gathering for an informal birthday party.

There would be special guests such as Malcolm Forbes, men of medicine and commerce, sporting friends like British amateur golf champion John Cook, hairdressers and jewelers, painters and jurists. Close friends also, like army chief General Mohammed Medbouh, and relatives like the king's brother, Prince Moulay Abdullah, and other members of the royal family, would gather for conversation, golf, perhaps a swim. Leaders of the diplomatic community would be on hand for the festivities.

But, by the time that birthday party came to an end, more than one hundred people would sprawl dead, slaughtered in the courtyard. The Belgian ambassador, Marcel Dupret, would die in the arms of the French ambassador, Claude Lebel. Famous French cardiologist Jean Himbert, wounded, would be callously machine-gunned to death as he bravely crawled across the courtyard to try to give aid to a seriously injured party guest. Military aides would be machine-gunned at the entrance to the palace complex as they rushed to the defense when the attack started. Fate saw many people arbitrarily butchered, others equally arbitrarily uninjured. Malcolm Forbes would come through the day unscathed.

Skhirat, some fifteen miles south of Rabat, is less a palace than a very grand seafront villa. It occupies land between the Casablanca road and the gently sloping Atlantic Coast beach. A golf course separates the palace buildings from the main road by a quarter mile, and at the northern end of the course is the lightly guarded main entrance and a car park. The palace is unfortified—the golf course separated from the road only by a hedge fence.

King Hassan is an avid golfer. Several American, Moroccan and European golf pros were in the royal retinue. Casual wear, sports clothes were the dress, and nothing more arduous was demanded of the guests than that they attend and enjoy themselves swimming, sunbathing, trap shooting or whatever. It was a stag affair; in keeping with Muslim custom there were no invited women guests.

Looking across the golf course down the road toward the palace and the ocean, a passerby could see only the buildings, the tent that housed the bar at the far side of the golf course, and a couple of antique railroad coaches and veteran automobiles that the king has collected.

The first guests began to arrive. Ordinary guests and lesser dignitaries would have their cars turn in at the main entrance and sweep into the car park nearby. The guests would then walk the quarter-mile up the drive alongside the golf course to the main building entrance.

Malcolm Forbes had spent the night in the Rabat Hilton, a gaunt place on high ground well removed from the city center. The Hilton's "Moroccan" touches are less Arabic flourishes than examples of American kitsch, but then it is there to serve Americans, not Moroccans.

In many troubled—and even relatively tranquil—parts of the world, the chauffeur is more than a mere car driver. Gray-suited and leather-gloved he may be, but often his jacket is never buttoned, and that bulge near the belt on his shoulder is not his wallet. Chauffeurs of high government officials—and this is especially true in places like Morocco, and Iran, and Indonesia—often are recruited from the security forces. In many countries highly placed individuals—in government, finance, politics, labor or the underworld—are driven by combination chauffeurs-bodyguards. These are not men whose duties revolve around keeping the Cadillac, Rolls-Royce, Mercedes, Daimler or Bentley shiny, and getting the master home to Old Greenwich in time for the 6:15 P.M. martini.

Malcolm Forbes often is chauffeured. From among his retinue of personal aides and attendants—men who fill a variety of jobs around his office, his estate, his yacht and his outposts—Malcolm selects his irregularly commissioned chauffeurs. The waiter in the New York townhouse doubles as chauffeur; the chief of his office security services—a former New York policeman who is licensed to carry a pistol, and does—also lives on the Forbes Far Hills estate, thereby fulfilling a second equally important role.

A man who may have started with Malcolm as valet, chauffeur, boathand, or estate hand, is expected to—and does—function at a variety of tasks: ballooning, bag carrying, valeting, general factotum and bodyguard. Malcolm has not traveled alone in almost ten years. The actual, but never articulated role as bodyguard—Malcolm has referred to them as "my guardians"—is one among many for some of Malcolm's employees. Malcolm expects his sons similarly to turn their hand to whatever needs doing—for him or for the business. It is when he is traveling that Malcolm is at his most commanding, and demanding.

The invitation to the king's birthday party was for Malcolm alone.

Back at *his* palace there was a party in full swing, one Patrick O'Higgins in *Town and Country* summed up like this:

There was a great crowd but Forbes himself was nowhere to be seen: he had been summoned by the King of Morocco to Skhirat, a royal golf course near Rabat, for a little stag party. Forbes' third son, Kip, a dark-haired youth who also happens to be an art historian, acted as host, suitably aided by both a current *and* a future wife!

We were fed a sumptuous, traditional meal of couscous, tagine, and pigeon pie. And the service was impeccable even if the plates were cardboard.

"Our china hasn't yet arrived," Kip Forbes explained. He didn't seem remotely perturbed until the Chief of Police appeared. *He* looked perturbed, however. It seemed there had been an attempt on the King's life at Skhirat, and Malcolm Forbes—along with sixty other distinguished guests, diplomats, celebrities—had been murdered!

Malcolm wasn't dead.

Malcolm on the day of the party, once inside the palace, looked out for familiar faces. Not a golfer, less than interested in trap shooting, sunbathing or swimming, Malcolm walked and talked among the guests, drink in hand. It was a colorful scene, free of the usual diplomatic formality of similar gatherings elsewhere.

Mao suits of the Chinese ambassadorial staff contrasted with the gray-suited formality of the Yugoslavian ambassador, a cultivated Communist of a different ilk.

Malcolm was soon chatting with U.S. Ambassador Stuart Rockwell and General Mohammed Oufkir, minister of the interior, who had been entertained on the *Highlander* many times.

At one end of the courtyard an orchestra played traditional Arabian airs, and, viewed through the glass-walled esplanade, out at sea three vessels of the Moroccan navy stood ready to fire a twenty-one-gun salute signaling His Majesty's birthday.

The king's personal guest that day was Habib Bourguiba, Jr., son of Tunisia's premier. After mingling and chatting with his several hundred guests, the king let it be known that the visitors were to help themselves to food from the splendid buffet, and to find themselves a pleasant table under one of the tents, taking as their dining partners whoever happened to be there.

Shortly before 2 P.M. as the guests were standing waiting—not quite with poised forks—for the king to sit and begin eating, thus signaling the start of lunch, the 1200 armed military cadets aboard the dozens of Moroccan army trucks hurtling up the Casablanca road were checking their automatic weapons.

The king took his seat beside his eldest son, seven-year-old Crown Prince Sidi Mohammed. The leading trucks swung in through the palace gates and headed up the drive to the main palace door. Other trucks halted alongside the golf course and the cadets jumped out, automatics ready. Already there was gunfire. As the army trucks came into the VIP parking lot those chauffeurs who also were bodyguards realized what was happening, and opened fire. They were quickly cut down with several bursts from automatic weapons.

To the relaxing guests, the firecracker noises beyond the building, somewhere on the golf course, sounded like the beginning of a fireworks festivity—part of the celebrations.

Malcolm Forbes thought so. So did Ambassador Stuart Rockwell. They were at tables fairly close to one another, about one hundred yards away from the king's table. Ambassador Rockwell was alongside the French ambassador, M. Lebel. No one was paying much attention to the noise until people started running into the courtyard through a small door that led to the golf course.

Malcolm saw them clutching parts of their body, stumbling or falling as they reached the courtyard. A hand grenade lobbed over the wall exploded. Shrapnel struck several guests. Ambassador Rockwell saw people in the courtyard being struck by bullets, screaming and falling to the ground.

"Let's get out of here," the Moroccan consul-general said to Malcolm, leading the way to the esplanade. Once at the esplanade the consul took a huge chair and smashed one of the windows, and quickly dropped the ten feet or so to the sand below.

The courtyard was filled with gunfire, smoke, screams and confusion. People were running everywhere, anywhere, senselessly and without any thought in mind. Some dropped under tables for cover, only to be seen there and to slump, dead, as bullets riddled their bodies. Others were caught in the open, their death coming in slow motion, as automatic fire ripped into their bodies, causing them to first slow, then to drop. Wounded people tried rolling out of the way, in any direction they considered safe. Some pleaded for mercy, but died just the same. British Ambassador Thomas Shaw followed the Yugoslavian ambassador—an old Tito-era World War II guerrilla fighter—and took split-second pointers in survival from him. The Yugoslav dived down behind a low parapet that bordered the swimming pool, and pulled a chair over his head. Recalled Shaw: "So I lay down beside him and did likewise."

China, crockery, glassware, cutlery sang a weird, shrieking descant to the screams and gunfire as tables crashed to the ground, or bullets sent silver trays skittering onto the courtyard tiles.

The pandemonium was rising to a crescendo. The group immediately around and responsible for the king were pushing him toward the door leading to the throne room. They kept pushing until, finally, the king and others, swept up in the protective rush to save the king, were all crowded into the lavatory area off the throne room.

Malcolm's first thought as the consul-general disappeared over the wall was, "I don't have to worry, I'm a foreigner." He stayed close to Ambassador Rockwell, reasoning that foreigners and diplomats had a "sort of immunity" in affairs such as this.

"But once it became perfectly apparent that the bullets weren't discriminating between foreigners and Moroccans, and that diplomatic immunity wasn't bullet-proof, I had second thoughts." Malcolm Forbes, too, took the exit route opened up by the consul-general, and jumped down onto the sand. Dropping down alongside him were other guests such as the Austrian ambassador. All snaked on their bellies along the beach below the esplanade wall toward the golf course, hoping to escape detection and death from the flying bullets.

When they emerged they were still inside the palace grounds, near a corner tee. Several others, including the king's caddy, were there first, crouched down behind the green-clad hillock of land.

The new arrivals and those already there worriedly asked: "What's going on?" but neither group could enlighten the other. Periodically, someone would daringly stick a head out for a fleeting glimpse of the palace to see if it was possible to figure out what was happening.

This was not an attempt to assassinate the king; it was a determined effort to replace him. And it had behind it one of the king's most trusted advisers, General Mohammed Medbouh, the king's personal military adviser, an officer and gentleman of courtly ways and liberal disposition. Medbouh was, of necessity, in league with Commandant Manousi of the Ahermoumou cadet school, and Manousi's second-in-command, Colonel Ababou, who displayed his talents as a brutal killer.

The attack at Skhirat, it seems, grew out of Medbouh's feeling of shame. Medbouh had been visiting Washington earlier in the year. He had been informed by the U.S. government that members of the Moroccan elite were systematically trying to obtain bribes from U.S. firms doing business in the country. In particular, a leading member of the Moroccan elite had sought a $1.8 million bribe from Pan American Airways with an offer to influence Moroccan government

disposition toward the building of a new hotel in Casablanca. Medbouh had been forced to be the bearer of bad tidings back to Rabat.
He was filled with personal shame and with indignation over the
image of his country abroad. The king's sacking of the ministers of
tourism, education, commerce and finance apparently did little to
assuage what Medbouh considered an affront to the nation's dignity.

Medbouh's actions culminating at the birthday party had served
to pull a variety of complaints into a single attempt at change. But
the several major manipulators of events wanted different results.

Medbouh wanted Hassan to abdicate and leave. Many military
leaders willing to participate in the plot may have wanted a Libyan-
style military junta. Ababou wanted power. The teenage cadets
hurled along with the bullets such venom-filled lines as "You didn't
have to come here to wallow with these pigs," to a frightened-for-his-
life Parisian hairdresser, and jeers such as "dirty profiteers," "long
live the revolution," "socialism has arrived."

As events turned out, socialism had not arrived.

The shooting died down, except for sporadic fire.

Those crouching behind the tee at the corner of the golf course
were seen. "Soldiers were sent to bring us in," said Malcolm Forbes.
"We were marched back to the palace. We passed by the VIP's
chauffeurs lying dead where they had fallen, then we came into the
courtyard. Hundreds of people were lying down, motionless. 'My
God,' I thought, 'they've killed everybody.' But they had not, and we
too were forced to lie down along with the others."

An hour already had passed. Another would pass, guests numb
with fear or pain, thirsty and racked with doubt about their future,
forced to remain perfectly still. From the Casablanca radio station,
already in the rebels' hands, a broadcast was telling Moroccans: "Attention. The army has just conducted a revolution for the people.
The royal regime is abolished. Remain vigilant. Long live the republic."

But the king was not dead, nor even captured. While Malcolm
Forbes and hundreds of others remained motionless, the king was
still crowded into the restrooms with the others.

Medbouh had known for hours where the king was. But he
wanted the king ousted, not murdered. Having witnessed the car-
nage that Ababou was inflicting, Medbouh had kept quiet, but had

slipped quickly into the throne room and spoken to the king in the adjoining restroom. Would the king pardon Ababou if the revolt was stopped? The king would not.

Medbouh left. Ababou's anger at being unable to find the king could not be placated. Yet such was the confusion that when Ababou demanded to know from Medbouh where the king was, Medbouh calmly replied he had sent the king to Rabat under escort to announce his abdication over the radio. That remark saved the king's life, but cost Medbouh his. In his fury at not having the king in his grip, Ababou ordered Medbouh shot. General Medbouh, chief of the royal army, a man who wanted to save Morocco from itself, seconds later collapsed to the ground, dead.

Ababou's departure for Rabat left many cadets at Skhirat, but without a regularly deputized leader. The next gamble was Hassan's. A group of cadets discovered the restrooms off the throne room, and in doing so apparently recognized the king. He dared them to challenge his authority, but those cadets were among the hundreds who had been told they were rescuing the king, not killing him. They submitted.

Malcolm Forbes, still lying on the ground, heard the call for General Oufkir—also among those who had been rounded up. "He got up, he was lying quite close to us, when the cadets announced the king wanted to see him. The revolt was over. Oufkir was being made dictator of the country.

"The cadets told us to get to our feet and leave. There would be cars taking us back to Rabat."

Hassan had leaders of the revolt executed. When other governments protested, Hassan retorted: "I don't give a royal damn." He rebuffed protests by saying his father had instructed him: "Morocco must be ruled from horseback, not from a throne."

After the immediate reprisals had died down, the affairs drifted out of the public eye, and the lessons learned by Morocco's elite that day slowly were forgotten. Almost exactly a year later, in August, 1972, the king's Boeing 707 was attacked by his Air Force in a second assassination attempt. The king foiled that attempt by broadcasting as if he were the mechanic and that the king was dead. The plane was allowed to land; the king fled into nearby woods and avoided capture as military fighters strafed his Rabat palace and the Rabat airport. Hours later loyalist troops again had the situation in hand. This time the assassination attempt had been masterminded by another close friend, the king's most trusted soldier, the gaunt Berber from the Atlas who had crushed so many earlier revolts: General Oufkir. Reports said Oufkir committed suicide.

Just as the afternoon at Skhirat was not Hassan's only brush with death, neither was it Malcolm Forbes' only close call. Though Malcolm wasn't keeping count, it could be argued that it was about the fifth time in his fifty-one years he had escaped with his neck from a danger-filled situation. In another five years, Malcolm would challenge his maker three more times, using up eight of his nine lives—if that's how many he has.

Machine-gun sergeant Forbes had been shot in the closing days of World War II. He had single-handedly scouted an area to ensure that his men and his machine-gun post were not being flanked by the enemy. His reminder is the rolling gait caused by one leg being slightly shorter than the other.

On another desperate occasion, to be certain not to miss a plane flight from the United States, Malcolm captained his yacht through dense fog *across* the shipping lanes of the St. Lawrence Seaway. His third close call was at sea, with Malcolm attempting to take *Wings* to Labrador and back. Near miss number four was on a battleship. Malcolm had just landed by helicopter—accompanying an admiral—on the deck of the USS *Forrestal.* The whirlybird crashed on take-off after the twosome had stepped out.

Life number five was cashed in at Skhirat. Six, seven and eight would be used up as Malcolm declined to be called to his reward by electrocution, when his balloon crashed into high-voltage wires and blacked out the Saturday-afternoon football game for a major portion of the state of Virginia; by drowning, when that same balloon landed out of control in Chesapeake Bay; and by being burned to death when his instantaneously-ignitable liquid oxygen bottles, strapped outside his transatlantic balloon capsule, *Windborne,* threatened to be smashed open on the tarmac of the U.S. Marine base at Santa Ana, California.

But all of this was in the future. The Moroccan incident did not deter Malcolm from making plans for the Arab world. He'd wanted a palace. Now to make it pay its way, or at least earn its keep. Why not an Arabic edition of *Forbes?* As Hal Lavine wrote:

> Malcolm is a gut businessman . . . on his return he called in editor James W. Michaels and said: "What do you think about putting out the Jan. 1 (Forbes annual report on American industry) in Arabic?" Michaels talked with several Middle East experts and reported back to Forbes: "There are only a few hundred people in the Middle East who'll read it." "Let's do it," said Forbes. The issue was a smashing success. Everyone rushed to buy advertising, because those few hundred people are worth tens of billions.

To reach his increasing outposts of empire Malcolm bought the ultra bijou: *The Capitalist Tool,* his personal airliner.

The first *Tool* had quite a reputation. It was a Convair 580 turboprop that once had belonged to Malcolm's school chum, near neighbor, and—briefly—political rival, Charles Engelhard. As the head of Engelhard Mining and Chemicals Corp., which included the Philipp Corp., a precious metals company, Charles Engelhard was a little-known member of a very exclusive club—he was a multimillionaire of incredible wealth with close connections to the near-monopoly gold and precious-metals market.

Engelhard's dealings were intertwined with those of Harry Oppenheimer of South Africa, whose Anglo-American company virtually controls the free world diamond market and has a firm grip—through not total control—on much free world gold production.

Engelhard had decided to give up the gold-colored Convair 580 and it had gone down to the Flying W ranch in southern New Jersey, an airport facility catering to private pilots and aircraft owners.

Vice president of customer relations at Flying W was William Meade Thornton, black, balding and able in a wide range of duties connected with flying. Bill Thornton, a bridge player, tennis buff, and collector of bone china, was fully qualified as an in-flight steward. Malcolm Forbes and he liked each other from the moment Malcolm first began dickering for the Convair. And, when the deal for the lease-purchase was struck, it was on condition that Bill Thornton be part of the deal—as second officer on *The Capitalist Tool.*

Bill Thornton had experience dating back to running an officers' club at the Philadelphia air station during World War II, and enough savvy to know the broad spectrum of business entertaining and in-flight organization. Startled guests on the *Tool*, catnapping during a trans-U.S. flight, or spread out fast asleep on a divan during a transatlantic jaunt, would awake to find their shoes gone. But the shoes would reappear shined, Second Officer Thornton anxious that all disembark from the aircraft as smartly turned out as they had stepped aboard.

Guests, backs stiff from a long trip, would find masseur Thornton's firm fingers quickly eliminating a crick in the neck. Ham-and-egg sandwiches from the galley at two in the morning for the hungry; Dramamine for the queasy; aspirin for the boozy; a range of good wines for the choosy—all are distributed by the extremely obliging second officer. Some people demur at having their shoes shined; some wince slightly at the way Malcolm barks out orders once aboard —but William Thornton is an entity unto himself.

Valuable, like most of Malcolm's men, Thornton is invaluable in being able to ease passage through crowded airports, putting guests at ease, and in anticipating the needs of a demanding aircraft owner.

One of Malcolm's sometime ventures was in the antiques business in London. Already living in London was a young former Far Hills resident, Warner Dailey. Warner, a tutor, had been introduced to Malcolm several years earlier when invited to a film show at Timberfield. Malcolm and Warner had exchanged pleasantries, Warner casually mentioning his interest in antiques. Within a couple of years Warner was living a somewhat Bohemian life in London— trading in antiques, shopping around for bargains in the greater London area and "punting" (selling) anything of value in the auction houses, Christie's and Sotheby's particularly.

By the late 1960s, Malcolm Forbes was becoming active in buying art and antiques in Britain. It says much for Malcolm's alertness that he had not forgotten Warner, and tracked him down to his Addison Bridge Road home. Warner, sartorially careless, wearing old clothes and, often enough, brokendown shoes, had developed a successful feel for the London antiques game. That much was apparent to Malcolm as the two of them talked on the transatlantic telephone. Would Warner be interested in acting as Malcolm's agent in London? Would he buy and sell on Malcolm's behalf? Warner was indeed interested. *The Capitalist Tool* was in Europe; would Warner fly back on it to the United States to discuss terms, accepting $100 a day stipend for his trouble and traveling time? Indeed Warner would, and did.

Unperturbed by his own casual appearance, and with pieces of cardboard jammed into his shoes where they had worn through the soles, Warner threw a few items, antiques included, into a bag and joined the *Tool* at London's Heathrow Airport. On the twin turbo-prop Convair it would be a long trip—reminiscent of the pre-jet fourteen-hour Douglas DC-6 turboprop Atlantic flights. But it was free, and an adventure.

The *Tool* refueled at Iceland and Goose Bay, Newfoundland. Warner finally dropped off to sleep. He had thanked Bill Thornton for the offer to have his shoes shined, but had declined. He never polished them. But Warner Dailey had not reckoned on Bill Thornton's persistence. Two hours out of Newark Airport, where the *Tool* was a regular feature at Butler Aviation, steward Thornton wakened everyone for breakfast, his inflight bacon-and-scrambled-eggs special.

Warner looked down at his feet. No shoes. But there they were, at the side of his chair, shined—and with brand-new cardboard soles cut out and slipped inside to cover the holes.

Warner did set up a Forbes International antiques business. He had a full-time assistant, Astrid, a quiet young German girl, and became a more regular feature of the auction rooms. With Warner operating from home, expenses were low, and with Warner operating shrewdly, the stock of valuable merchandise grew. Many items were bought and shipped back to the United States.

Warner's home became a tourist attraction in itself, but only for those most "in" of tourists, people somehow connected with Malcolm, his children, or Warner himself. Just inside the Addison Bridge Road red brick, itself a treasured London antique, stood Charlie, the stuffed crocodile, tray in hand. Spread all over that front room were oddments, curios and antiques to entertain and dazzle the curio seeker and the bric-a-brac fiend. There was an old glazed bowl which later would bring $5,000 at auction—"I thought it might be worth about $40 when I bought it for $20," said Warner.

In one bedroom was a complete Elizabethan corner bed, later used by the British Broadcasting Corporation in an authentic setting for a BBC sequence. He has collected old model steam trains, carved wood, pictures made of ivory, large pieces of furniture and small pieces of Victorian jewelry—the utilitarian and the trivial, plus the exotic from other ages, other lands.

In the dark and dingy kitchen, Warner would eat off an odd plate of fine Spode chinaware, perhaps stir his coffee with a silver spoon from a long-gone Cunard steamer. The kitchen table itself is a mass of carvings, regular visitors being expected to execute a sample of the woodcarver's art in its soft pine surface. A complete place setting is carved into one spot.

Oil lamps and nineteenth-century carbide bicycle lamps illuminate cast-iron trivets and parchment and delicate crystal filled brimful with "plonk"—the British term for cheap red wine. Into this house ebbed and flowed people who bought and sold antiques for a living, or who occasionally picked up a piece of something for pleasure. Through Warner, a particular piece of furniture could be tracked down.

Flitting in and out of the auction rooms was fun. Malcolm and Warner had that in common. Warner "tried to guide Malcolm's taste"—but Warner was no more successful at it than anyone else had been.

Back in New York some *Forbes* employees wondered if Malcolm was buying paintings by the yard rather than by the item. Huge, heavily gilt-framed oils from several centuries began to crowd each other in Forbes, Inc. corridors and offices.

Her Britannic Majesty's government has a taste for taxes and likes to relieve the higher income brackets of the major portion of their gotten gains, as much as 80 percent or 90 percent. Capital gains are taxed almost to the point of extinction, and H.M. Inland Revenue is well aware that capital gains are more likely these days in the auction marts than they are on the London stock market.

So it was that Forbes International was requested by the British government to make some declaration of what it was up to in Britain. Tax collectors like to see figures. Malcolm Forbes is adamant on that score: "No one sees the books."

Once, when being interviewed by a New Jersey newspaper reporter, Malcolm pointed to the paper shredder on his desk "and smiled wickedly as he fed it some papers: 'This is our company balance sheet.'"

Rather than discuss details with the British Inland Revenue Service, Malcolm closed down the antique business interest. Warner was able to buy the accumulated stock on very generous terms, and Malcolm limits himself to occasional appearances at the auction rooms, but as an American with an external bank account, not as a U.S. entity doing business in Britain.

Warner is still blocking the street with his three Packard coach-built limousines. Vintage cars and motorcycles accumulate dust on top of their rust around back. Down in the basement kitchen, coffee still is stirred with Cunard spoons and plonk is sipped from Venetian crystal amid the dust and debris of a bachelor's quarters. He still has holes in his shoes.

The original *Tool* was followed by the DC–9, which, like its predecessor, would never be hangared: "It's great publicity having it sit there on the tarmac for everyone to see," says Malcolm.

With *"The Capitalist Tool"* on its nose, the Forbes motto, "Grace Me Guide" on its tail under the Forbes clan emblem, a stag's head, the DC–9 *Tool* was the ultimate in twentieth-century mobility and luxury. Not even *Playboy*'s Hugh Hefner has been able to maintain that high a lifestyle. *Playboy*'s DC–9 *Flying Bunny* was put up for sale in 1975. The *Tool* was sold to Westinghouse late in 1976. But while it lasted—now that was fun, even at $3000 a day.

Much of Malcolm's spending is, as Chris Welles commented on Malcolm's art collecting, "partly a device to soak up some of his company's burgeoning cash reserves."

It was a mix of available cash and a new fun toy that got Malcolm into the motorcycle business. His first ride was on an employee's bike at his Far Hills estate. Malcolm liked that enough to want one for himself. Again, one thing led to another—initially to Hank Slegers' Whippany, New Jersey, showrooms, and then into a business venture as Slegers-Forbes.

Before long this business too was newsworthy. As expected, the millionaire motorcyclist was good copy for *Cycle, Cycle Sport, Cycle World,* and the like—but then reports spread to the *New York Times* and the area dailies, including the Newark *Star-Ledger.*

Always one with a quip for the reporter needing a quote, Malcolm said of his knowledge of a bike engine: "If I kick the starter and it [the bike] doesn't go, I kick the bike and call for help."

Even Malcolm's biking adds to his legend. Leaning into a bend in the Rif Mountains of Morocco on his 1000-cc. Honda at something in excess of 70 m.p.h., Malcolm never thought there might be a cow wandering across the tarmac further around the bend. There was, Malcolm hit it, was thrown from his bike, and traveled on his face for twenty yards, cutting himself very badly, going into momentary shock, and ending up with a permanent memento or two, facial scars and an out-of-shape little finger on his right hand.

While son Bobby took photographs of the scene, including shots of the blood pouring down his father's face, gymnast and guardian Kip Cleland—for both youngsters were not far behind Malcolm on their bikes—patched up "the boss" and flagged down a car. It was filled with Soviet diplomats.

The diplomats got Malcolm to the doctor who lives close to his Tangier palace, and then Malcolm—no longer in shock, and with a wicked sense of gratitude—had Bobby show the diplomats over the palace, show them the film of the balloon events, and take them out to the airport. There, the Communist diplomats were given an inspection tour of the gold-colored DC–9. They could scarcely miss the legend, or the implications, of the name on its nose: *The Capitalist Tool.*

Malcolm was ordered to bed for forty-eight hours, but instead was host at dinner the following night, chiding his steward for not keeping the ice cream frozen, noting that there really didn't appear to be enough lamb chops for everyone, and wincing because only one tray of the two-tiered cake stand had any cookies on it. (All this, yet conscious enough—as always—of his guests to send along his personal Water Pik to a house guest who had forgotten hers.)

Malcolm freely admits to interesting other corporate executives —including townhouse lunch guests—in biking. New York advertising agency director Paul Gaynor read in *Forbes* that Malcolm was into bikes. Gaynor called up and ordered a minibike.

Malcolm, for a lark, brought the bike himself into Manhattan in the back of his Mercedes-Benz limousine. His chauffeur dropped him off at the office block housing Gaynor offices. The elevator operator had to be talked into allowing Malcolm upstairs with the bike—he fibbed it was going to be used for advertising photographs.

Once Malcolm had the bike up to the Gaynor floor, he wheeled it out into the corridor, cranked it up and went roaring into Gaynor's office to make a personal full-throttle delivery.

Monarchs seem to like jewels. Malcolm, with his tax-deductible monarchy, is no exception. The bediamonded novelties made for Czar Nicholas II that Malcolm owned had been an early attraction.

"When I was very young I read with horrified fascination an abundantly illustrated volume on World War I," writes Malcolm in the foreword to the Forbes Fabergé catalogue. "Its chapter on the Russian revolution and the massacre of the Romanov family included a picture of a Fabergé Imperial Egg to illustrate the prewar extravagance of Russia's rulers."

Malcolm's own view of Fabergé is that "one man's decadence is another man's creative art."

Malcolm collects with enthusiasm when there is "money to match desire." The sealed boxes in the Forbes lobby walls contain sparkling examples of non-utilitarian extravanganzas in miniature: a mother-of-pearl-lined miniature gold sedan chair with crystal windows; a gold-and-diamond ostrich-feather fan; miniature ornamental trees to hold tiny Easter eggs worth thousands of dollars; and the chanticleer egg, a clock which, on the hour, produces a cockerel on top to nod its head, flap its wings and crow.

Malcolm can justifiably crow that the $3 to $5 million worth of Fabergés has been a sound investment up to now. And with them he almost lives up to his reputation of making everything serve double service. But the Internal Revenue Service refused to allow the Fabergé collection as a deduction in the face of the Forbes Inc. claim that it is used in *Forbes'* advertising program, which it is. Not even the redoubtable Malcolm Forbes and his financial right-hand man Leonard Yablon could swing that one past the IRS.

The IRS keeps close watch. Malcolm keeps a closer watch. Every visitor entertained in the townhouse, yachted up the Hudson or jetted around the world, is photographed and logged. That way when the Internal Revenue Service comes calling, Malcolm can *prove* that the expense was business related. If Forbes, Inc. is sensitive, it is because a front-page story in the old *Herald Tribune* once stated that new tax laws would sink yachts such as the *Highlander II*, pictured above the story.

The *Highlander* was not sunk; the *Tool* was not grounded. The *Tool*, that DC–9, was quite a jewel.

When the DC–9 *Tool* landed at Tangier airport, sometimes the *chef du cabinet* was on the tarmac to greet Malcolm. The locals, customs and immigration officials, knew him and the plane by sight: "Mr. For-bess, Mr. For-bess" they would call in greeting; Second Officer Thornton would have already taken care of passports and formalities. *Tool* captains Wimmer Coder, formerly with Gulf & Western's Charles Bluhdorn, and Joseph Eberhardt, formerly U.S. Air Force, logged their flight time around the world. From Nadi Airport in Fiji, to Marrakech in Morocco, from Papeete in Tahiti to Deauville in Normandy, "the big golden bird," as junior members of the family called it, was a well-known sight. The *Tool* ranked high in Malcolm's affections though perhaps not with the IRS: $1 million a year in air fares? DC–9 number FM 64 went up for sale.

"The château is not for sale." Madame Myriam Bénédic, the former Myriam de Balleroy, descendant of the Marquis de Balleroy, watched the helicopter getting smaller as it receded from the château and village of Balleroy. She and her husband, Hubert, had spent hours with this American. They had flown in his helicopter above the château; they had shown him through the château, explaining its history, its architectural significance. Now they had sent him on his way.

The Château de Balleroy, in Normandy, is one of France's architectural jewels. The young architect François Mansart began in 1626 by carving its setting out of the lightly wooded rolling Normandy Hills. To complement the setting he carefully designed the château in red and gray stone; to complement the château he built the village. Monsieur Bénédic, a French businessman with interests overseas, in places like French Guiana in South America, where there was some gold and diamond mining, was well born, and the Bénédics were comfortably off financially—but not to the point where it was possible to keep the château as a residence.

So the new invaders were the prospective purchasers. Monsieur and Madame Bénédic were discriminating sellers even though they needed to relinquish the château. It was a national monument, the home of a great number of oil paintings important in French history. The American had been invited for lunch at 1 P.M. He had arrived by helicopter at 3 P.M. with the curt announcement: "We've already eaten."

Once the helicopter had placed the Bénédics back on their own turf, Madame Bénédic looked the American straight in the eye. "The château," she told Bernie Cornfeld, creator-manager of Geneva-based IOS, a soon-to-disintegrate $2 billion mutual fund, "is not for sale." Cornfeld departed, eventually to languish in a grim Geneva jail. He never would be master of Balleroy. That distinction would go to Malcolm Stevenson Forbes, whose magazine, as early as 1966, had warned American investors against Cornfeld.

Once Malcolm took possession of Balleroy at a cost of less than $350,000, Hubert Bénédic commented, "The future is in good hands."

When word got out to the French press that Malcolm was re-modeling inside the château, some of the information published slightly overstated the case. As one French journal ran it: "He has already equipped the château with 17 bathrooms. The village will be at the top of the cleanest built-up areas in France. Bravo USA!"

Malcolm has not added seventeen bathrooms. Just four. His own followed the pattern of all his bathrooms: sunken tub, gold fittings, sauna, wallpaper and drapes in brocades and moquettes, with some of the same tones carried into the master bedroom, with its thirty-foot ceiling and fourteen-foot-tall shuttered windows.

To the private quarters Malcolm had added an extremely important feature: additional central heating capacity to ward off the centuries-old chill in that stone-wall château, moist from centuries of damp air blowing in from La Manche (the English Channel). The château is not a monstrosity, and it is small enough to appear home-like for a large family. When the Forbes children and friends are there, the building rings with voices. The little sitting room with its fireplace, the ubiquitous photographs of the Forbes family and possessions, stamp the château undeniably Forbes. It is a pleasant spot. Filled with family it seems to lose its size and much of its historic importance.

Its aura of permanence, like that of the small chapel at the perimeter of the château grounds, is its charm. There are other charms, but the most homelike feature is the front door key. When the occupants want to go out in an evening, perhaps to see the fifteen- and twenty-year-old French-dubbed Hollywood technicolor epics in the cinema at Deauville, the key to the front door of Balleroy is hidden under the footscraper at the side of the front door.

The Château de Balleroy, for all its historic claims to fame, has had thrust upon it Malcolm's own claim to fame for it, the Château de Balleroy balloon museum. If dozens of tourists make their way to the historic château, and thousands make their way to the war museums of the nearby Normandy beaches, then surely hundreds, at least, would want to see a balloon museum. Surely they would want to see the handsomely remodeled stables, complete with balloon artifacts and illustrations, with exquisitely made dioramas from ballooning history—like the model of the journalists escaping by balloon during the Prussian siege of Paris in 1870.

"What is the difference between men and boys?" asks Malcolm Forbes. And he answers, "Men's toys are more expensive." With the balloon museum at Balleroy, Malcolm Forbes is letting his little-boy romanticism run away with him as with his toy-soldier museum in the Palais de Mendoub in Tangier.

Land, Malcolm was discovering, can be made to turn a profit.

Two of the Forbes family holdings are owned by the family, not the corporation—the 4–Bs cabin at Jackson Hole, Wyoming, and the twenty-square-mile ranch in Montana bordering Yellowstone National Park. When Malcolm is globe girdling, Montana is where his wife, Roberta, spends her time, supervising the Black Angus herd.

"One of the more colorful characters to move into Park County in recent years, at least part-time is Malcolm S. Forbes," cheerily editorializes the Livingston, Montana, *Enterprise*. "Forbes and his family have owned a large parcel of mountainous land north of Gardiner for some time, and have built a large new home on the crest of one of the hills. The ranch is managed year round and visited periodically by the clan. Much of the local Forbes activity, like the editorials in his magazine . . . exhibit a unique family flair for living."

Malcolm once appeared on the program of the Montana Stock Growers' Association's annual convention. Cattlemen take their business seriously. As one reporter covering the convention noted: "No one wore jeans."

It was as a result of his Montana ranch that Malcolm fell for another new hobby, having dioramas created. A local high school principal, Harold Guthrie, had made a diorama of the Park County town of Electric in its early days. The model so delighted Malcolm he asked Guthrie to make a model of the town of Aldridge, which is on the Forbeses' Montana property. Dioramas for the balloon museum at Balleroy were a natural follow-up.

The Montana ranch is small and personal, however, compared to the Forbes, Inc. Trinchera ranch, the 260-square-mile spread 200 miles south of Denver. The Trinchera, as any piece of Forbes, Inc.'s literature on its Sangre de Cristo ranches will confirm, is part of the 1843 Sangre de Cristo grant made by Governor Manuel Armijo to favored applicants.

A succession of owners brought the ranch into this century until, in 1938, it became the property of Mr. and Mrs. Arthur G. Simms, who used it as a private home—not a ranch—and as a private game reserve. The Simmses owned the ranch for thirty years. But death brought inheritance taxes, and reportedly that was the reason the ranch went up for sale in 1969.

The National Forest Service was anxious to annex the land to its other holdings in the area—and the Alamosa, Colorado, *Valley Courier* reported that valley residents were hoping the Forest Service would obtain it.

But Malcolm got it, paying between $3.5 million and $4.5 million for the 174,000 acres, on which the annual land tax was $8,000.

Malcolm ordered $1 million worth of fence. He would fence the Trinchera and turn it into the world's most exclusive game-hunting preserve. Soon beautiful four-color brochures with maroon borders were inviting riflemen to "Hunt the Trinchera—guided hunt fees are $1,000 for bull elk, $1,250 for bull elk and bull deer, $500 for buck deer and $1,000 for black bear . . . we will make every effort this year to accommodate all our hunting guests in the Forbes Trinchera Lodge. The daily rate, American Plan, is $50."

But the legislators of the West were out gunning for Malcolm to shoot down his commercial hunting plans. The state of Colorado ruled that Malcolm could fence in all his acres—but not all the animals because they belonged to the state. Possibly tongue in cheek, the state ruled that if Malcolm removed all the state's animals from his 260–square–mile tract he could perhaps restock with his own animals.

Malcolm ended up with $100,000 of already-delivered fence on his hands. If Americans couldn't hunt his fenced land, they could buy it, some of it.

The stocks of burgundy-colored "Hunt Trinchera" brochures with the magnificently antlered buck elk on the cover were replaced by blue-sky-and-grassland brochures, featuring a father and his two children—all three on horseback. "Your own land in the Old Southwest. Sangre de Cristo Ranches, division of *Forbes* Magazine." Many of the magazine's editorial staff shuddered when they saw that.

But everything has to do double duty and, on the first page inside the brochure, the land of "majestic mountains, grassy meadows, cascading waterfalls and bubbling streams"—a description of "Colorado, a state of incomparable beauty"—was intertwined with the magazine, "this prominent and highly reputable business publication."

This promotion was so thorough that the reader was informed, "equal in size to 20 city lots, five acres contains 217,000 square feet of land." All that for only $3500—payable monthly because Forbes wants cash flow, not lump sums. The price would move up to $5000 and beyond for better five-acres. The promotion took hold and the buyers wrote in for their bargains, their "investment for all time— for all seasons," their own stake "in the land and the sky," and their own directions telling them "how to get to your ranch."

The arithmetic made sense. Malcolm would spin off at least 40,000 acres of Trinchera as five-acre lots. He would run a no-nonsense campaign—$35 a month would buy the land and guaranteed money back if not satisfied—selling the five-acre lots at between $3500 and $5000, depending on the site. The land could bring in $20 or $30 million—and that's a lot of $1000-a-bear hunting fees and $50 American Plan breakfasts.

But why would people buy them? Leonard Yablon is Forbes' Brooklyn-born $150,000-a-year executive vice president and financial jack-of-all-trades, nationally and internationally. Despite the stuffed front half of a tiger in the glass case in his office, the smartly groomed, mustachioed Yablon knows more about the asphalt jungle than about the great outdoors. And he figured that people who live in the steel-and-glass cliffs above the asphalt want a piece of that big American outdoors "way out west."

Maintained Yablon, as the sales promotion began to pick up, "People like to be able to say in a casual way at the cocktail party, 'Yeah, I've got a bit of land out West myself.' "

Overseeing the land promotion is one of Yablon's prime responsibilities, along with having to find the money whenever a new idea bursts upon Malcolm. To Yablon falls, too, the uneasy task of having to discover how the latest pursuit can be deducted, at least in part, as a business expense to the satisfaction of the Internal Revenue Service. But that's what the $150,000 is for. In the meantime he grazes his "CSY" brand herd on the Forbes Trinchera and, Malcolm-like, gives out minibikes as gifts.

When things go wrong, like the $250,000 cost overrun at Old Battersea House, where the dry rot eating up the woodwork was quickly eating up Malcolm's money, Yablon has to solve the problem. The Old Battersea House problem is most particularly Len's—he was the strongest advocate of a stately stake in London.

Or, as Steve Forbes put it, "Len's got to worry about that one." The Depression born Yablon, who has been with Forbes since 1962, has come up through Forbes ranks.

Magazine owners sometimes are at one another's throats; other times they are a clubby lot. When they are clubby they jointly protest postal hikes and run advertisements mentioning all their names in each other's magazines (stating that magazine advertising gives a better rate of return than television advertising). It is not surprising to see *Time* magazine selling some of its Time-Life products on *Forbes'* pages—at no cost to Time-Life because in one of Time-Life's publications somewhere is a Forbes advertisement for, say, Sangre de Cristo ranch lots.

The glossy advertising and colorful prose about the Sangre de Cristo ranches caught the imagination of the *National Lampoon.* Malcolm, with the politician's belief that any publicity is good public-ity, reprinted the parody:

"Room to Live, Room to Laugh—at Wise Acres."

The acquisitions had been continuing apace. The *Gallagher Re-port* summed them up:

International land grab underway. Company presidents eye historic monuments as potential money makers. Acquire buildings at minimal cost. Renovate properties. Cover costs by conversion into luxury hotels for well-heeled executives. Major potential in property appreciation. Forbes Inc. President Malcolm Forbes bought 170,000-acre Trinchera

Ranch (Colo.) 16 months ago. Acquired 30-room French castle (Balleroy) near Normandy. Plans to renovate Saddi-Daimi palace in Tangier (Morocco). Has title to 1.2 million acres Australian "outback" region near Alice Springs. . . . Forbes' goal—to acquire, renovate maximum 20 similar properties.

As for those 1.2 million acres in Australia, the option was never exercised. The only way Malcolm could have gone into the Australian livestock business would have been by obtaining leases to Australian government lands adjoining the acreage he was considering to make the spread large enough to be economically feasible. (Australian antiforeigner sensibilities preclude foreigners' renting Australian-government property. But that type of attitude is not limited to Australia —American presidential candidates in the 1880s ran on a like-minded Alien Land Bill plank—to ban foreigners from owning U.S. property.

The Forbes Trinchera ranch still guarantees an elk for $1000. Nor is that as difficult as it seems. Elk graze in the same general areas each evening. Pull the truck into a cluster of trees and wait: Eventually the elk, who can react anxiously to the smell of man but apparently ignore the smell of trucks, go bounding past for supper. Bang. One trophy.

Managing the Forbes ranch, wildlife biologist Errol Ryland keeps an active eye on timber, wildlife and ranch sales, while head cowboy O. D. Fleming keeps his eye on the herd. Both the land sales and the ranch are flourishing businesses. Cattle graze in the meadowlands until early summer, then are driven in two days up to the pastures at nine thousand feet. Summer grazing up there permits the meadowlands to grow tall and to be mown for winter feed. The thousand miles of roads and trails throughout the ranch and the Sangre de Cristo development abound in what the brochure offers: bear, elk, porcupines, cattle and horses.

The main ranch lodge no longer exists. Once a showpiece, its walls hung with seascapes and ship paintings of endless variety, its mantel holding cases with clockwork ships that bobbed up and down through paper waves, and mounted on the wall, hundreds of pieces of presentation silver, it was destroyed in a fire.

Presentation silver is the commemorative bibelots Europeans were forever handing to one another: silver-plated cups for winning the village cricket match, watches awarded to young World War I army officers by their troops at a reunion, the precious-metal (thinly plated) memorabilia of early ages. Still at the ranch are a few rescued pieces: an old Russian peasant guiding a horse pulling a heavily-laden sled: "From the confirmation candidates, St. Petersburg, 1899." There is the 1932 winner's cup from the Coupes de Glaciers mountain automobile race. And on the walls there are oils still with their auction-room stickers on.

There is a new lodge going up—at about 9000 feet. Built of interlocking cedar logs, with huge plate-glass windows to take in the panorama, as far as the eye can see to the furthest mountain peak, Mount Trinchera, 13,109 feet ahead. There will be solar panels for heat, and water is being piped in up the hillside from a mile or so away. In winter, the approach roads will have to be plowed out—but for those who like a white Christmas, Colorado's Sangre de Cristo ranches can practically guarantee it at that altitude.

Malcolm, when at Trinchera, loves to sit on the porch reading, a drink in his hand, the glass having the Forbes Trinchera Ranch brand on it: FT with the bottom of the T lengthened, and broken to the left. He has tried to use the small mountain A-frame at 12,000 feet, but each time has returned to lower altitudes during the night because of splitting headaches. Others who have tried it have experienced vomiting or dizziness. The average altitude of the Trinchera ranch is about 8000 feet—sufficiently high to give some lowland folk a slight dizziness or a minor headache for a day or two until they adjust to it. But the night at that altitude—sky filled with stars, coyotes howling and the forests filled with wildlife—gives the promise of the brochure for those buying the wooded plots.

The hard sell of Sangre de Cristo is a rather light touch. Buyers can change their minds in sixty days or, if they visit the ranch site within a year and do not like its location, they can trade for a location they do like. There is 6 percent simple interest on the money.

After avoiding being stuck with 176,000 acres and turning it to incredible profit, Malcolm showed what a cool gambler he is. He plays life as he plays bridge, weighing first every player, then every card. And he plays life and bridge well enough to succeed at both. (Malcolm Forbes' bridge hands are sufficiently well calculated to make the Chicago *Daily News* bridge column, "Aces Bridge," run by

Ira G. Corn, Captain of the Aces. Not surprisingly, and quite in character, one headline read, "Getting Down to Business, Forbes Tackles Slam Bid." Advised Corn, "Witness his careful play of today's trap-ridden slam deal." He could have been describing Malcolm's approach to life or business.)

Malcolm in the 1970s is no longer the "slender, bespectacled publisher" the *New York Times* had described during his political heyday in 1957. He fights, and sometimes loses, the battle of the bulge—but he is not fat, though fleshier than he need be. His jowls are not sufficiently loose to shake with laughter. And the muscles are still close enough to the surface so that in moments of danger or anger—neither of them rarities in his life—the jaw sets firm, the eyes narrow, the mouth forms a snarl. But the moment passes and the return to the earlier mood is accomplished with equal speed—the muscles relax, the eyes widen and the large mouth and jaw, with strong white teeth evident but not flashing, make the transition back to amusement, entertainment or conversation.

In the early 1970s, he could look back on eight years of personal ownership with some degree of satisfaction. The magazine was booming—its circulation and number of advertising pages eclipsed *Fortune;* its profitability eclipsed everything but *Playboy*—at that date still a privately held company too.

It was said that only *Forbes* and *Playboy* really knew how to make money—charging enough for the magazine so that most of the expenses were met out of the subscription price. Many newspapers, periodicals and magazines have to subsidize their circulation and editorial costs out of their advertising revenue.

By the end of 1972, with *Forbes* circulation at 625,000 (well ahead of *Fortune's* 550,000), subscriptions alone were generating $4.5 million. That was enough to cover the costs of circulation, promotion (no mean expense) and the editorial department, and still leave enough over to run the *Highlander*.

Advertising was bringing in $8 million, and with rents from 60 Fifth Avenue, from the stock-market course and special-situations service, revenue was over $13 million. Less than $200,000 was set aside for taxes.

If revenues seem minor, especially when compared to Malcolm's lifestyle, this was before the big money started rolling in from the

Sangre de Cristo ranch exploitation. In these years the Trinchera, Sangre de Cristo, and the international showcases were draining the kitty. And there was still the *Tool* to run. When everything had been evened out, Malcolm had to set aside money for federal corporate income taxes—plus his own income taxes out of the $150,000 annual salary he paid himself. Malcolm maintains he pays annually "six figures" in taxes. He may well some years—the idea is to get close to costs equaling expenses, but not to the point when one hits zero; otherwise the taxman cometh with a vengeance. No wise millionaire really wants to end up paying no taxes—the Internal Revenue Service cannot help but get out its fine-tooth combs. Furthermore, the publicity of a low-tax existence in a life lived in one's personal Aladdin's cave can turn sour in the public mouth.

Malcolm was giving the IRS something new to think about. He was about to get into ballooning—as a business expense.

9

The Balloonatic

By the time . . . his balloon finally touched down in Chesapeake Bay, Malcolm Forbes was almost as familiar to Americans as Evel Knievel. Needless to say, Malcolm Forbes the promoter, publicist and pitchman had as much to do with this as Malcolm Forbes the balloonist. With all the resources of *Forbes* magazine and Forbes Inc. at his disposal (he is sole stockholder of both) he had inundated the press, radio and television networks with PR kits, films and advance men all touting the wonders of the epic cross country flight. The promotion was obvious, but the public loved it.

Sports Illustrated

Three little white Renault cars bobbed and swayed as they rattled along Victor Hugues Boulevard in Kourou, French Guiana, a humid, unpleasant land of rain forest, mangrove swamp and occasional stretches of open savannah.

A fourth white Renault, its tiny engine straining, its tinny body vibrating, gradually caught up to the parade of three. The car edged its way past them. Horn tooting dramatically, with an arm waving wildly out of one window, the fourth Renault flagged down the other cars and pulled jerkily to the side of the road.

These Renaults, tails sticking up in the air like bustles on *belle époque* dames, painted the institutional white of CNES (Centre National d'Études Spatiales), the French space agency, are familiar sights in this inhospitable corner of northeastern South America. It was to sparsely populated French Guiana that France had moved its rocket and missile test sites after the colonial French government had been ousted from Algeria.

The driver's door swung open and a bearded Frenchman

jumped out of the car. He ran to the lead car in the trio he had halted. Face aglow with pride, the Frenchman said in careful English: "I have the hats." He smiled expectantly.

"Great," said Malcolm, stepping out of his car as all three vehicles emptied, their passengers anxious to see what was going on. "I'll take them all. How much?"

"You may have only two," replied the Frenchman, opening his Renault's tailgate. "The others, too, have ordered them. Fifty francs each."

From a box jammed into the small space behind the rear seat, the Frenchman produced two French Foreign Legion *képis,* the stiff white pillbox caps with shiny black peaks, instantly recognizable and internationally known.

"Wow, these are great," said Malcolm. He ripped the plastic covering off one cap and jauntily jammed the *képi* down around his ears. He turned for approval, eyebrows raised, a characteristic slight flush of mixed embarrassment and pride reddening his jowls, cheeks and what could be seen of his forehead. Approval Malcolm got from all. The Frenchman beamed. It was a lot of fun pleasing this madcap millionaire from North America.

Only the previous day he had bought up all that remained of an entire box of French Foreign Legion T-shirts, white with the green inscription: "Legio Patria Nostra 3 Rei," with the Third Regiment's catlike emblem embroidered on the left sleeve.

The T-shirts, like the *képis,* had been quietly acquired from persons unnamed at Third Regiment headquarters scarcely a half mile down the road from *Les Roches,* Kourou's only occupied hotel. At $10 for a *képi,* $5 for a shirt, the dealings were profitable. Certainly both items were being retailed on Victor Hugues Boulevard— named after a benighted French Guiana governor of the 1800s—at a price that included a handsome markup for every set of hands through which they passed.

Malcolm returned to his car. In his white *képi,* his red shirt and yellow slacks—colors of the Forbes Magazine Balloon Ascension Division—he cut a bizarre figure.

If Malcolm's appearance was bizarre, his reason for being in Kourou was even more so. The French space agency had agreed to test launch a series of helium-filled plastic balloons, similar to those

Malcolm Forbes was going to use in his attempt to be the first man to balloon successfully across the Atlantic.

Kourou, French Guiana, is one of the few places on the globe that regularly experiences zero wind.

French Guiana is one of those countries which, when first mentioned, people think might be in Africa—renamed Zambola, or something—or possibly exist as an island paradise somewhere far off the coast of Australia or New Zealand or Fiji. As one of the passengers on *The Capitalist Tool* remarked boarding at Newark, "I didn't really know where we were going until my wife got out the map."

French Guiana squats, a fetid land, with a population scarcely in excess of forty thousand, between the borders of Brazil to the south, and Surinam (Dutch Guiana as was) to the west. It is known on the books of some travel agents as a place to send tourists who have been everywhere else. There are genuine never-seen-by-white-man natives upriver, and in the local stores postcards of fertility rites. Whether the photographer had a great imagination, or whether in fact some of the goings-on nakedly portrayed on the glossy full-color five-by-sevens actually still go on, no one seems to know.

Malcolm Forbes' connection with the French space agency came through his companion for the proposed flight, Thomas Heinsheimer, an astrophysicist now playing Passepartout to Forbes' Phileas Fogg. After his first-ever trans–United States hot-air balloon trip, Malcolm had his eyes on *the* big challenge for balloonists: the Atlantic. The dream already had cost four lives—one in the preceding twelve months. Malcolm's attempt would be the thirteenth. But he dismissed suggestions of a superstitious nature.

Malcolm's ballooning activities had gone from a $150 trial flight in 1972 to a $120,000 cross-country trip in 1973 to a prospective Atlantic crossing attempt initially budgeted at $750,000 and already on its way to a $1.35 million final price tag.

But it would all be worth it, providing the money could come out of Forbes Inc.'s pretax income as a justified expenditure, and shown to be worthwhile as a business-promotion expense in the eyes of the Internal Revenue Service. It would be worthwhile if the balloons finally landed somewhere on the other side of the Atlantic, and if the romance enkindled by boyhood memories of Lindbergh's ticker tape worship and total national recognition came true. It would be worth it—to be recognized, and to have achieved that great death-defying first.

Malcolm's entry into ballooning came by way of a small advertisement in a magazine. He was nestled back in the cushions of his huge maroon Mercedes-Benz limousine, on the way from rural New Jersey into Manhattan, when he read of the trial balloon flights.

As *Sports Illustrated* reported it:

> "It sounded like a cool idea," he says, "so I talked my chauffeur into going up with me. The next thing we knew we had both signed up for lessons."
>
> Since then, Forbes has participated in every major balloon race in the U.S., established the world's first Museum of Ballooning, acquired more than a dozen hot air balloons—several of them valued in excess of $25,000—and last year became the first person to cross the continental U.S. in a single balloon. En route he set six world records, in addition to wiping out a row of parked cars ("How can you explain to the insurance man," said one victim, "that you were hit by a balloon?").

Malcolm, the writer who had learned to identify with his audience, figured they'd enjoy hot-air ballooning as much as he did. He figured that the readership would fill letters with "so that's where all the hot air comes from to keep balloons up" and similar letdowns, so he used the jokes against himself first.

Nonetheless, when readers disagree, they do use the balloon metaphor as a first verbal line of attack: "Asinine. Go out and play with your balloon. . . ." "We finally learned where the hot air comes from that you use in your big balloon."

The cross-country trip, for Malcolm, was more than one more escapade—it was a saga. And a bruising one at that. "The price wasn't all financial—about $100,000," wrote Gordon Cruickshanks in *National Aeronautics* magazine, "it was physical, too. For 34 days Malcolm Forbes took the beating of his life. Meeting him for the first time at the Showboat Motel right after the Casper, Wyoming, landing, Malcolm was black and blue from high on the chest to down to his calves."

As Cruickshanks summed it up: "Twenty-one hops and 141 hours and 30 minutes air time after its Coos Bay, Oregon ascent, the *Château de Balleroy* (Bal-luh-wah) found the pot of gold at the other end of the rainbow—at Gwynn Island on the east coast. Forbes the argonaut had set one of aviation's greatest records—a FIRST! And six world records en route."

Malcolm, who described ballooning as "the most frivolous endeavor man can enjoy," as usual was attracting plenty of publicity. *Newsday* sent Dennis Duggan on the trans-U.S. trip. The *New York Times* was in from the beginning, atop the Forbes building for a pre-attempt inflation of the *Château de Balleroy.* "It's up, up and away for Forbes," headlined the eighteen-inch story that mentioned everything from the motorcycle agency in Whippany to the ranch lots being sold off at Sangre de Cristo. Even pre-launch the "Bal-luh-wah" was paying her way.

Once the saga was ended, Malcolm wrote a fifty-thousand-word narrative, dedicated to "Bob Forbes, intrepid photographer, cool son, warm human." One publisher approached with the manuscript commented: "Malcolm can't write."

After the trans-U.S. success, Malcolm was preoccupied by a possible transatlantic trip. Colonel Thomas Gatch had recently perished somewhere near the Azores in a United States–to–Europe attempt.

Malcolm had been talking to Raven Industries, the company that had built his earlier hot-air balloons. He had said he wanted balloons like Gatch's, but bigger ones that would take him above weather. Could they do it? Yes, they could.

Raven also built balloons for Tom Heinsheimer, a California-based scientist who worked with superpressure gas-filled balloons for the government. Heinsheimer learned about Malcolm's interest and cabled him saying he had some expertise in the field.

Malcolm was excited when he got the cable in his office.

"Mary Ann," he asked his secretary, "please get this Mr. Heinsheimer on the phone." Miss Danner tracked Heinsheimer down at work.

"Mr. Heinsheimer, this is Malcolm Forbes of *Forbes* magazine. How are *you?* Great. I'm into ballooning. I made a hot-air balloon trip across the United States last year, you may have read about it. Raven Industries tells me they make high-altitude balloons for you. I'm thinking about trying the Atlantic, you know, like Gatch did, but above the weather, that sort of thing. Well, Raven says you're the best man there is. I'd like to hire you, you know, retain you to handle all the preparations. Would you want to do it?"

"Oh, I don't know, Mr. Forbes. I someday hoped to make the same trip myself, but it takes money to do it. If you would build two balloons we could duplicate everything."

"That's a big expense. It sounds foolish to build two. Is it possible to set up a system for a two-man thing?"

"Yes, it is, that could work. We'd have to design a system to accommodate the payload, one man or two men."

Would Mr. Heinsheimer fly east at Mr. Forbes' expense to talk it over? Could he come that day? The next day? Two days later Tom Heinsheimer was a guest at the Forbeses' New Jersey estate and an adventure was born. "We just hit it off," said Malcolm. "He made an enormous impression on me. We signed a contract, an agreement. I figured his interest in it would be pretty thorough if he was in the gondola too."

Heinsheimer was quickly exposed to hot-air ballooning and soon had his balloon pilot's license. Malcolm was quickly exposed to estimates, the enormity of the expense, the complexity of the undertaking. Given the life-support systems necessary, the precision planning required, the altitude at which the attempt was to be made, the *Windborne*—as the gondola would be called—was to go on nothing less than a space shot.

It was a first-generation American space spectacular: Malcolm, son of an immigrant Scot; Heinsheimer, son of an immigrant Viennese musician, an expatriate from Hitler-threatened Austria. But it was a very American undertaking: scientists and engineers soon were moonlighting from the Southern California space industry as word of the project spread among friends and fellow space enthusiasts. Most of those involved were people with side ventures, one-man businesses and big dreams—technological and financial.

Now, months later, the project had reached its pre-launch trials.

That morning, as the mosquitoes ceased their stinging and equally vicious biting jungle insects took their place, an elegantly choreographed launch had taken place. The "balloon" of transparent Mylar had been slowly inflated into life as the helium traveled through a corrugated umbilicus not unlike an old-fashioned vacuum-cleaner tube.

The chilled Mylar, for the pre-dawn temperature in the small hangar had kept the plastic fairly stiff, crackled and snapped as it opened its folds. Once the balloon had swelled a little, it was moved outside. A "cap," a snood-like affair, was draped over its top. From the snood dozens of lines hung down. These lines carried weights and —as the balloon filled—the weights all around the balloon were sufficient to keep it from becoming airborne.

Precise measurement allowed that once the helium in the balloon correctly offset the total downward pull of the weights, then the correct amount of helium had been pumped in. Naturally the balloon was nowhere near swelled to its maximum capacity—allowance had to be made for the helium's expanding as the balloon rose thousands and thousands of feet into the thinning atmosphere. Only then would the balloon become a sphere. At the level of mere earthbound mortals, the Mylar bag was the shape of a single dip of ice cream on a cone —rounded top, narrowing down to the point at which the helium had been pumped in.

This balloon was carrying an electronics payload, automatic sensors and payload "snippers" of the type which—during the *Windborne* descent months ahead—would allow the aeronauts to release balloons electronically from inside the gondola.

Miles of nylon rigging and electrical wiring would be involved in the final thirteen-balloon *Windborne* craft.

This single balloon was launched. There were confusion, shouts and calls as the balloon moved up more rapidly than expected, jerking and tugging at its payload as each team let go in choreographed order.

Within seconds the balloon and its payload were beyond reach. "Someone should have led the applause," said NBC documentary maker George Heinemann.

"A precipitous launch but apparently nothing broke," said Tom Heinsheimer.

"If the balloon doesn't break we're in business," said a pleased Malcolm.

"We'll follow it on the radar," said Tom, watching the reflection from the sun as the Mylar cone rose thousands of feet. "We can get a prediction of the climb-out. It's going up at something like ten feet per second."

"What happened?" asked writer Joan Bender. "She was being launched smoothly then jumped ahead a little from the pressure before you were ready for it?"

"That's because we have a much bigger balloon than the adapter is used to," said Tom. "The adapter [a small winch] was not up to it. Since we had rehearsed the thing yesterday we knew what to do and we just followed through. When that thing [the balloon] gets going it moves like an express train. If you hold on to your line you can get that feed line jerked and it will do a lot of damage. The only guy that got caught was at the very end. His line jerked so the very last payload dragged on the ground a little. It shouldn't do any harm."

Heinsheimer's work with the French space agency, CNES, and some delicate negotiations between Heinsheimer (on Forbes' behalf) and the agency, were making possible the cooperation the *Windborne* project was receiving from CNES. With a no-expense to CNES formal agreement between Malcolm and CNES, the French scientists were using the *Windborne* to gather additional information for their own purposes, while the Forbes project benefited from the French agency's skills and services.

Dr. Jacques Blaumont headed the CNES team in Kourou at the morning launch. Thin-faced ascetic, with thin-rimmed glasses and authoritative Anglo-French diction, a priest lecturing acolytes, he had given briefings the previous afternoon. Next came Jean-Pierre Pommerau, a broad-shouldered and handsome Basque, a good-looking rival to the younger members of the Forbes Balloon Ascension Division who, like tomcats on the prowl, spent most evenings seeking a frolic. Pommerau, a respected scientist and astrophysicist, was in charge of the launch tests, and would be in final command on the day of the launch itself.

Pommerau's presence, his curt, Gallic authority, his occasional moments of relaxation and laughter, his constant reaching for cigarettes—an aura of Gauloise Bleu—were a reassurance and restorer of order throughout *Windborne*'s entire development.

The three white Renaults by this time had pulled up at the Kourou harbor. A young Frenchman wearing the local tennis club T-shirt pointed to a boat chugging off downriver into the distance.

"It left without you," said the young man, unsure of what reaction his comment would bring. Malcolm, eyes peering downriver from under the *Képi* peak, frowned, then looked at his watch. "They were told to wait." He grimaced and looked around at the little group of disappointed faces. He hated these moments, to have a cheerful entourage suddenly turn sour; to be at the peak, then come crashing down. And, when he was responsible for such *divertisse-ments* as a trip to Devil's Island, he did not like the criticism—real or imagined—when things did not work out. His mood blackened but he prevented himself from lashing out verbally at anyone. He was temporarily caught short, and uncertain what to say. He looked quickly, trying to read the mood of the group.

There was George Heinemann, the balding, round-faced fiftyish producer of the NBC documentary on the transatlantic balloon attempt, assigned by Malcolm's friend Robert "Bobby" Sarnoff, then chief executive officer of RCA (which owns NBC) to do the documentary.

There was Tony Halik, also fiftyish, hawk-nosed, long fair hair slicked back, truly an eccentric, and NBC's chief cameraman, based in Mexico City. Halik knew he was a character, and was comfortable in the role. In his jungle suit, with silver-dollar belt holding cans of film, a colorful silk scarf and big onyx woggle at his throat, Halik can run at full speed with a thirty-five-pound camera, filming all the while, and still be able to tumble like an acrobat, rolling onto his back to suddenly switch camera angles and get an upward climbing shot. Halik, dubbed by the Kourou team "the white rhino," author of books about big-game hunting with camera, an expert on the Matto Grosso and the Amazon, slipped easily into conversations in the three languages of the Kourou group: French with the French space scientists; Spanish with his sound man, Roberto; and English with Malcolm and his entourage.

Joan Bender, nervous about jungle insects but confident as a freelance director-writer, working with Heineman on this project, had many television documentary hits to her credit. She was the New York media professional and freelance, charming and capable, plus, she was *writing* the documentary.

George Heinemann's pert, dark-haired wife, Helen, deliberately a face at the edge of the crowd, was quietly watching, quietly smiling and quietly keeping her own counsel. Belinda Neushul's husband, Peter, was an employee of Malcolm's building the transatlantic gondola in his Glendale, California, workshop. The Neushul premises usually turned out such prosaic items as hospital laundry carts and luggage pods for airliners. The chance to build a space capsule—in what still stands as the world's only one-man-funded free-enterprise "space shot"—came from his friendship with Tom Heinsheimer.

Heinsheimer believed that Neushul could produce the *Windborne*'s sphere. Malcolm was prepared to take project director–traveling companion Heinsheimer's word for it. It was Heinsheimer's neck too.

At this moment, while the group was gathered at the Kourou dock, Tom Heinsheimer was still working alongside the French space technicians out at the launch site tracking this day's 6 A.M. trial balloon launch.

On the Forbes Inc. payroll at $50,000 a year for the duration of the balloon epic—and an equal sharer in any glories that accrued from a successful Atlantic crossing—Heinsheimer was still getting acclimatized to the pressures and pleasures of being caught up in the moneyed maelstrom of Malcolm's entourage.

If Julie Heinsheimer was enjoying it, she wasn't showing it. She was in the harborside group. Slim, thin-faced, she had been with Tom in his various assignments, his years in France, so that she too now spoke the language like a native. She had settled on the fringes of the California aerospace community, in Rolling Hills, the almost suburban wife—but with sufficient animals around to keep suburbia at its worst at bay. With two children, Julie had adjusted to the role of wife, mother and farmhand. But what was staring her in the face every day as this balloon trip got closer and closer to becoming a reality was the prospect of being a widow.

That was why Julie Heinsheimer was not smiling with the crowd, reflecting the grin Malcolm now was flashing. She was still adjusting to Tom's new place as Malcolm's employed scientific confidant and co-pilot, and she had not yet convinced herself that she liked what the future held.

Back in New Jersey, Roberta had similar concerns to mull over. She was accustomed to Malcolm's unpredictability, but even for Malcolm this was madness. She was opposed to it. But it didn't do any good to say anything. He would just go ahead with it anyway. He always had, with any project, and he always would no matter what anyone had to say about it.

A huge gray patrol boat came around the bend from upriver and headed for the landing stage. *This* was the craft Malcolm had arranged for the Devil's Island trip. He realized it instantly. The open sided island-hopper now out of sight downriver was the local commercial ferry.

Back in Kourou that evening the worst was known. Malcolm and some of the others had taken *The Capitalist Tool* to track the balloon in the air, and it had soon become apparent that the test was not going as planned. The balloon did not reach the expected altitude, and in fact began to fall, remaining aloft for only part of that day.

As the refugees from Devil's Island and the long day's launching gathered over seafood and wine at Kourou's Vietnamese restaurant late that evening, there was a rather solemn air. Malcolm arrived late and said little. Joan Bender not punning, summed up everyone's feelings: "Poor Malcolm, he's deflated."

Was Malcolm having second thoughts about risking his neck under a cluster of plastic Baggies that were expected to stand the stresses of the upper atmosphere for a week or more?

Next morning the returns were in. Professor Blaumont summed up: "We operate at a constant level of disappointment. If you cannot stand disappointment stay out of the technology business. We are at the frontiers of technology. If we have no failures we have over-designed."

Soon it was Tom Heinsheimer's turn at the green board with a chalk in his hand. Apparently they knew what had happened to the previous day's balloon. One of the plugs in the Mylar holding the electronic snippers must have been tugged out during the jerky launch ceremony. The rate of escape of helium was exactly calculable to the amount that would escape from such a plug loss. Despite the outcome, then, the balloon had contributed to the test series.

There were to be more launches, more calculations and briefings, more gatherings and get-togethers. The mulatto sipping Coke at the bar at the hotel looked in wonder and some envy at these North Americans, grinning, wealthy, relaxed and highly intelligent, and their French companions. In the boy's eyes one could read his own assessment of life ahead—no matter what he did, no matter how hard he worked, he never would be as these men were: successful, wealthy and white.

It is unlikely that Malcolm's restaurant guide would have given Les Roches Hotel's cuisine a single star. Most of the North Americans felt the same way, and the last night in Kourou—especially for the

NBC team—was time for a change of dining venue. The steak at a different establishment that night was good, the wine acceptable, the surroundings neat and clean. The fact that it was also the local whorehouse did nothing to diminish the quality of the food. Diners were not obliged to make their way through to the sexy inner-reaches. And, in fact, decorum prevailed.

At 4 A.M. the Forbes party was up and heading by car along jungle roads—replete with the occasional squashed monkey—to Cayenne and the flight back to the United States. The convoy of cars was missing one passenger. His prowling had led him into the boudoir of one of the more attractive female guests at Kourou—but no one was certain which guest, or which room. His early-morning alarm call could not be delivered without awakening the entire hotel.

It was all aboard *The Capitalist Tool.* There would be a stop at Puerto Rico to drop off cameraman Halik and sound man Roberto. The DC-9's engines were warming up, the door about to close, when across the runway, racing for his life, came the missing passenger. He'd made it—but only just. Malcolm laughed and watched as the reprobate made his way aboard, red-faced but unrepentant. Was Malcolm reminded of Orly airport, twenty years earlier, when he too narrowly avoided missing his flight?

On Tuesday, September 24, 1974, the Forbes Atlantic Project was formally announced at a televised press conference in the Hilton Room (formerly the Empire Room) of New York's Waldorf Astoria. It was the same room in which, twenty-seven years earlier, Malcolm had formally unveiled *Nation's Heritage* magazine.

The Atlantic Project press conference was an elaborately staged affair that had two major purposes to fill: it was to gain publicity for the Forbes project, but had to show—through scientific displays of what was involved—that this was a serious venture and not just one more Malcolm Forbes publicity stunt. In the weeks in Kourou and leading up to the Waldorf unveiling Malcolm had been particularly anxious to get the message across to the media that this was more than just a Forbesian stunt.

The array of scientific information and specimens around the Waldorf room did just that. Reporters from newspapers and magazines looked at the life-support systems with the respect usually reserved for exhibits at the Smithsonian. They fingered the samples of Mylar in wonderment at the risks involved—and they flipped open the volume of *Fact and Comment* that was being given out free of charge to each person attending the conference. (Sales had been positively sluggish).

Malcolm was on hand to chat informally with visitors before the conference started. Roberta was there too, trying to stay in the background. At the head table Malcolm would be joined by co-venturer Tom Heinsheimer, and such worthies as friend Robert W. Sarnoff.

Malcolm learned that when the events got under way Tom Heinsheimer would be closer to the television cameras than he would. He switched the place cards around.

Where the suspicious New York media are concerned Malcolm has to work hard to undo the self-publicist image. Once the press conference had started, Malcolm's handling of the questions and his references to the scientific aspects of the trip began to make a convincing case for the seriousness of the undertaking. He was just about convincing the skeptics when a scantily dressed hireling came running into the room shouting, "Mr. Forbes! Mr. Forbes!" Malcolm was nearly transfixed in bewilderment and with barely-concealed fury. It looked as though he had staged some silliness and that the New York media's worst suspicions were confirmed.

The damsel distressing Malcolm delivered her message. It was a good-luck greeting from W. F. "Al" Rockwell, Jr., chairman of Rockwell International, a friend who, at that moment, Malcolm cheerfully would have choked. After muttering that the interruption was most unexpected and that he had nothing to do with it, Malcolm resumed the question-and-answer session. It says much for the complexity of the Atlantic Project as outlined that Malcolm got good media notices.

Malcolm that day, in fact, probably turned the corner in changing his public image. Whether it was the fact that he was calmly prepared to risk his life, or whether he was able to convey a sense of earnestness about the undertaking, a slightly different, somehow more respectful public image of Malcolm Forbes has begun to emerge since September, 1974.

This was strictly pioneer work, life-and-limb risking, on the part of Malcolm Forbes and Tom Heinsheimer. Superpressure balloons had been known to turn brittle at high altitude and drop like pieces of confetti to the earth or sea below. The miles of electrical wires that would connect the sphere with the balloons, reporting back on temperatures and providing the eventual snipping device for return to earth, were first-time developments.

As scientists like Heinsheimer, Blaumont and Pommerau were quick to tell any listener, this was an experiment in which the test flight was also the real flight. All systems had to work the moment they were tested—that is, when the *Windborne* was launched.

Man had never ridden in the jetstream at the stream's own speed, doing experiments inside it while being carried along by it at speeds of up to two hundred knots. Among the many scientific quids-pro-quo the *Windborne* was carrying, the research into what is going on inside the jetstream was the most original. But two men in a ten-foot-diameter sphere at forty-thousand feet were placing their lives in the hands of their earthbound engineers to an even greater degree than had the Apollo astronauts. *Windborne* possessed no motive system—it could not be made to go in a particular direction. Poorly calculated jetstream currents could see *Windborne* sent down into the jungles of South America, or shifted out into the Pacific, not across the United States toward the Atlantic.

Once they were aloft it was possible the jetstream could branch off in any of several directions, sweeping the *Windborne* up over arctic Greenland, or south to the Southern Atlantic or Africa. There were no guarantees. That meant the inboard systems *had* to work. Pressurized inside the car (the balloonists' term for the gondola) Malcolm and Tom were at the mercy of the efficiency of thermodynamicist Hugh Haroldson's insulation, Hart Smith's bonded joints, Roger Edelmann's electronics, Peter Neuschal's construction skills, the life-support oxygen-recycling system, and the monitoring stations globally tracking the private-enterprise microdot spacecraft.

Within the ballooning fraternity there had been some hard feeling toward Malcolm after his successful record-breaking trans-U.S. attempt. *Sports Illustrated* touched the sore point this way:

> Not everybody in that fraternity is amused by the swath Forbes has cut through the sport. Bob Hilton, of the International Professional Balloon Pilots Racing Association, becomes apoplectic at the mention of the Atlantic flight. "It's a travesty," he says, "an insult to the sport and to

serious balloonists." Others point out that the coast-to-coast flight was supported by a ground crew of some 30 people, plus an airplane, a bus, several cars, a motor home and extensive electronic equipment. The fact that Forbes spent most nights in motels and three times flew home for weekends arouses further ire. Forbes is nonplussed by such criticism.

"The reason my flight succeeded and other failed," he says, "can be summed up in one word: money. The flight could never have been made without ground support such as I had. I was willing to pay for it. No one else has been."

James C. Fletcher, administrator of the National Aeronautics and Space Administration, however, called the *Windborne's* plans for the transatlantic flight "most professional, and coupled with the information I got from our brief discussion in Salt Lake City, I am impressed by the degree of planning that has gone into the project."

For the technically-minded, the experiment payload on *Windborne* would include "quadrantid meteor spectroscopy, infrasonic noise measurement, aeronomy (for French space agency CNES), IR environment and gradient wind." Those experiments were not mere dressing to cover up a Forbesian superblimp. They were serious; they were Heinsheimer's personal claim on *Windborne,* its scientific fall-out.

Heinsheimer twice had applied in the 1960s to the National Science Program as a scientist-astronaut. Eight years later he could look back at not having made it with the comment that while it would have provided professional cachet at the time, "it turned out to be nothing. There were astronauts who wasted their lives by getting involved in something which could not result in any achievement. Quite to the contrary, they trained to do a lot of things that were unnecessary and useless. Probably most of them ruined their professional careers."

Heinsheimer, who has his own small company, Atmospherics, Inc., was prime contractor to the Forbes Atlantic Project. But for him the *Windborne* was more than the construction and the flight: "We can show it's serious when we do make good measurements and make observations that are worth having." And that, along with surviving a death-defying "first," would be reward—professional and personal—enough.

As a piece of entertainment, *Windborne* also had its attractions.

NBC knew it would be a fascinating television documentary.

Second-eldest Forbes son, Robert, was producing and directing a documentary of the *Windborne*, backed up by John Ehrendon and Dale Whitman, that, if successful, might be released nationally to cinemas. Having made the film, the sons would have to get out and hawk it around the movie-house sales circuit—one way Malcolm inculcates in his children the harsher business realities.

Other cameramen interested in the *Windborne* included John Ott, the veteran stop-motion cameraman who developed the movie technique for Disney of flowers opening and plants growing. Ott's camera would be strapped under the *Windborne* and its in-flight record would become part of the NBC documentary, carrying pictures of oceans, plains and mountains.

Alpine balloonist Dolder was asking Malcolm and Tom—by mail —the sort of questions balloonists wanted answers to:

> a. How can you make the balloon descend if you want to land?
> b. How can you steer the balloon over ground if you fall into turbulent area or toward a dangerous obstacle?

There was an answer for the first. None for the second. The aeronauts would be taking their chances on a blind safe landing. Dolder reminisced his own answer to the first question: "Audoin and Charles Dolfuss lifted off with a cluster balloon in an open wicker basket to 7,500 meters for astro-research. For descent he killed one of the balloons with a pistol!"

Pistols aside, what *Windborne* was attempting was risk-laden. Every Atlantic attempt had been.

The first announced attempt in 1859 ended in disaster "for Messrs. Haddock and La Montaigne after a brief, but fatal ascension, from Watertown, New York." Thaddeus Lowe, in 1860, was planning an attempt but his balloon perished on inflation in New York City's Reservoir Square.

Promoters entered the picture when the New York *Daily Graphic* sponsored the 1873 launching of Captain W. H. Donaldson, George Ashton Lunt and Alfred Ford. The trio came down in New Canaan, Connecticut, having provided nothing other than an alternate form of suburban commuting.

In St. Louis, Missouri, Gateway to the West, Samuel King and John Wise in 1878 announced their Atlantic project and began construction on a balloon. But their *Atlantic*'s test ascension warned them off the idea, that and the high cost of repairing it after the initial trial.

Not for eighty years did anyone attempt the Atlantic. Then in 1958, Britons Tim Eiloert, his son and two companions tried an east-to-west crossing, lifting off from the Canary Islands. Fortunately their gondola also was a seaworthy craft, and they traveled further across the Atlantic by water than they did by air.

A decade later another Briton, Francis Brenton, made two unsuccessful east-to-west attempts, and in the same year as Brenton's first try, 1968, Canadians Mark Winters and Jerry Kostur attempted a west-to-east voyage from Halifax, Nova Scotia. They were pulled from the sea fifty miles off the coast of Nova Scotia.

Britons Malcolm and Pamela Brighton and Rodney Anderson lost their lives when *The Free Life* went into the Atlantic off Newfoundland during a heavy rain following their Long Island launch in 1970. A five-day search recovered only a picnic cooler.

Bob Sparks took off from Bar Harbor, Maine, airport on August 7, 1973 in *Yankee Zephyr*. Severe thunderstorms led to his abandoning the flight within twenty-four hours after launch. He was rescued off Newfoundland by a Canadian icebreaker.

The ill-fated attempt by Colonel Thomas Gatch followed six months later, by which time Malcolm had already decided he was going to attempt it himself. And, even as preparations were continuing, the twelfth attempt, and seventh loss of life, came with Robert Berger's launch from the Naval Air Station at Lakehurst, New Jersey. Berger's helium balloons apparently burst apart in the air, plunging him into Barnegat Bay.

Why were they doing it? The question does not need to be answered. Berger, who launched into the New Jersey skies only to die in Barnegat Bay, had been a member of Gatch's ground crew. "What got me into it," he said not long before his launch, "was the challenge and the glory, and I felt there might be some fame and fortune in it for me." He was extremely frank, and foolhardy—he had never previously piloted a balloon.

With all of this in mind, the Forbeses celebrated Christmas, 1974, in Far Hills, New Jersey, and the Heinsheimers in Rolling Hills, California.

December 26 was departure date for Los Angeles and Santa

Ana. Soon it was the small hours of the morning, Newark Airport once again with *The Capitalist Tool* warming her engines and the entourage arriving by twos and fours ready for the take-off.

If Malcolm were to meet his end in the *Windborne,* what then of the family and descendants of the late Bertie Charles Forbes? Adelaide had died in 1974. To the end, she was a woman of striking appearance, opinionated and outspoken. She and Bertie had been on speaking terms before his death, but they knew they were better apart.

In the years after the separation, Adelaide had realized—contrary to her earlier suspicions—that there never had been any sort of dalliance between BC and Miss Weiner. So Adelaide and Gertrude Weiner would meet, cordially and without tension, to talk over old times.

Bruce and Duncan were dead. Bruce's only child, Bonnie, also was dead. Ruth, Bruce's widow, lives in Manhattan, but maintains no links with Forbes Inc.

Gordon, vice president at Paramount Pictures, never was part of the Forbes Inc. picture. When Gordon with his wife, Claudine, and children drove down from Hollywood to Santa Ana to inspect the *Windborne* prior to the launch, the children referred to Malcolm as "father's brother," rather than their uncle.

Wallace, president of Standard Research Consultants, a division of Standard & Poor's, lives a quiet family life with his wife and three children. Wallace's interests run to the trusteeship of Anatolia College, Thessaloniki, Greece, being a director of the Near East College Association, and serving as a director of a mutual fund owned by Swiss Re, the big Helvetian reinsurance company. After leaving *Forbes* and IAI, Wallace had formed his own company (providing a discretionary investment management for private portfolios of up to $150,000), but sold out in 1972.

In the company Bertie Charles founded, there would be, if Malcolm died, just Steve, Christopher and, perhaps, Bobby. Steve had followed closely, maybe too closely, in his father's footsteps. At Princeton he too had founded a magazine, *Business Today.* After graduating *cum laude* from Princeton, Steve joined *Forbes* as a reporter-researcher. In that, as in everything else he tackles around Forbes Inc., Steve was diligent and hardworking.

A retiring person with the editorial staff—with whom he tends to wear his eyebrows as exasperation marks—in the business offices he is much more the corporate executive. While he has earned his spurs in editorial, moving up first to staff writer, then associate editor, Steve simultaneously has been carrying additional burdens, taking care of a wide range of Forbes Inc. empire details his father increasingly tends to leave to him.

Some *Forbes* writers feel Steve should have worked elsewhere for a spell before coming to *Forbes*. He knows his stuff, but he lacks, they would say, the rounded and sound experience of not being the boss's son.

Steve has a good mind and brain. He is as demanding as his father, as industrious, and certainly more intense. Playing understudy to Malcolm could make anyone intense.

As vice president and controller of all the voting stock in the event of Malcolm's death, Steve could, overnight, become one of the most powerful young publishing tycoons in the United States. He could handle it.

Steve has understudied carefully and will bring his own character into the act in time. He admires his father: "He is quick, he's bright. I would rather bounce my ideas off him than anyone else I know," says Steve. "When I feel I'm right, we disagree, we knock heads. I'm interested in things he is not interested in; I watch the things he doesn't: circulation, some of the editorial trends. He's not interested in the intricacies of money. I am."

Steve admits he is learning about promotion. When Malcolm's balloon exploits were first getting under way, many employees of Forbes Inc., particularly those connected with the more exotic possessions—the aircraft, the yacht, the global real estate—were worrying about their future. Their assessment was that, if Malcolm got killed, Steve would regard some possessions as "lavish" and sell them off.

"I will keep the yacht," Steve says. "I can see the value of the promotion. This magazine would not have been where it is today if my father had not taken it over, and done what he did."

Not surprisingly, Steve's cool assessment of himself and his father will emerge only as he is given more control over the enterprise. "My father would not long keep an albatross around his neck. He says he is not making money on motorcycles. If he wasn't, he wouldn't keep the business." And of himself Steve says: "If I am retiring, I *am* learning." Steve and Malcolm never fly together on the same aircraft. The loss would be too severe for the organization.

The Forbeses' second son, Robert, by contrast, long has been his father's aide-de-camp and traveling companion. His assessment of his father is not the jest he inscribed in the book on toy soldiers in the Tangier toy-soldier museum ("To the proto-fascist in all of us"); rather, with a wave around the *Tool*, Bobby once said: "This is my father's *shtick*. He's good at it." Bobby regards his father as *"very* demanding. But what he does works."

Kip is a very different character. Shy too, like Steve, but refusing to let it show, he comes across as the socially-at-ease Beau Brummell. Where Steve listens intently to what is being said, Kip is as likely to use the setting to stimulate a rapid-patter conversation. If Steve watches to concentrate, Kip watches to score points. And certainly he is cutting a wider social swath than Steve. Being curator of the *Forbes* magazine art collection, Kip has been able to exert some influence on his father's buying habits.

As a Princeton undergraduate in the sixties, Kip became interested, then fascinated, by the Victorian painters. He persuaded his father to let him start building up a collection of twenty "essential" Victorian artists, constantly upgrading the Forbes collection examples of their works. Kip was smart in that he began this before Victorian paintings and artists were in vogue—and indeed his actions may have helped stimulate that vogue. Much of the romantic nonsense of the Pre-Raphaelites and other sweetness-and-light Victorian artists were, in *Newsweek*'s words, the "wrong" sort of art.

Kip, working with a wicked smile that shows him his father's son, and with an ambition that to some extent makes him his spiritual heir, keeps his own counsel. Once, when Malcolm was looking for a possible castle in Italy, Kip wanted Malcolm to buy a particular estate because the owner automatically had the noble title that accompanied possession. Lord Kip bears a strong resemblance to magazine Lord Forbes, and mirrors some of his traits. Malcolm too was a third son.

In 1974 Christopher mounted his exhibition "The Art and Mind of Victorian England," at the University of Minnesota Art Gallery in

Minneapolis. In keeping with a true descendant of the tax-deductible monarchy, Kip had seen to it that printed on the RSVP cards for the Minneapolis showing was the legend:

Please make checks payable to The Victorian Society Scholarship Fund, Inc. All contributions are tax deductible to the fullest extent allowed by law.

Steve had been married in June, 1972, and Kip had followed him to the altar in December, when he married Sondra "Sandy" Irene Simone. "Sandy" was from a social milieu similar to Kip's, daughter of a senior partner in the French electronics industry; granddaughter of the president of Pittsburgh Ice Cream Company on one side, and of the Paris-born Simones on the other. The marriage did not last— not because it was a Roman Catholic–Protestant union (though historically in the Forbes family that had meant trouble).

Kip met his second wife, Astrid, a quiet German girl, when she was working for Warner Dailey in his London antique business. By the time Kip brought the exhibition "The Royal Academy (1837–1901) Revisited" at the Metropolitan Museum of Art in New York, in 1975, he was divorced and remarried.

He was twenty-three, Astrid thirty-eight.

Timothy and Moira, Malcolm and Roberta's two youngest children, are not yet really part of the public Forbes family. Timothy may never be, if the assessment of his older brothers is correct. The budding moviemaker may be the family maverick.

Moira too is an entity unto herself. Her public appearances have been limited to Balleroy and similar family affairs. She is not usually in on the public family peregrinations. And, still away at school, like Tim she is not easily drawn into those Forbes family things that also are Forbes Inc. things.

When the Christmas cards are mailed, they include, always, the latest family photograph. Roberta writes all the cards out, nearly a thousand of them, by hand, in green ink. The 1972 Christmas card was a classic.

Steve had just married Sabina Beekman, daughter of the retired rector of St. Paul's American Episcopal Church in Rome. Christopher was married later in the year. When the card went out it had photographs of both weddings on the cover. When it was opened up there was an inside photograph: Malcolm and Roberta at their wedding.

One *Forbes* staffer who growled about Malcolm using his family so much, and most of all as his Christmas card, went to work for the Los Angeles *Times*. The *Times'* owners, the Chandlers, he found out, send the same sort of cards.

If a member of his family is involved in a project, Malcolm is careless at times of others' contributions. His book *Fact and Comment*, a compilation from the magazine of twenty-five years of ingenious two-liners, ingenuous hardliners, sentimental softliners, owed its existence much to the efforts of senior editor Ruth Gruenberg, who for years has handled Malcolm's columns, editing out the more-garbled syntax and reworking the general idea without killing the MSF style. Ruth had worked up a format for the *Fact and Comment* book, and provided the earliest input.

Malcolm's son Steve took over the project and worked hard from that point on to see it through the printers and into the hands of what turned out to be an unreceptive public. The credit for the edit went to Steve. Ruth's labors went unnoticed, unacknowledged.

To the casual observer, Malcolm's apparent domination of his wife and children looms as one of the least-attractive elements of his very demanding personality. But behind the public glimpses is an esprit and organization quite familiar to those who know the lifestyle of, for example, the English upper classes—most particularly those destined for or hoping for acceptance into the aristocracy.

The family "front" is as old as primogeniture. Malcolm demands, and gets, the public support of all family members in furthering the family "cause"—the magazine. Roberta appears in public, detests it. When duty calls, she is there. But, whether sitting quietly sipping a drink in the late evening as the *Highlander* returns to the 79th Street yacht basin, or alongside Malcolm being photographed on his latest motorcycle, she appears to be under a strain.

Alone with the family, her reserve and wan appearance are gone. Relaxed, among the children on the *Tool* or with the family in Far Hills, she can assert herself. Photographers taking pictures to accompany articles on Malcolm all say how difficult it is to catch Roberta smiling or "natural." With the family alone, or on the ranch in Montana, her preferred possession, she is "natural."

And, when she does smile, it's worth the wait. Her face lights up and she looks in private life something she never appears in public: happy. What makes her happy? At one Forbes veterans' party for the five-years-service-and-more employees, Trinchera ranch boss Errol Ryland flew in. He was wearing western clothes and boots, his normal everyday clothes.

Dozens of people were milling around on the lawn at Far Hills when Roberta saw Errol in his boots. "Your western boots make me feel homesick for the ranch," said Roberta, dressed as customary in a well-cut but plain dress. "Why don't you change, then?" suggested Errol.

Roberta went into the house and came out later in blue jeans and boots, and with a big grin on her face. That was her way of enjoying herself hugely.

If Roberta has taken the line of least resistance in acceding to Malcolm's wants without complaint, the boys, periodically, have complained. The most united front came over the bagpipes, which all the Forbes boys have played since an early age.

In the 1960s, on tour with the *Highlander,* they had been on deck, reeds in lips and bags under the arms, to pipe guests aboard. Now, boys becoming men, Malcolm still expected them to change into kilts and do their Scottish thing whenever he needed them. He had a minor rebellion on his hands over the Old Battersea House opening but, finally, they had performed when Malcolm had taken title in a blaze of publicity.

The final showdown over bagpipes came in Tangier. Timmy and Kip flatly refused to play. Malcolm still won. He said that if they played at the Palais de Mendoub reception he would not expect them ever to play for him publicly again. They haven't.

But all members of the family—in-laws, too—are expected to take their turns at the public entertaining that is part of Malcolm's business. In no setting is the family front more marked than on the now traditional autumn weekends up the Hudson, when Malcolm's special guests travel on the *Highlander* to the West Point football games.Forbes' fall football program has settled into a comfortable tradition after fifteen years. Throughout the fall, guests, potential or actual advertisers, visiting dignitaries, the occasional journalist spend a Saturday on the yacht.

The day begins very early at the Manhattan 79th Street Boat

Basin, long before the guests have to make their 9 A.M. appearance. The Forbes family already are aboard, standing by appointed stations as hosts for the day. Today it is Malcolm and Roberta, Sabina, wife of Steve, Bobby, Kip and his wife Astrid.

The scene is set: small jetties and catwalks right-angle off the broad boardwalk and jut out into the Hudson River. To these jetties are tied dozens of yachts, from the tiniest ten-footer to the fifty-foot standard symbols of having arrived yachtingwise. Stretched out, her elegant lines dominate every other craft in the basin: the 117-foot *Highlander II* is an oceangoing beauty in white and varnished teak. Among big yachts the *Highlander* is no mean vessel.

On a typical brisk September Saturday morning the day's guests are arriving. The crew, Captain Alexander F. Pfotnhauer in command, are smartly turned out. Chef Richard Caward already has coffee and Danish ready and a day's menu prepared that would entice even the finicky eater—from a lobster and champagne lunch to an evening buffet dinner featuring chicken breasts stuffed with crab. Discerning palates will be rewarded by selections from Malcolm's 12,000-bottle wine cellar at the New York townhouse, Margaux a specialty.

Many of the guests have flown in from around the country the evening before. They come aboard two by two, dutifully mounting the gangplank onto Malcolm's ark. Here is Malcolm, the actor-manager, at his most superb—creating an elegant way of life for a day, tugging at the Walter Mitty in every new arrival. It is easy to tell who doesn't own a luxury yacht, or who has not been aboard the *Highlander* before. At some point, when no one is looking, those being inducted for the first time into a day on the *Highlander* surreptitiously stroke their hands along the varnished mahogany guard rail.

Few corporate executives run to yachts this size. But occasionally even Malcolm gets put down. The executive vice president of Hertz, at a lunch aboard the *Highlander* one weekday, was being pressed by Malcolm—following the statutory tour of the craft—to say how much he liked her. He demurred, but Malcolm insisted. He looked Malcolm straight in the eye: "I don't like stinkpots." There are those who travel on the yacht, stay in the château, relax at the palace, hunt at the ranch, munch at the townhouse who know it's all part of the game. The end result is business. Advertising. Money.

There are those people who go to the theater and never overcome the fact that they are watching a group of people playing parts on the stage. The illusion of what is being enacted never envelopes them. For such people—those whose critical eye surveys, who never let their guard down, whose judgment and awareness are conscious that this is all an act—a day on the *Highlander* can be amusing, but never relaxing. These are the people who know instinctively, in advance, what an egress is—no matter how skillful the Barnum.

Malcolm's choreography is superb, the organization is impeccable.

As Roger Manvell quotes Ellen Terry on Irving:

An egotist—an egotist of the great type, *never* "a mean egotist," as he was once slanderously described—and all his faults sprang from egotism.

Malcolm *instinctively* understands good theater—which may be why he never goes. He knows that the ticket holder gives up control over reality for the length of the play. The theater is dominated by the actor-manager. The audience is compliant, willing to be entertained, enthralled, amused, even criticized. The theater is alien territory wherein the playgoer expects to come under the thrall of the producer, director, designers, playwright and, not the least, the actors and actresses themselves. Criticism comes accompanied by bitter resentment if those performing the play do not live up to expectations, for the theatergoer is relatively defenseless once inside the actor-manager's setting, the theater itself.

So too with those spending a day on the *Highlander*.

Malcolm, smiling and convivial, is the barker out front. Smiling and informative, he shows the new arrival to a seat. Smiling and obviously captivated for the moment, he explains the day's program. Storyteller-narrator-actor, he signals the start of the entertainment, and the *Highlander* reels in her cables and points her stately nose up the Hudson.

Malcolm is entertaining, charming, as he, on his own decks, produces, directs and ushers on the various acts. One moment the jester, another the leading player. For those impressed by public personalities this day, he introduces Mr. and Mrs. Morton Phillips. He is a businessman, she is Dear Abby of the "Dear Abby" column, mother-confessor to the lovelorn. Seated aft on the half-moon of cushions around the curve of the covered-over stern, a semicircle of admirers talks to the diminutive Abby, a busy-bee in yellow-and-black, sharper in the tongue than with the pen, taking a quick reading of the questioners and knowing almost exactly the questions that will be forthcoming.

The free-form theater-in-the-round is progressing nicely. Now the affable John D. deButts, chairman of the mighty American Telephone and Telegraph, chortles as he reveals that the investment of a modest $750 for a public pay telephone in a strategic Manhattan location can generate as much as $150 a month, cash. As John muffles a guffaw, Malcolm swaps tidbit-for-tidbit, line for line, laughingly explains that he wishes the *Forbes* employees would enjoy the "psychic rewards" of working for Forbes Inc., treasuring the uniqueness of the enterprise as part of—and perhaps instead of—pay increases. Muffled guffaws.

The coffee-and-cake stage of the morning is passing and the first round of drinks is being offered. People swap seats, wander about the *Highlander,* enjoy the warming sun and admire the landscape. The conversations now are less stilted, more informal and relaxed. The passengers, hosts and crew group and regroup in informal vignettes. The wife of an insurance-company chief looks at the wife of another corporate giant and gasps softly, "That's her third. It's not even lunchtime." As she sips her midwesternly-moral pre-lunch Scotch and water, which has been replenished only with ice cubes for the previous hour, her eyes move on to the next observation.

Sabina now is chatting to Abby—Sabina, mother of twins, and Abby, twin sister of columnist Ann Landers.

Malcolm, eyes watchful behind the glasses, mind checking off the immediate needs, converses easily with a manufacturer and his wife, while sending the steward to assure the chef that lunch should be ready on time as arranged. Roberta, dips again into the cigarette box, tête-à-tête with daughter-in-law Astrid, then the two of them, with Kippie, fan out among the guests. Robert pours a drink while the steward is occupied, offers a light to an unlit cigarette. All is grace and smoothness, one more performance by the Forbes family in a fall ritual repertory that adds faces to the cast as the boys marry and bring their wives within the Forbes sphere of influence. (Voices off: "Forbes men are hard on their wives," muttered in brogue by a

Buchanite in Scotland who watched two Forbes generations. "The Forbes boys want wives who are wives like their mother. And they are as demanding as their father," comments an East Coast voice.)

In a setting such as this, the actor-manager must be instinctively, unflinchingly obeyed. One system, patriarchal, supports the other, financial.

At the West Point dock there is an old bus to take the *Highlander* guests to the game. Kippie walks up and down the aisle taking money from the gamegoers—there is to be a lottery. Whoever guesses closest to the combined scores of the day wins the money. Malcolm is up front gently haranguing the assembled with the clever insults of the expert comic—"if you get lost, and the bigger the businessman the better his chance of getting lost, make your way to this bus." He knows his audience well enough from experience to realize that some people always need to be herded.

The game. The downpour. A yellow balloon hundreds of feet into the air at one end of the stadium. The bus back. The lottery winners. The *Highlander.* An evening of good food, good booze, fine wine, cut-throat bridge, a movie, more conversation—and Malcolm rings down the curtain at the Manhattan Boat Basin. Show's over, folks. Applause gracefully accepted. The last guests depart. The actor-manager is now the manager. Malcolm goes over the day's takings—how many pages of advertising it may all be worth. The advertising men will be expected to close those pages as firm deals in the days and weeks ahead. The stagehands and actors relax for a moment. Some unguarded critiques and comments about the day's guests, and a few family jokes. Light bantering with the crew. The theater is closed for the night.

The show is over—but only until the next curtain.

The dirigible hangar at the U.S. Marine Corps base, Santa Ana, 60 miles southeast of Los Angeles, is reputedly the largest wooden structure in the United States, a King Kong–sized quonset hut standing 120 feet from floor to ceiling, and long enough to hold the *Queen Elizabeth.*

It hasn't seen a dirigible in years, and the cluster of tiny—by comparison—fully inflated 30-foot-tall Mylar balloons for the *Windborne* project were simply decor in one corner of a hangar otherwise filled with helicopters brought back from the wound-down war in Vietnam.

Malcolm was inside the *Windborne*'s sphere. Launch would come any day now—after a week of waiting, scrubs and contrary weather. He was sticking his head out the main hatch while yet one more batch of photographers fired away. First Malcolm, then Tom, then the two of them together. No more press conferences now—those days were gone. It was briefings. One had just ended. Even the journalists had just about stopped asking the two hardy annuals: "How much is it costing?" "How do you go to the john?"

The answer to the first Malcolm shuddered to think—though $1 million was already in sight.

There already had been a meeting on costs. In the same *Forbes* boardroom in which *Forbes* writers have to defend their story ideas, the subcontractors on the *Windborne* had felt Malcolm cracking the whip on prices as he asked them to defend their cost overruns.

There was a smile on his face, but none in his voice as, eyebrows raised, he told them pointedly: "This ordering without regard to cost has got to stop. Now." He leaned back in his chair, knee against the table edge. "This project is already well over budget." Arguments that high technology means high costs did not remove the chill from Malcolm's voice.

His voice was to take on the same tone when he found, in the week ahead, that the work was not progressing at the rate needed to make the launch schedule a reality.

Malcolm had engaged more than once in a little mild fun-poking as technicians connected with the Forbes Atlantic Project had tackled the food, flatus and so on problem:

> Dear Tom:
>
> Re reference to "diets which reduce the mass of feces and the volume of flatus" . . . since neither is a problem for the Army ground forces I don't imagine the tasty dishes we tasted that are being prepared for the Army would take these factors very much into account. Can't we get specific data from NASA on the subject?

The final diet was closer to space food than boot-camp hash.

Early suggestions were made that the aeronauts "modify their diets for two weeks prior to the flight." If anything, Malcolm had added to the rubber tire around his middle, and he was enjoying his food as much as ever: risks yes; personal privation, no.

In fact, at the pre-launch weighing ceremony Malcolm at 184 pounds was found to have exceeded his anticipated weight for the *Windborne's* payload. He turned to Tom Heinsheimer with a smile and told the diminutive scientist, a spare 131 pounds, "You have to lose some weight, Tom." Originally the *Windborne* was to have had four clusters of three balloons: an extra balloon, a thirteenth, already had been added.

If Malcolm was going to die in an aluminum-foil ballbearing suspended beneath thirteen helium-filled bags, he was going to do it on a full stomach with the taste of a good wine and a stiff drink either on his lips or within recent memory. Death he could face, self-discipline for the sake of science—never.

The first of the California press conferences had been held on Friday, December 27, in the Santa Ana Officers' Club. U.S. Marine brass watched as the whole media performing circus got under way —this time with an NBC documentary crew filming Malcolm being filmed and interviewed. The launch would be attempted six days later, in the early hours of Thursday, January 2.

News teams would have to be kept standing around for six days. Malcolm didn't like that idea because he was concerned that editors would lose interest.

Editors know nothing about ballooning. When a reporter goes out on a story he is supposed to come back with one. Bad weather can delay something for a day and an editor will grumble but understand. But, as the extra days mount up, and the stories become repetitive, editors become dyspeptic and start to call their newshounds back to the editorial kennels.

Malcolm was becoming anxious lest the waiting throng was able to wait no longer. Even the NBC crew head, George Heinemann, watching the motel bills mount with every passing cancellation, was getting restless. The two Winnebago motor homes—one serving as executive headquarters, the other as a crews' mess during the on-site hours away from the Newporter Inn, were adding to cost at the rate of $350 a day.

At its peak, NBC had a seventeen-person crew in attendance. As the launch cancellations followed one after the other, December 30, 31, New Year's Day, January 2, 3, 4, those on the periphery of the

Windborne project were beginning to count the costs. How much longer could the dozens of journalists, the dozens of moonlighting or part-time aerospace workers, be kept interested? Malcolm's costs were escalating daily, too. Some of the Forbes balloon ascension division team were on the Forbes Inc. payroll. But several dozen others were an out-of-pocket expense that even a big pocket was finding costly. Once the launch was on, the running costs quickly would drop off, then cease.

The immediate risk was that the media would drop off. Newspapers would follow any bizarre story—for a while. After all, Evel Kneivel had worked a motorcycle stunt act into a multi-million-dollar spectacular largely on the basis of the media providing the coverage. The media usually pick up whatever kinds of risk-laden inanity men are capable of. At the very moment Malcolm was preparing to go into space, an Anglican priest, Geoffrey Howard, was attempting to push a Chinese wheelbarrow, with a sail and a five-foot-diameter single wheel, two thousand miles across the Sahara, from Béni-Abbès, Algeria, to Kano in Nigeria. Why? "It's something I must do. It's never been done before."

Those stories grab the readers' and viewers' attention, but only in passing; they can't be maintained day after day. Malcolm didn't want delays. He had arrived in California the day after Christmas to find the project behind schedule. Within twenty-four hours he was cracking his own organization whip, urging the various subcontractors into more rapid action. The project had lacked a strong hand, a "chief whip," who could bark at everyone to make sure deadlines were met, that difficulties were quickly smoothed out.

Only at that late stage in the Atlantic Project, launch week, did Malcolm take full command, urging on with the authority of one picking up the tab. And the media moved in.

By New Year's Day, 1975, Malcolm was the focal point of space scientists, tracking stations, television crews from several lands—the Germans, British and French had brought their cameras to compete for space and light with the NBC documentary makers. And he was hoping to maintain the interest and presence of the dozens of newspaper and magazine journalists flocking around the place, but becoming increasingly dismayed as delay added to delay. By the end of the first week in Santa Ana, Malcolm was his own project director:

smoothing, urging, cajoling. The pace quickened, tempers tightened, but the work progressed.

On New Year's Day another launch date was set: January 4. When the evening of January 3 arrived, yet one more briefing was called in the Marine pilots' ready room that the *Windborne* project was using. The green chalkboard carried the message: "Forbes launch—January 4."

Scientists, technicians, riggers, electronics experts, newswriters, launch crew members, all crowded into the dismal green-gray operations center with its decrepit rows of old seats long since expropriated from a military movie house. Once everyone was in place, cigarette smoke filling the crowded room, Malcolm again had to give out the bad news:

"We're just not ready technically. We could be ready by tonight, but we could not be tested out as a launch team for the 4 A.M. launch. There is no way we can finish in time and simultaneously test all the systems." Disappointment, even ill-concealed anger, were showing through, but Malcolm did not want to vent his temper in front of an audience. "Jean-Pierre? Or, if you want to add anything, Tom?"

"No, Malc," said Tom, "you've covered it."

Jean-Pierre Pommerau quickly went through the changes that would be made in the launching dry-run. Originally the inflated balloons, linked together by miles of nylon rope, one cluster to the next, were to have been battened down onto flat-bed trucks. The trucks would slowly be driven out of the dirigible hangar onto the helicopter launch blacktop. Clusters were to be released slowly, one cluster at a time, then with increasing speed as the lift of the helium made the balloons anxious to soar aloft.

Those flat-bed trucks had been scrapped. Weighted-down laundry carts from the Neuschal workshops were to be used instead. Rather than huge winches and drums mounted on top of the heavy motor trucks, smaller handbraked winches had been mounted on the carts. These rough-and-ready vehicles were showing up faults—loose wheels, winch brakes not working. There could be no launch unless the carts were ready, Jean-Pierre said. He talked to the men who would be handling the nylon harnesses between the carts; there was to be a final rehearsal.

There were problems of people straggling onto the work site and taking an hour to get going; time was being wasted, that had to stop. There were only a few weeks of weather each year when a balloon system such as this could be launched. Valuable time already had been lost—when the right weather came, *Windborne had* to be ready.

"I can promise to have the Forbes people here at 4 A.M. for the practice launch," said Malcolm firmly, then added with a laugh, "and that's the most difficult promise of all. Who's going to guarantee that the engineers and the launch crew will be here?" He pointedly looked around the room, fixing an unsmiling eye on his subcontractors. Promises were given: everyone would be present and on time. The briefing ended. For all but a few people there was little else to be done tonight. Engineers concerned with the electronics and life-support systems were still busy, and those laundry carts had to be made ready and reliable.

Malcolm was buttonholing people now, asking what their particular delays and holdups were. The publicist in him was waiting for a good-luck telephone call from Evel Knievel. The small boy in him was reveling in the adventure, the flurry, the complex technicalities. And the man in him was anxious to face the challenge—and get it over with.

Pre-dawn on January 4. An eerie promenade beneath the glaring lights of the dirigible hangar. Black, moonless night outside, while inside a spectral procession made its way slowly the eighth of a mile *inside* the hangar from the end furthest from the launching site. The huge electrically operated doors—each 120 feet high by 50 feet wide, were slowly opened. The balloons were anxious, living things as they tugged at the harnesses when a chance breeze wafted through the open hangar doors. This was only the rehearsal; the balloons, too, wanted to be up and off, windborne and free.

The camera teams panned this slow-motion procession as the transparent ice-cream-cone-shaped Mylar balloons were eased along their route toward the hangar doors. Pommerau barked orders in a mix of French and English, watching vigilantly, trying to anticipate from this dry run what might go wrong the next day, January 5, the day of the launch.

The balloons reached the end of the hangar—they were not being taken outside; the risks were too great, the wind too strong. It was a partial test—the thirteen cones slowly were returned to their moorings at the east end of the hangar.

January 5 looked possible but uncertain. Meteorological reports could not promise that the winds would be calm enough at ground level, or in the correct direction in the upper atmosphere, to allow the *Windborne* to proceed.

Malcolm's impatience was showing. Would he push the launch into action against the meteorologist's advice, and against the wishes of his launch director?

By that time the *Windborne* was part of the life of an inspired and industrious team of men who, like Malcolm, were stretching their minds and abilities to the limits to create a fully viable spacecraft.

Perhaps the prize catch was John Hart Smith, an Australian specialist in bonded and bolted joints and composite structures. A McDonnell Douglas employee, Hart Smith was the epitome of the dedicated scientist-engineer. So dedicated that he personally drilled the 20,000 holes that put together the .025-inch-thick aluminum sphere in which the aeronauts would live. So dedicated that when Hart Smith felt it possible that Malcolm might demand a premature launching—in order not to disappoint the waiting media throng—he developed a plan to sabotage and delay the launch rather than waste the thousands of man hours involved.

Unbeknown to any other member of the team, Hart Smith had decided that if Malcolm overruled Pommerau on the launch—ordering a launch when Pommerau was opposed to it—then he, Hart Smith, would sabotage the *Windborne* gondola. The technique was simple, he intended to drill a hole through one of the three-quarter-inch-thick acrylic windows. He then intended to point out what he had done, and why he had done it.

More acrylic could be obtained, but the purpose—to delay a risky launch—would have been achieved.

Malcolm knew none of this. He had not seen the other side of the *Windborne* project. He did not know that much of the *esprit* had come from people in the aerospace industry, enjoying themselves because of the rare challenge. He did not know that many engineers were giving far more than was required in terms of dedication—because they were engineers and scientists. This was their thing too.

Many of the men working at the project were taking time off from jobs with big corporations or the military. They had made their own arrangements, willingly. They had come together as a team from their own "grapevine"—and Malcolm did not realize the stresses he added when he reached into their milieu through the Secretary of the Air Force, having things done from the top that previously had been arranged at the bottom. Malcolm was able to get people temporarily seconded from the largest corporations—whose chairmen and presidents lunch with him in townhouse and on yacht. And there came a time when he needed to. But hackles bristled when there was any suggestion that the scientists and engineers were just doing a job for money. They weren't. They were putting everything they believed themselves to be capable of on the line.

From his steely dark, closely cropped gray hair, now allowed to curl slightly at the sides and nape, to his determined, plodding, practically flat-footed gait, Malcolm was still the performer. Organizing all the while, he was reading the audiences and events. He was playing to the crowd, or to the audience of one, with equal skill, adroitness and dedication.

The time was set. At 4 A.M. on January 5, the balloons began their journey out of the hangar once more, ready for launch as soon as the sun cast its first red light over the low hills southeast of the air base.

Members of the Forbes family had arrived two days earlier. Roberta, impassive most of the time, trying to smile when spoken to, worried and admitting it, also was attempting to keep out of the public and media glare. Except for her rosy cheeks, she was pale.

Malcolm already had infuriated her once. When giving an ABC television interview, he had stepped from camera range and eased his wife into the camera's eye and into the interviewer's clutches. She answered quietly, but stepped out quickly to tell Malcolm: "Don't you ever do that to me again." Malcolm smiled broadly, as if indulging her, and both knew full well that if it suited his purposes, and if the opportunity presented itself again, he would attempt it again.

For Roberta this was like a return to being the political candidate's wife. She hated it. There was the additional worry, deepseated and heartfelt: this time he really *was* risking his life. She was afraid. Malcolm wasn't.

Tom Heinsheimer's smile had been extremely wan for the past

twenty-four hours, but Malcolm was working up to a great euphoric kick that kept his worries well below the public surface. Julie Heinsheimer's anxiety was written in her eyes; her staccato answers gave witness to her preoccupation—Tom's life.

The hangar doors were open now; the launch team and harness crew were in position. The onlookers were in position too, and in the upper reaches of the dirigible hangar cameramen focused down on the surrealistic promenade of the Mylar balloons, little ants of men beside them.

It was a Sunday, but the days had long since lost individuality for those connected with the *Windborne* project. The night sky was calm, but with some slight evidence of wind, which, it was hoped, would die down, if not die away. To those waiting on the dark tarmac apron, looking into the hangar watching the balloons appear larger ever larger as they got closer to the door, the site was ethereal. Yes, it was being done, but look at them, thirteen plastic bags on laundry carts.

The minutes ticked on, the balloons got closer to the hangar door. The wind was picking up. Meteorologists were giving their final statements. The currents weren't right, the ground swells too strong. The *Windborne* should not launch. Pommerau consulted hurriedly with Malcolm and Tom. No launch. No launch. Malcolm agreed. The bitterness came and went. The word quickly was passed around. The balloons on their carts were backed toward the far end of the hangar. Another impromptu press conference. In camera glare, controlled and cajoling, resigned but attempting to keep interest levels high, Malcolm explained the scrub.

John Hart Smith had not needed to drill a hole in the *Windborne's*'s window.

They would try again the following day, said Malcolm. They did. It was a disaster. Not fatal, but a disaster nonetheless. The laundry carts were not equal to the task of holding the living, tugging balloons in check. Like inflated Gullivers tugging at the puny restraining bonds of the Lilliputians, the balloons mocked the men's efforts as they snapped restraining cords, bouncing the weighted carts on the tarmac like someone shaking a spider at the end of his silken thread.

Roberta watched horrified—NBC director George Heinemann with his arm protectively through her arm—as the gondola was torn loose from its moorings and bounced harshly onto the tarmac. Launch director Pommerau coolly risked his life to save that of the aeronauts, for if the external liquid oxygen bottles fastened atop the bouncing gondola had cracked, the *Windborne*'s life sphere would have been a mass of flames, Malcolm and Tom incinerated in seconds.

Athletic and alert, Pommerau leaped up toward the careening gondola and grabbed at the balloon release handle. He got it first time. *Windborne* immediately was earthbound. The balloons cracked and snapped and shot up rapidly into the dark sky, the movie camera strobes and spotlights following their thousands-of-feet-a-minute climb now that their restraining payload had been snatched from them.

Weeks later Malcolm sat on a couch in George Heinemann's apartment overlooking New York's East River. The NBC producer was showing the final sequence on his videoscreen. There was Tom, his final wave, and Malcolm, his wave, as they disappeared into the sphere.

All eyes were on the screen following the camera's eye as it watched the first cluster of balloons begin to follow the lead balloon aloft, slowly, away from its cart. Pommerau's voice echoed through the apartment from out of the speaker, calling orders, urging caution.

Suddenly, confusion was filling the screen. Some balloons were tugging loose. The laundry carts were beginning to dance. The camera's eye swung to the gondola—it was being pulled off its launch platform. Desperately the camera was trying to capture everything going on—but the frenzy was too great as the camera looked now at the balloons, now back at the gondola. Follow the gondola. There's Pommerau, the screen is jerking but Pommerau is shouting and running toward the bouncing sphere. He jumps up on the sphere as it half rolls. The balloons are free and the camera follows them only for a brief second before returning to the sphere, now motionless practically on its side. Men are milling around it, blocking the camera's prying eye.

Malcolm, on the couch, moments before intense and concentrating, now was only mildly interested. He took another sip from his glass, and waited for the lights to be switched back on.

Just for a moment the balloon had pulled him back to it; the

Windborne project had exerted her old spell. But at the precise moment that Malcolm had emerged from the dented million-dollar sphere on the Santa Ana tarmac, the spell had effectively been broken. That was it.

There would have to be a wind-down, statements about trying again, and new techniques and materials to be developed. But Malcolm knew himself well enough to know that it was over. Done. His was the thirteenth attempt. It had ended in failure. He would not try again.

The "fiasco" at Santa Ana was similar to the malfunctioning at the test launch at Kourou, French Guiana. The restraining winches on the laundry carts simply were not capable of withstanding the tremendous forces being exerted by the gravity-defying balloons. As the first balloons had started to be released they began to pay out faster than the system needed; a line jerked and may have snapped, the winches unable to stop the launch, which "came through like an express train." That sudden jerk to the system had the lightweight laundry carts dancing on the tarmac as a chain reaction of chaos set in. Dennis Fleck, Forbes' full-time balloonist, muttered darkly. "I told them those laundry carts would not work. No one would listen." He was furious that the decision had been made to change from large winches mounted on flatbed trucks.

Those carts may have saved the lives of Malcolm Forbes and Tom Heinsheimer. A successful launch might have resulted in death. When the balloons were recovered miles away in the desert it was apparent only five balloons had survived the launch. *Windborne* could not have stayed aloft with full payload with fewer than eleven. The sudden loss of four or six or eight balloons would have sent Malcolm and Tom plunging to certain death.

Seated on the couch in George Heinemann's apartment, he regarded the *Windborne* as a historic event; his romantic self was already fitting out the schooner *Jessica,* to be renamed *Laucala,* readying her for a sail in stages from Antigua to his island, Laucala, in the Fijis.

The next adventure was all systems go. The *Windborne* was already just one more item for the balloon museum at the Château de Balleroy. *Windborne* made it across the Atlantic, "in the belly of a jumbo jet."

For an entire summer, daughter Moira and one of her school

friends would work in a Forbes building back office pasting the clippings from newspapers and magazines around the world into a dozen scrapbooks.

And was it all worth it? Could Malcolm justify it financially? Just for a brief moment, the television news cameras, the radio stations, the documentary makers and the world press were alert to a silver ball on the tarmac at Santa Ana Marine base, California, U.S.A.

During a London press conference, Malcolm had been asked if he was "as nuts as Evel Knievel."

Malcolm replied: "I don't know how nuts Evel Knievel was. He was making money on his trip and I am losing money on mine." It was good press-conference banter if slightly disingenuous. By Malcolm's count the *Windborne* covered about twenty feet all told. At $1.35 million for the project, that comes out at nearly $6000 an inch —one of the most expensive voyages in history.

Malcolm would have loved the success, but the failure was nothing to lick wounds over. While the media of the western world were busily extracting romance out of ballooning, Malcolm was busily extracting commerce out of romance. In the four weeks prior to the balloon launch alone Malcolm Forbes—therefore *Forbes* magazine, Sangre de Cristo Ranches and the Malcolm persona—had been featured in spreads across *Sports Illustrated, Newsweek* and *People.* Everyone knew Malcolm was promoting and, for once, no one seemed to mind.

Prime-time television costs $120,000 a minute. The Forbes Magazine Balloon Ascension Division's "Windborne" Atlantic Project cost $1.35 million. That much money would buy twelve minutes and thirty seconds prime-time television.

Was *Windborne* worth it? Ten times over.

Will there be another attempt? Malcolm occasionally will allow himself the little white lie that he might just try again. But he won't. That scrapbook has been filled, and closed.

Now there was another adventure, less public, less profitable in promotion terms, but enjoyable in its own way. The *Laucala* under full sail was heading across the Pacific, from the Galápagos to Tahiti and, eventually, on from Tahiti to Laucala.

Malcolm Forbes had doffed his Phileas Fogg hat. Its replacement was the weathered cap of the South Seas skipper.

Sailor he's not. After thirty-six hours of *Laucala* life, the tedium of being trapped aboard the schooner set in. He would never let *that* happen again. His simple summary of life before the mast was, "Well, I read a lot of books I otherwise wouldn't have had time for."

10

The Sun Never Sets . . .

> With all thy getting get understanding
>
> > For sixty years this quote has appeared above
> > the *Forbes* "Fact and Comment" columns.

In the shade of the banyan tree at the edge of the white sandy beach, instrumentalists of the Royal Fiji Army Band, red jacketed and wearing smart white tailored skirts, wet their lips and waited.

On the other side of a vast expanse of grass, the men of Laucala island, their backs to a blue South Pacific Ocean dotted with islands similar to this one, rustled restlessly in their palm-leaf skirts, nervously fingering their spears, axes and clubs.

The women of Laucala, seated on the grass in their fresh, colorful red-and-blue-print dresses, chatted among themselves, knowing that when it was time for the singing and dancing to begin they would be ready.

Other women, under the watchful maternal eye of Mrs. Flo Douglas, wife of Malcolm's Laucala plantation boss, Noel Douglas—himself an island plantation owner—were busily preparing food in the plantation house. The squealing pigs of yesterday had been cooking slowly in the big earth pit of stones and embers since two in the morning. The whole island had been up practically all night, partying and preparing. There was to be a *meke*.

The children of Laucala had the previous afternoon off from school to pick litter off the beach and from around the houses, while their fathers with bulldozers and tractors dragged washed-up tree stumps and other heavy flotsam off the beach.

Malcolm wanted everything to be spic-and-span, nothing and no one out of place.

"Everything has to be just so when Mr. For-bess is on the island," said one of the Fijian workers.

At the edge of the expanse of grass, facing the ocean but away from the beach, was a tin-roofed reviewing area, shaded so that the dignitaries coming that day would not broil under the noonday sun.

Dozens of children in their Sunday finery sat in the shade near the old copra drying shed, or leaned against its peeling red-painted side. The children had not been so quiet earlier in the day. There was a ritual for the children whenever Malcolm arrived down at the beach in his two-seater Cushman track-laying "mini-tank."

"Mr. For-bess, Mr. For-bess," the children would squeal, their eyes wild with delight. Malcolm, his eyes equally wild, that wide grin getting wider, would gun the Cushman engine.

Off would shoot the children, as fast as their bare feet could carry them, Malcolm in hot pursuit with his tank as they hared around the copra shed. A few brave ones would try to make it home —and the man old enough to be their grandfather gleefully would swing the tank after them, chasing them right up to the gate of the patches of garden around their plywood or tin-sided houses.

From these shacks, only a few dozen yards from the water's edge, the children can rush to the beach. Malcolm is building new housing further inland, modern tile and masonry housing that the Fijian Minister of Housing would dedicate—and praise Malcolm for —later in the day. But the islanders cannot see the sea from there, or feel the fresh onshore breezes that dries the clothes on their clotheslines outside their back doors.

Right now the huts were "home" for the delighted children Malcolm was pursuing. Beneath his grin, muscles tensed at his firm jaw, was a high degree of control, not abandon.

Malcolm played the game safe. His eyes were never still as he kept constant track of the half-dozen or so children he was chasing. His strong hands gripped the controls, ready in a split second to whip the machine into reverse or a sharp curve should a child stumble or suddenly freeze in panic.

As abruptly as the game started, Malcolm peeled away and disappeared up the steep slopes to his mountaintop home on Laucala's peak, a house with a breathtaking view of the Pacific from its north and south sides.

On a nearby knoll is the earthworks of an old island fort. Archaeologists will be visiting Laucala at Malcolm's invitation to learn more about the fort. To the islanders, Malcolm is courting bad luck by tampering with it, and by building his mountain retreat nearby. They won't go near it.

The morning chase was now just a memory for the children. And Malcolm was a half mile away on the airstrip waiting for the official guests to arrive. There, in cool cottons, he with Roberta impatiently waited as the light aircraft bringing the Fijian prime minister, Ratu Sir Kamasese Mara, his wife, Adi Lady Lala, and other government ministers touched down.

Laucala is more than an hour's flight from Fiji's main airport, Nadi, on the major island, Viti Levu. Malcolm bought Laucala from the Maurice Hedstrom trading company in 1970 at a period when copra prices—coconut is the island's sole product—were low. Hedstrom was delighted at what was then a record price. At first, he had been asking $1.25 million. Malcolm was interested, but the potential sellers wanted to see bank statements if the deal was not a cash deal. "No one sees the books." Malcolm responded with the successful $1 million cash offer.

Originally Malcolm's plan had been to subdivide part of Laucala as a getaway Bali Hai for the weary wealthy of Europe, the United States, Japan, Australia and New Zealand. On Laucala, amid the natural South Pacific beauty, on an island where the inhabitants had jobs that were not tourist dependent, the leisure class could go native.

But the Fiji islands are 1700 miles from Sydney, 5500 from San Francisco, 6800 from Tokyo and 11,000 from London. Even before oil embargo, those distances became very expensive air miles. Not just that, the Fijian government was insisting that Fijian subdivisions have roads and other appurtenances of modern suburbia. Malcolm saw Laucala's selling point as the idyllic simplicity and fun of having trails, not roads, in keeping with the surroundings.

Government wishes and high air fares deflected Malcolm from the original plan. For the time being he joshes about his hopes for developing the island's plantation, increasing the copra production, perhaps growing some lumber, but mainly to make "Laucala" coconut oil a brand name rather than a generic product. Or, at least, that is what he was to tell a press conference later that day.

The Australian journalists, flown in the nearly 2000 miles from Australia at Malcolm's expense, kept saying they couldn't understand why they were there.

As Malcolm relaxed in the South Pacific listening to them, he knew that even with good prices the copra sales that year would not bring in better than $36,000. But it didn't matter; to him Laucala already was worth much more than the $1 million cash he had paid for it.

He fielded their questions and explained that with Forbes Inc.'s "understanding of such things as promotion" Laucala-brand coconut oil could bring prosperity to the island. Malcolm, having bought the land for development, had to come up with something.

Ratu Mara, Adi Lady Lala and the other distinguished visitors arrived and traveled in Toyota pick-up trucks to the ceremonial site. The band played. On the beach the prime minister and his wife were welcomed with due respect. Whales' teeth, the traditional gift to the important visitor, were presented by warriors in leaf skirts. The local schoolteacher was the intermediary between warriors and prime minister.

Following the formal presentation of a pepper tree by the island men, the *kava* ceremony began.

Kava, a beverage that tastes like Elmer's glue, is made from the ground root of the pepper plant by men charged with its preparation.

One Pacific island journalist told the others, in an aside, "You'll *love kava*. It's great for hangovers, it's an aphrodisiac, it's a diuretic, and after a couple of drinks you've no feeling left in your tongue or any part of your legs below the knees."

First Ratu Mara, then Adi Lady Lala, then Malcolm, were presented with coconut shells filled with *kava*.

Tradition requires that the final drop of *kava* be spilled on the ground. The shell then is filled with water as a chaser. The *kava* ceremony was over, though the shells were refilled regularly throughout the afternoon without Ratu Mara displaying any weakness of the knees. The men and boys performed an amusing erotic spear dance, the details of which are best conjured up in the imagination.

The film crew Malcolm had brought in from Viti Levu were busily recording everything for posterity—and for a later showing to *Forbes* employees.

Malcolm, who had watched rehearsals the day before, beamed in satisfaction.

Soon it was the women's turn. Forming a single line, wearing blue-and-red cotton with matching hand-held hoops to wave, the women of Laucala began their pleasing song, moving slowly and gracefully in accompaniment. Their song was about Malcolm, the island, his yacht and his plane.

This was one man's empire.

As the women sang, Malcolm's yacht the *Laucala* unfurled her spinnaker on the horizon. The *Forbes* emblem, the stag's head, was bold against the orange-and-red sail. The women continued to sing. *The Capitalist Tool*, that gold-colored DC-9, made its flypast, dipping its wings in homage as the pilot gunned the engines to send the aircraft roaring over Laucala's peaks and out to sea again for a second flypast.

This was the pinnacle of Malcolm's rapid growth.

This was Kipling and Rider Haggard, this was fun. This was the audacity of it all—that a kid from Brooklyn, for Malcolm was born in a Brooklyn hospital, could acquire an empire on which the sun never sets.

No, this wasn't the White House. But no president of the United States was as free as Malcolm to follow his will or whim. Presidents only have *Air Force I,* the White House, Camp David and somewhere in the sun.

Malcolm had his golden bird, *The Capitalist Tool.* Today Malcolm was flanked by leaders of government. Malcolm on his *High-*

lander does entertain heads of state. In his Mediterranean persona he does give motorcycles to kings.

Malcolm had achieved not by dissipating an inherited fortune— but while acquiring a fortune. He'd done it having the time of his life —with the sheer exuberance of a "fifty-year-old adolescent" catching up on all his boyhood dreams.

The *Tool* made her second and final flypast. She dipped her wings for the last time. Now she could be put up for sale. Emperor Malcolm had a thin smile on his lips, then he broke into his wide grin. What a helluva trip!

Was he laughing at the world? He'd made it. He'd arrived. He was, as Paul Erdman had written, using a lot of money to make "lots and lots of money." Malcolm sat there, listening to his praises sung, witnessing his invitations answered by heads of state. His fortune was building up by the minute.

It is a very American fortune. Ted Morgan captured the Malcolmness of it in *Signature:*

"Are you an apologist for the capitalist system?" the reporter asked.

"No," Forbes replied calmly, "I'm a beneficiary."

How wealthy is Malcolm? The figures are fascinating not just as a clue to Malcolm's success, but as an indication how it's possible, with chutzpah, flair, opportunism and luck.

Forbes Inc. income from magazine advertising alone exceeded $20 million in 1976. Not much for a corporation, but not bad for a "one-man" business. Add in approximately $5 million from subscriptions.

Forty percent of all *Forbes* subscriptions are three-year subscriptions paid in advance. Usually, only 40 percent of advance subscription income for newspapers and magazines is taxable during the current year. In other words, from subscription income alone Malcolm could have annually an untaxed $1.5 million or so to invest in stocks, bonds, cattle, land or anything else he chooses.

The advertising revenues cover the costs of printing, promoting and advertising *Forbes,* and leave millions over for the tax man if they are not absorbed as business expenses. The *Tool* has gone, but the *Highlander* sops up $500,000 annually.

A château has to be refurbished; refurbishing can be a business expense, right down to buying oil paintings to include as part of the décor. Islands can be bought, and the upkeep, maintenance and improvements deducted as business expenses. Soon the expenses can begin almost to equal the revenues. Is Malcolm's income rising faster than his ability to find deductible outlets? Magazine advertising revenue alone shot up nearly $5 million in the twelve-month period ending December, 1976. The Sangre de Cristo ranches are on target. They generate $9000 a day in cash—better than $3 million a year. Under certain circumstances the first-year income in land sales need not be declared for tax purposes.

The 7100 Sangre lots already signed for mean that Malcolm already has sold $34 million worth of lots from a ranch for which he paid between $3.5 and $4.5 million. In the world of men of wealth, Malcolm's doing better than most.

And yet, even though the money is piling up, Malcolm's personal progress that day on Fiji was reaching a high point. The *Windborne* was but a memory, the *Château de Balleroy* practically history. The political bids were back in the recesses of memory, and *Nation's Heritage* was a museum piece. The *Tool* soon would be a sigh as Malcolm waited in line at the first-class ticket counter.

There, on Laucala, slimmed down from earlier in the year when he had realized his stomach was hanging over his belt, Malcolm could look along the line of VIPs on either side in the reviewing area and review most of his family. There are four grandchildren now. There is money enough in places enough so that financial disaster is almost impossible. Health and luck permitting, a comfortable old age is guaranteed.

In an age of 7 and 8 percent unemployment and continuing inflation, Malcolm seems increasingly sensitive to suggestions he is riding on the taxpayers' backs. The fact is he does what the law allows, permits and even encourages.

He is not insensitive to the swath he cuts. His father, writing in 1919, reprimanded the actress Mabel Gillman for parading in the $75,000 sable her husband had bought her. "This is the time for *not* flaunting $75,000 coats in the face of the masses," thundered BC Forbes.

Perhaps it isn't time for flaunting Fabergé and balloons, either. But that's for the individual to decide.

Malcolm may have done it for himself, but he did it legally. He did it with a grin in an increasingly grim world. He did it outrageously, audaciously, and very, very shrewdly. He is a character when there aren't very many.

He made it look easy, and it wasn't. That's the greatest trick of all. And he has had fun.

There is *plenty* of "fun" to look back on. He hobnobs with presidents of the United States. When he and Steve sat down with President Ford in 1975, commentators called it "Gerry Ford's interview of Malcolm Forbes." Malcolm could have taken an experienced interviewer, or prepped himself. Instead he was indulging himself.

There's the *Social Register* Malcolm has acquired and doesn't like to talk about. How's that for compensating for any snubs about "second-generation nouveau riche" suffered along the way?

The older boys—Steve excepted—are heading off into their own ventures. The head of this magazine clan isn't sixty until 1979—Malcolm's got plenty of motorcycling and ballooning left in him yet, if he's willing to do it.

The magazine is doing extraordinarily well, and there's a new bureau opened in Houston.

Everything couldn't be better. But it's too good. So Malcolm will sit and simmer, and travel and imagine and then, just when men are supposed to be willing to slow down and babysit with the grandchildren, Malcolm will be gearing up for one more "last fling."

BC will still be spinning in his grave. After all, in that first *Forbes* "Fact and Comment," BC opened with:

Business was originated to produce happiness, not to pile up millions.

But Malcolm went for both.

Index

Ababou, Colonel, 136–138
Adamson, George, 29
Addison Bridge Road, 141, 142
Adi Lady Lala, 198, 199
Advertising Age, 75, 108
Ahermoumou, 131, 136
Alamosa, Colorado, *Valley Courier,* 150
Albert Frank-Gunther Law, Inc., 108
Aldrich, Winthrop, 78
Aldridge, diorama of, 150
American, 13, 22
American Brands, 93
American Foundry Company, 73
American Institute of Public Opinion, 83
American Telephone and Telegraph, 80
Anceny, Charles, 44
Arizona *Republic,* 2, 112
Associated Press, 83
Atmospherics, Inc., 171
Auction, 126

Balloon Ascension Division, *Forbes* magazine, 164, 194
Ballooning, 156–160, 162–173, 183–193
  as advertising, 161, 194
  early Atlantic attempts, 172, 173
Balloon Museum, 149, 160, 193
Baltz, Evelyn, 84
Barton, L. M., 39
Bateman, Raymond H., 95
Bender, Joan, 163, 165, 167
Bénédic, Hubert, 147, 148
Bénédic, Madame Myriam, 147
Bernardsville Borough Council, 78
Bernardsville *News,* 94
Be Something (poem), 22
Biel, Heinz H., 97
Biossat, Bruce, 83
Black Friday, 1929, 47
Blaumont, Dr. Jacques, 164, 167, 170
Boer War, 21, 22, 24

Boston *Herald,* 13
Bourguiba, Habib, Jr., 134
Brady, Ray, 119
British Broadcasting Corporation, 142
British Inland Revenue, 143, 144
Brown, Helen Gurley, 109
Bryn Mawr, 89
Buchan, 7, 15
Buchan *Observer,* 18
Burns, Robert, 38, 103
Burns Society of New York, 32
Burt, David, 4
Business Week, 10
Butler General Hospital, 72, 73

Capitalist Tool, The, 3, 5, 140, 141, 144–
  147, 159, 167, 168, 174, 200
Caplan, Basil, 123
Capriccio (Burt), 4
Carnegie, Andrew, 22, 41
Casablanca, 137
Case, Senator Clifford P., 91
Castle Forbes, 15
Caward, Chef Richard, 180
Centre National d'Études Spatiales, 157,
  164
Chamberlain, Joseph, 22
Chase Manhattan Bank, 114
Château de Balleroy, 160, 161, 202
Château de Balleroy, 147
  balloon museum at, 149, 150
  furnishings of, 148
Chemical Bank, 13
Chesterton, G. K., 11
Chicago *Daily News,* 154, 155
Chicago *Tribune,* 102
Churchill, Winston, 23
Cities Service Oil Company, 113
City of Dunc Weekly News, The, 50
Cleland, Kip, 145
Cleveland *Press,* 101

Clifford, Walter, S., 80
Cohen, H. Freeman, 25, 26
Columbia University, 68, 84
Commercial and Financial Chronicle,
    33, 34
Connoisseur, 2
Cook, Jim, 124
Cornfeld, Bernie, 148
Cosmopolitan, 109
Craig, Cleo F., 80
"Criminal Railroads, The" (B. C. Forbes),
    34
Cruickshanks, Gordon, 160
Cycle, 116, 144
Cycle Sport, 144
Cycle World, 144

Dailey, Warner, 141–144, 177
Daily Duffle Bag, The, 72
Daily Princetonian, 58
Danner, Mary Ann, 161
Depression years, 47, 48, 50, 51, 59, 65,
    66, 67
Detroit, 58, 59, 87
Dewey, Governor Thomas E., 88, 100
Direct Mail Advertising Journal, 108
Doddsworth, John W., 30, 32
"Doers and Doings," 35, 36
Doherty, Henry L., 49
Douglas, Flo (Mrs. Noel), 196
Douglas, Noel, 196
Drey, Walter, 36, 65
Drey's Listing Service, 65
Driscoll, Governor Alfred E., 81
Duggan, Dennis, 128
Dundee, 21, 27
Dundee *Courier and Weekly News,* 19,
    20
Dunn, James, 103, 105
Dun's Review, 67, 119
Dupret, Marcel, 131

Eagle Scout, 8, 51
Ecuador, 2
Edelmann, Roger, 170
Edison, Thomas A., 80
Ehrendon, John, 172
Eisenhower, Mrs. Dwight D., 81
Eisenhower, President Dwight D., 80,
    81–84, 88, 103
Englehard, Charles W., 96, 110, 140
Englehard Mining and Chemicals, 96,
    140
Englewood, 40, 43, 44, 47, 50
Englewood Board of Education, 68
Englewood Junior High, 51

Erdman, Paul, 10, 201
Esquire, 124

Fabergé collection, 4, 9, 146
"Fact and Comment," 5, 6, 33, 38, 75, 91,
    98, 102, 106, 116, 125, 169, 178, 196,
    203
Fairfield *Times,* 60
Family Album, 50
Fifty Men Who Are Making America, 36
Fiji Islands, 198
First Presbyterian Church, 45
Flaherty, Robert, 67, 124
Fleck, Dennis, 193
Fleming, O. D., 153
Fletcher, James C., 171
Flying W Ranch, 140
Forbes, 1, 2, 13, 37, 75
    advertising slogan for, 1, 101
    Arabic edition of, 140
    Balloon Ascension Division, 157, 164,
        194
    beginning of, 36
    business lunches, 103–105, 127
    circulation, 93, 96, 97, 102
    company yacht, 91, 92
    during the Depression, 47, 51, 65, 66,
        67
    under dual management, 91–93
    effect of corporate stories, 112, 113
    employer-employee relations, 114,
        115, 116
    Fabergé collection, 4, 9, 146
    fiftieth anniversary, 109–111
    first issue, 38–40
    "Forbes Program for 1918," 41
    freedom of writers for, 117
    history of, 4
    January 1 issue, 79
    the large "Forbes family," 50
    liquor advertising under BC, 46
    London office of, 2
    major advertising campaign, 101–103
    Malcolm becomes head, 10, 101
    ownership of, 87, 100, 101
    possessions of, 118
    postwar condition of, 10, 75, 76, 97
    postwar growth of, 97
    research department, 4, 94
    "Sidelines," 107
    60 Fifth Avenue, 4, 98, 104, 155
    Special Situations Service, 76
    staff responsibilities, 118, 123, 124
    stock options, 124, 125
    suits against, 112, 113, 128
    thirtieth year gala, 79

Forbes (Continued)
wine cellar of, 104, 105
women's section of, 40
Forbes, Adelaide (Mrs. B. C.), 34, 41, 45, 49, 54, 70, 77, 128
death of, 174
description of, 46
separation from BC, 62, 68
Forbes, Astrid (Mrs. Christopher), 177
Forbes, Bertie Charles, 4, 8–10, 13, 70, 71, 203
birthplace of, 7, 15
brothers and sisters of, 16, 46, 71
Cousin Dora, 23, 24
Cunnieknowe, 15, 71
death of, 86
"Doers and Doings," 35, 36
early years, 15–16
"Fact and Comment," 5, 6, 33
first jobs in New York, 30–33
first newspaper job, 18, 19
funeral of, 64
as immigrant, 28, 29
on labor, 41
last visit to Scotland, 85
letter from Hearst, 28
marital problems, 53, 54, 62, 63
marriage, 34
national tour, 42
newspaper experience in Scotland, 19–21
as a parent, 43–46
poker, 34, 74, 76, 77
on the Rand *Daily Mail,* 25–27
religion, 45, 46, 63
on rich industrial figures, 42
on salesmen, 57, 58
separation from Adelaide, 62, 63, 68
in South Africa, 21–27
views on the Depression, 66
work habits, 7
Forbes, Bruce Charles (son of BC), 10, 40, 45, 49, 50, 53, 55, 57, 61, 71, 82, 85
death of, 99
in Detroit, 59, 87
magazine ownership, 87
management responsibilities on magazine, 91–93
in New York, 87, 88
personal qualities, 115
in Scotland, 50
Forbes, Christopher (son of Malcolm), 89, 174, 176, 179
as curator, 176, 177
marriage, 177

Forbes, Duncan (son of BC), 10, 36, 43
death of, 48, 49, 50, 54
Forbes, Gordon (son of BC), 44, 71, 87, 100, 174
Forbes, Inc., 7, 12, 101
Forbes, Malcolm (son of clan chief), 15
Forbes, Malcolm Stevenson, 1, 71
ancestors of, 16
in antiques, 141–143
attitude toward money, 130, 203
ballooning activities, 12, 156–173, 183–193
birth of, 13
bridge game, 77, 154, 155
brushes with death, 139
changed public image, 169
early publications, 8, 48, 50, 51, 54, 55, 58
early years, 8, 14
education of, 7, 51, 53, 54, 58, 59
"Fact and Comment," 5, 6, 33, 75, 91, 98, 102, 106, 116, 125, 169, 178, 196, 203
family life, 10, 43–45, 49, 50, 102, 177–180
first career venture, 60
"guardians," 133
Investors Advisory Institute, 76, 87
in Lancaster, Ohio, 8, 59, 60, 68
magazine ownership, 87, 100, 101
management responsibilities on magazine, 91–93, 98, 106, 107, 109
marriage, 74, 75
in Morocco, 129–139
office of, 5
personality and description of, 6–9, 11, 12, 43, 46, 51, 105, 115, 126, 127, 129, 155, 165, 178, 203
in politics, 8, 78, 80–84, 88, 90–92, 94–96
at Princeton, 58, 59
promotion and public relations, 106, 107, 109
in real estate, 129, 149–154, 156
religion, 4, 45, 46, 61, 75
Slegers-Forbes and biking, 144–146
Time current events prize, 56
travels, 91, 101, 108, 147
war decorations, 73, 74
wealth of, 201–203
in World War II, 10, 60, 71–73, 89, 139
Forbes, Malcolm Stevenson, Jr. (son of Malcolm), 77, 103, 152, 174–178
Business Today, 174
Forbes, Moira (daughter of Malcolm), 94, 177, 193, 194

Forbes, Mrs. Malcolm Stevenson, 8, 74, 75, 89, 149, 166, 169, 177–179, 190, 198
  Christopher, 89, 174, 176, 177, 179
  education of, 89
  interests of, 90
  Malcolm S., Jr., 77, 103, 152, 174–178
  Moira, 94, 177, 193, 194
  Robert, 78, 145, 161, 172, 174, 176
  Timothy, 177, 179
  in World War II, 89
Forbes, Robert, 78, 145, 161, 172, 174, 176
Forbes, Robert (of New Deer), 15, 16
Forbes, Ruth (Mrs. Bruce), 88, 100, 174
Forbes, Sabina Beekman (Mrs. Malcolm Stevenson, Jr.), 177
Forbes, Timothy (son of Malcolm), 177, 179
Forbes, Wallace (son of BC), 44, 49, 62, 71, 79, 87, 100, 174
Forbes Atlantic Project, 168, 169, 171–173, 184
Forbes collections, 4, 9, 50, 103, 104, 144, 177
Forbes International antiques business, 142, 143
Forbes Investment Portfolio, 97
"Forbes Program for 1918," 41
Forbes Resturant Guide, 127–129
Forbes Stock Market Course, 99
Fortnum and Mason, 2
Fortune, 10, 58, 102, 120, 155
Freedom Foundation, 80
Frelinghuysen, Peter Hans, 94
Frick, Henry C., 36

Galápagos Islands, 2
Gallagher Report, 152, 153
Gallup, Dr. George, 59, 83
Gatch, Colonel Thomas, 161, 173
Gavin, James, 102
Gaynor, Paul, 145, 146
Glasgow, 49
Goldsmith, Oliver, 38
Gould, George Jay, 39, 40
Grammick, Andy, 86
Grant, T. W., 19
Grey, Zane, 2
Greig, Gavin, 17, 18, 85
Grieg, Mary Jane, 17
Gruenberg, Ruth, 178
Guthrie, Harold, 149

Hackley Eagle, 54
Hackley School, 7, 53, 54
Halbrooks, Norman E., 106

Halik, Tony, 165, 168
Haroldson, Hugh, 170
Harvard Law School, 57
Hassan II, King of Morocco, 130–138
Hearst, 34
Hearst, William Randolph, 7, 13, 28, 33, 35, 37, 68
Hearst papers, 67
Heath's Hotel, 26
Hedstrom, Maurice, 198
Hefner, Hugh, 144
Heimann, Robert K., 78, 84, 85, 93
Heinemann, George, 163, 165, 185, 191–193
Heinemann, Helen (Mrs. George), 165
Heinsheimer, Julie (Mrs. Thomas), 166, 191
Heinsheimer, Thomas, 159, 161–164, 166, 167, 169–171, 185, 190–193
"Hero of Poverty Flats, by Bruce Charles Pere, The," 40
Highlander, 5, 155
Highlander II, 5, 101, 118, 127, 146
  business use of, 183
  personalities aboard, 181, 182
  trip description, 179–183
Hook, Charles, 73
Hooper, Lucien O., 97
Hoover, Herbert, 88, 103
Houston, David F., 37
Humphrey, Hubert H., 110
Hutchinson, Edith, 89

Institutional Investor, 119
Internal Revenue Service, 9, 12, 146, 147, 152, 156, 159
International Business Machines, 40
Investors Advisory Institute, 76, 87
Investors League, 68
Irving, William, 77

Jambo (Smith), 11
Jameson, W. A., 55
Javits, Ben, 68
Javits, Senator Jacob, 68
Johannesburg, 25, 26, 29
Johannesburg Standard and Diggers News, 25
Johnson, Percy H., 13, 14
Johnson, President Lyndon B., 50
Jones, Alton, 49
Journal of Commerce and Commercial Bulletin, 30, 31, 32

Kava ceremony, 199, 200
Kennedy, President John F., 94
Kennedy Eagle, 55

Képis, 158
Kerrigan, Joe, 88
Key Largo Anglers Club, 88
"Keys to Unlock the Door of Success," 39
Kinney National Service, Inc., 112, 113
Kinzel, George, 71
Kline, Richard, 67, 96, 97
Knievel, Evel, 188
Knudsen, Semon "Bunky," 88
Kouron, French Guiana, 157, 158, 164, 167
Kremlin, 4

Laidlaw, Henry Bell, 74
Laidlaw, Roberta Remsen. *See* Forbes, Mrs. Malcolm Stevenson
Laidlaw & Coggeshall, 74
Lalli, Frank, 119, 121
Lancaster, 8, 59, 60, 68
Lancaster *Tribune*, 60
Landon, Alfred M., 56
Lane, Margaret, 6, 26
Laucala, 2, 193–195, 200
Laucala island, 2, 196–199, 202
Lavine, Harold, 2, 112, 125, 129
Lawrence, The, 55
Lawrenceville, 7, 55–57
Lawrenceville *Lit*, 55
Lawrentian, 56
Lebel, Claude, 131, 135
Levy, Carol, 119
Life, 58
Lindbergh, Charles, A., 44
Litton Industries, 112
London, 1–3, 32, 141, 152
London *Daily Mail*, 24, 25
London Sunday *Telegraph*, 115
Lurie, Sidney B., 97

Mack, Byron, 90, 93, 94, 96, 98
Magazine of Wall Street, The, 36
Mahoney, David, 88, 100
Mansart, François, 147
McCarthy, Senator Joseph, 85
McCleland family, 32
Medbouk, General Mohammed, 136–138
Men Who Are Making the West, The (Forbes), 44
Merrill, Harewood, 67
Metropolitan Life Insurance Company, 113
Meyner, Mrs. Helen, 110
Meyner, Robert, 110
Michaels, James Walker, 5, 10, 96, 98, 101, 107, 112, 114, 116, 117
  abilities of, 118–121

as editor, 123
education of, 122
experience of, 122
war service, 122
Modern Industry, 67
Montana Stock Grower's Association, 149
More, 126
Morgan, Ted, 1, 201
Morocco, 130, 138
  revolt against King Hassan, 131–138
Motley, Arthur, 77
Mount Trinchera, 154

Nassau Sovereign, 8, 58, 78, 93, 98
Natal *Mercury*, 23, 24
National Aeronautics, 160
National Aeronautics and Space Administration, 171
National Association of Manufacturers, 75
National Cash Register Company, 40, 113
National Forest Service, 150
National Lampoon, 152
National Magazine, 35
National Science Program, 171
Nation's Heritage, 8, 78, 80, 93
NBC, 185, 192
Neushul, Peter, 165, 166, 170
Newark *News*, 89
Newark *Star-Ledger*, 81, 82, 110, 144
New Deer, 16, 17, 45, 50, 80
New Jersey Ike-Nixon Clubs, 81
New Jersey National Guard, 95
New Jersey Republicans for Eisenhower, 83
Newsweek, 40, 121, 124
New West, 119
New York, 28, 32
New York, 5, 105, 118, 119
New York *American*, 13, 28, 33, 35, 68
New York *Daily News*, 129
New York *Herald Tribune*, 58, 68, 78, 146
New York School of Interior Decoration, 89
New York Stock Exchange, 33, 91
New York Times, 1, 62, 102, 125, 144
Nixon, Richard M., 95, 103

Ode to a Financial Columnist (poem), 52, 53
O'Higgins, Patrick, 10, 126, 133
Old Battersea House, 3, 152, 179
  party at, 3, 4
O'Neel, R. W. N., 13

Opinion Research, 119
Oppenheimer, Harry, 140
Ott, John, 172
Oufkir, General Mohammed, 134, 138, 139

Palais de Medoub, 4, 9, 129, 130, 179
  toy-soldier museum, 149
Palm Springs, 69
Pan American Airways, 136
Parade, 77
Paramount Pictures, 174
Paramount Securities, 52
Patterson, J. H., 40
Pauly, David, 121
Perth, 20
Peterhead, 17, 18
Peterhead Sentinel, 18
Pfotnhauer, Captain Alexander F., 180
Plainfield Courier News, 88
Playboy, 144, 155
Political Almanac, 83
Pommerau, Jean-Pierre, 164, 170, 187, 189, 192
Princeton Tiger, 58
Princeton University, 7, 57

Queen Elizabeth, 50
Quickel, Steven, 124

Rabat, 132, 137–139
Rabat Hilton, 132
Racquet and Tennis Club, 87
Radio Corporation of America, 43, 116, 165
Rand Daily Mail, 25, 26, 29, 32, 115
Ratu Sir Kamasese Mara, 198–200
Raven Industries, 161
Reddig, Bill, 124
Rhodes, Cecil John, 24
Robert the Bruce, 15
Rockwell, Ambassador Stuart, 134–136
Rockwell, W. F., 169
Roosevelt, President Franklin Delano, 47, 48
Rudnitsky, Howard, 124
Rugg, Harold, 68
Ryland, Errol, 153, 179

St. Cecilia's Church, 45
Salesman's Diary for 1938, The. Daily Pep Pellets, 57
Sangre de Cristo, 9, 150–154, 156
Sarnoff, David, 43
Sarnoff, Robert W., 165, 169
Saunders, Dero, 120, 124

Schad, Tennyson, 117
Schiff, Jacob H., 36
Schultz, George P., 50, 102
Schwab, Charles M., 35
Schwartz, Kenneth, 119
Scribner's, 58
Shankland, Elmer M., 97
Shaw, Thomas, 135
Shipley School, 89
Sidi Mohammed, Crown Prince of Morocco, 134
Signature, 1, 201
Silver Bears, The (Erdman), 10
Simms, Mr. and Mrs. Arthur G., 150
60 Fifth Avenue, 4, 98, 104, 155
Skhirat, 132, 134, 136, 139
Slegers-Forbes, 144
Smith, Anthony, 11
Smith, Geoffrey, 124
Smith, John Hart, 170, 189, 191
South Africa, 21–27
Special Situations Service, 76
Spirit of St. Louis, 44
Sports Illustrated, 157, 170, 171
Srodes, James, 115
Stevenson, Tom, 116
Stock, Emma, 101
Suzy, 5, 129

Taft, Senator Robert, 78, 79
Taft Committee on the Economy, 1947, 78
Tahiti, 2
Tangier, 4, 129, 179
  toy-soldier museum, 149, 176
Teachers College, 68
Thornton, William Meade, 140–142
Timberfield, 110, 141
Time, 40, 56, 152
Times-Tribune, 60, 61
Town and Country, 10, 126, 133
Trenton Missourian, 67
Trenton Times, 83
Trinchera ranch, 2, 126, 150–153, 156
Truman, President Harry S., 79

Underclassmen's Voice, The, 54
United States, 21, 27, 28
University of Michigan, 57

Vail, Theodore N., 80
Victoria, Queen, 16, 21
Viti Levu Island, 2, 198, 200

Waldorf Astoria, 31, 34, 78, 168
Wallace, Edgar, 6, 23–26, 98

Wall Street, 30, 32, 52
  1929 crash, 47, 64
  1931 crash, 64
Wall Street Journal, 5, 9, 102, 113, 125, 129
Watson, William, 20
Watt, Alex, 18
Webster, John, 85
Weiner, Gertrude, 52, 55, 68–70, 73, 86, 87, 91, 100, 101, 103, 174
Welch, Wayne, 119
Welles, Chris, 126, 144
Whitman, Dale, 172
Wilson, President Woodrow, 37

Windborne, 162–164, 170–172, 183, 184, 186–194
Wings, 84, 85
World War I, period before and during, 35
World War II, 8, 10, 60, 71–74, 89, 139
Wren, Sir Christopher, 2

Xerox, 112

Yablon, Leonard, 146, 151, 152
Yama Farms, 49

Zalaznick, Sheldon, 118, 119